George Grindle lived alone in one of the miner's stone cottages. He spoke the old Somerset which, for a while, caused me problems. When I called to see him he sat by the fire and fixed me with his piercing eyes. Then he spat inaccurately in the direction of the flames. He missed.

"What is it, George?" I asked.

"You'm darctor. You tell oi."

He undid the top button of the clothing that encased his chest and neck. It revealed about four inches of skin.

"I need a bit more clothes off," I said.

"Want oi to ketch me death loikely," he said and coughed again. I dodged and undid as much of his clothing as I could without actually engaging in fisticuffs with him. He was feverish and had fairly severe bronchitis and it was obvious that he needed to go to a hospital, but that meant the poor law institution four miles away.

"I think we'll have to get you to hospital, Georgie. You've got bronchitis."

"Oi bent gwine to no orspital! Yew give oi zum vusick loik Doc. Ballard useter. Brown and strong wi' plenty o' garlic."

I did my best to persuade him but it was a losing battle. The Union, as the poor law institution was called, was where you went to die, and finally I had to leave, giving him a prescription and determining to ask the local district nurses to look in on him.

Then I went home and began the routine for ridding myself of fleas.

Five days later Georgie's daughter arrived from Canada – and trouble really began ...

Diary of a Medical Nobody
Kenneth Lane

CORGI BOOKS
A DIVISION OF TRANSWORLD PUBLISHERS LTD

DIARY OF A MEDICAL NOBODY

A CORGI BOOK 0 552 12033 2

First publication in Great Britain

PRINTING HISTORY
Corgi edition published 1982

Copyright © Kenneth Lane 1982

This book is set in 10/11 Plantin

Corgi Books are published by
Transworld Publishers Ltd.,
Century House, 61–63 Uxbridge Road,
Ealing, London W5 5SA

Made and printed in Great Britain by
Hunt Barnard Printing Ltd., Aylesbury, Bucks.

This book is affectionately dedicated to my brother, Professor Ronald Lane C.B.E., who became a medical somebody.

I have made extensive use of diaries kept by my wife and have drawn as true a picture as I can of family practice in the 1930s.

Almost all the patients mentioned – as well, alas, as my first partners – are long dead. No actual names have been used except those of my own family and where specifically stated. I have written about my patients with love as well as laughter but wherever there seemed a possibility of embarrassment to relatives of patients the circumstances have been changed to avoid recognition.

K.E.L.

1

In August nineteen twenty nine I took the train for the West Country. For the first twenty three years of my life I had lived in the South East of England and the journey to Somerset was like a venture into a foreign land. It was true they probably spoke a language not unlike our own 'down there', but all I knew about the West Country was that they lived on cider and cream and rode seven on a horse to Widecombe Fair.

I was brought up in Kent and had spent the last five years at medical school in London, so the countryside that rushed past when we were twenty minutes out of Paddington was new to me. For half an hour I sat alone in my third class carriage looking out of the window expecting something new and different but it all seemed remarkably like the flatter parts of Kent and I began to lose interest. I tried to look carefully at it, to analyse its features but as my interest flagged the image of a young woman in her early twenties with black hair and brown eyes kept replacing it in my field of vision. We had been engaged for three long years, we were very much in love and we desperately wanted to get married.

You didn't marry in those days until you had a good income and a secure future. This would have been easy if I had had the money to buy a practice but I had none. I had borrowed eight pounds from my brother to pay for my one decent suit and owed three hundred and twenty pounds to the Kent Education Committee in payment of a loan on my education. Apart from this I was fairly solvent.

So the girl smiled back at me through the window. I didn't want her to go away. The countryside could look after itself.

In nineteen twenty nine a newly qualified doctor had very few chances to establish himself unless he had capital. If you wanted to specialise you needed a private income or else a great deal of patronage from the giants of the profession, or both. A start in general practice also required money to buy the practice. Without it you were doomed to remain an assistant at about five hundred a year for the rest of your life, unless some kindly principal indulged his charitable instincts in your favour.

I had scoured the Eastern counties looking for the right spot to spend the rest of my life, always hoping to find a practice where they were not absolutely wedded to money and would consider taking on an energetic young fellow who had no capital. At the interviews I usually got on quite well with the principals looking for a junior partner but then sooner or later would come the punch line. 'How about capital?'

'I haven't any,' I would say, whereon the jovial manner would change quite suddenly, sometimes with regret but always decisively, to a chilly indifference.

My brother had trodden the same road before me. We both went to Guy's and in doing so squeezed my father's resources to the limit, taking from him half his income for ten years. He could do no more. My brother undertook a three year assistantship on the verbal promise of a partnership after that. At the end of a year, having no capital, he could see no prospect of the promise being fulfilled and left general practice for good. The move led him eventually to a university chair but it was traumatic at the time.

With his experience in mind I was determined to run no risk of this sort and to choose a practice where money was not the central factor. This of course limited my choice enormously. Life was hard for those with no capital . . .

It must have been between ten and eleven in the morning when I emerged from Bath station. I was to be met by Thomas Wyburn the junior partner of Drs. Symonds, Beverley and Wyburn and he was to take me to the senior partner's house for lunch. I looked round expectantly, but no one looking remotely like a young doctor was anywhere to be seen. I walked up and down several times. I began to consider what I

10

should do if no one turned up. Then after what seemed like a couple of hours but was probably only a few minutes I noticed a youngish man sitting at the wheel of a car in the car park. He seemed to be in a trance and when I walked up to him he still looked straight ahead, his features expressionless. I passed and repassed him and then with a sudden burst of decision, accosted him. 'You wouldn't be Dr. Wyburn?' I asked.

He looked as though he was coming out of a dream, stared at me and then light began to dawn. He got out of the car and held out his hand. 'I do apologise. You are Lane. I thought your train wasn't due yet.'

We shook hands and got into the car. It was a very fine Austin with leather upholstery and all the solid worth of a British car of the nineteen twenties. As we drove south out of Bath he changed gear with impressive silence, timing the double de-clutch with perfect precision, then removing his hand from the gear lever with a flourish like a dandy of the eighteenth century completing his bow.

He drove me round the little country town of Melbrook. The High Street was wide and quite attractive — so long as you looked at it from the Town Hall end with that building behind you. A pleasant stream dominated it and a few fine old buildings were interspersed among the shops. The Town Hall on the other hand was a massive structure of solid grey stone which had little to recommend it except that it would probably stand there till the crack of doom. I passed a flippant remark about it and suggested that a little surreptitious arson would be no bad thing. Dr. Wyburn was not amused and I made no further attempt at lightening the conversation. He told me that the architect had been a very nice man, full of charitable works and a pillar of society — also a good patient of the firm a generation ago. This settled the matter of one's approval of the building.

We drove round the town and then out to some pleasant villages. Two forces seemed to have been at work in the vicinity of the two adjacent small towns of Melbrook and Radwell. Nature had done well, filling the whole area with pleasant hills, valleys, woods and lush pastures. Man on the other hand had sunk several coal mines, scarring the countryside here and there with mountains of grey brown earthworks. The few fine old houses that existed seemed to be hiding themselves from the prominent rows of miners' cottages.

We drove on, between hedgerows and past green meadows to a village several miles out. 'You must forgive me,' Wyburn said, 'if I don't take you straight to John Symonds' house. He won't be free till lunchtime and in the meantime I have to call on old Lady Chepstow at the Manor. I thought you might like to see something of the neighbourhood.'

His speech was slow and deliberate, he was immaculately dressed and quietly pleased with life. When I discovered that he was a fellow of the Royal College of Surgeons and an ex-registrar of a teaching hospital, it was impossible not to be impressed.

It seemed to me after a while that he was driving very fast through the narrow winding lanes and my anxiety must have communicated itself to him in some way. Perhaps I was gripping my seat or holding myself in readiness for an imminent crash. 'You may think I drive rather fast round these lanes,' he said, 'but I know every inch of them so well that it is perfectly safe.'

The logic of this eluded me and something inside me murmured 'then you've been lucky, my friend'. I was silent however and merely pressed with all my strength against the floor boards on an imaginary brake. I couldn't swear that Wyburn was aware of my alarm but he seemed to put on speed and rush round the corners like lightning. Then he began to hum nonchalantly and I was half afraid he would break into song like Toad of Toad Hall.

The traffic in those days was only a tiny fraction of what it is today but as luck would have it we met in a narrow part of the lane a farmer driving an old bull-nosed Morris. There was about twenty yards between the two cars when each sighted the other and we seemed to be approaching at a speed of some hundred miles an hour. Wyburn's brakes were of course in perfect order and he stopped incredibly quickly. The two cars came to rest bonnet to bonnet some two inches apart.

'How remarkable,' Wyburn said in his gentlest voice. Evidently he had never before met another car in the lanes.

It was a sign of the attitudes of the time that the farmer got out of his car, beamed heartily and apologised profusely. 'Zorry Darc,' he said. 'Oi were in a bit of an 'urry. Oi'll droive 'er back to the gate yere.'

He did and we passed like royalty waving a regal hand to the proletariat. 'Sam Burrows,' said Wyburn. 'He drives too fast of course.' He was silent for some minutes after this.

Later he disappeared for half an hour and when he rejoined me he said, 'Charming old lady but a little apprehensive about pains in her abdomen.'

'Neurotic?' I asked innocently.

'She is very sensitive and has to take great care over her diet. Not neurotic.' He spoke so solemnly that I couldn't make out whether he was joking. I looked at him and realised that he was absolutely serious. Thomas Wyburn F.R.C.S. had been able to convince himself that the members of the upper classes were differently constituted from the rest of the community. They suffered more grievously by reason of nervous systems that had not been blunted by vulgar sufferings in childhood.

'Is there much upper class practice?' I asked.

'A fair amount. I confess I enjoy that part of the work. As well as the frankly working class. I am not so fond of the middle classes. They always seem to me too aggressive and demanding.'

Belonging as I did to the middle section of the bourgeoisie I felt mildly snubbed, though he could hardly have expected a duke or a dustman to apply for the practice vacancy.

Finally at lunch, I met John Symonds. Almost at once I decided he was a man I would like to work with. He was down to earth, competent and warm hearted. He was not impressive to look at, being below average height, slim with neat regular features, fair hair and pale blue eyes. A small well trimmed moustache gave him a slightly dapper appearance. He had been a better than average tennis player much in demand during his many bachelor years before his rather late marriage, but he would not have held his place even in a B class reserve team in the sixth eleven of a football side. He was, I soon discovered, a very good business man.

With some pride he showed me his books and accounts.

Each private visit was marked with the word 'iter' — the journey being apparently more important than the consultation. Each consultation in the surgery was marked 'visus'. I noticed a curious entry entitled 'telephone *visus*'. How I wondered could you see anyone on the telephone? He answered my unspoken query a few minutes later.

'We give good value for money here, Lane,' he said. 'I can say that without hesitation but we like to be paid for our trouble. That, you see.' He pointed to the cryptic 'telephone visus'. 'When someone consults me on the telephone — they often think they can get away with free advice if they don't come to see you — I mark it down as a telephone visus and charge them half a crown, the same as if they came to the surgery.'

He was so quietly confident and such a pleasant fellow that it never struck me that he was too keen on the money bags. I could never in my life bring myself to charge anyone for advice on the telephone though. Not because of my generosity but because I simply hadn't the audacity.

Dr. Symonds seemed something like the lawyer in the old doctor lawyer story. A doctor asked a lawyer on the golf course what he did when clients consulted him on social occasions. 'I send them an account for professional advice,' he said, 'and promptly too.' Next day the doctor had an account from the lawyer.

I am not saying that I got the impression that John Symonds kept too tight a hold on the purse strings. He appeared efficient and business like. Most of all he was a very successful family doctor. In nineteen twenty nine he must have earned over two thousand pounds — a large sum in those days — probably equal to forty thousand now in nineteen eighty. In theory I had always scorned people who were too much concerned with the importance of money and the remarkably pleasant glow induced in me by the possibility of joining a rich practice was mixed with just a slight tinge of guilt. This however was subdued without undue difficulty.

The same afternoon I met Bill Beverley the third partner. Apart from a fair sized general practice he was medical officer to a famous public school two miles from Melbrook. He was large but not fat, had a rugged face, grey eyes and limped because of a severe war wound in the hip. He gave the impression of waving his arms and legs about as he walked, rather like a windmill in a stiff breeze. He exercised his mind vigorously in research as well as in routine practice, doing everything with vast enthusiasm. On the rare occasions when he stopped talking he smoked a pipe.

I thought he would be as easy to know as Wyburn was difficult. They were both ten years my senior, had both been in the first world war and I liked them both on first acquaintance. Beverley was the only real family man of the three. He was thirty four and had three children. Symonds had no children and Wyburn was still unmarried.

I had been told it was as important to choose the right partners in medical practice as the right wife, but the difficulty was to assess the value of that first liking, the first impression.

I decided that first weekend that this was the practice for me. The next thing was to persuade the partners that I was the man for them.

'What do you think of the place?' John Symonds asked me before I left on the Sunday evening.

'I like it,' I said, 'and I would like to join you.'

'What about the purchase price?'

'You are selling a share worth a thousand a year nett for two thousand pounds, aren't you?' Then my mouth went dry as I added, 'Could I pay out of income? I have no money but we could live on five hundred a year and pay five hundred a year for four years.'

He pointed out the impossibility of this with easy conviction.

'You would have to pay income tax, rent or buy a decent house, buy a car, pay the interest. You can't put anything down?'

'I'm sorry. I haven't a bean.'

He didn't seem to condemn me out of hand but was cautious. 'That's disappointing. Well if you can raise the money or even part of it let us know. You see we have to pay out Ballard, that's the trouble. And Wyburn and Beverley are young and have a lot of expenses. We'll give you a week before we interview anyone else.'

15

I went back to London thoroughly disconsolate. The figures of the three partners kept passing through my mind in the train. Symonds, frail with a hint of steel beneath the surface, Wyburn quiet, reserved, polished and conservative, Beverley warm hearted, vivacious and very intelligent. And in the background another figure I have not mentioned — Hannah Woodruff the dispenser. I had only met her briefly but her dark brown eyes looked at me with disapproval. She seemed to stand stiffly like a wooden doll with movable eyes, enigmatic, vaguely threatening. I liked the partners and I thought they liked me but the West Country practice, the fine houses of the partners, the shining motor cars, the well equipped surgeries were only part of a disappearing dream. All I needed was two thousand pounds but I might as well have needed the moon. My father, a schoolmaster, was due to retire on a small pension. It would be cruelty to approach him or even let him know my difficulty.

Three days later I had a phone call from John Symonds to say they had agreed to offer me — subject to a few weeks locum — a partnership if I could put down five hundred pounds and promised to pay the balance over three years. It was something to have a definite offer and I redoubled my efforts. I tried my bank, my uncle and my godfather but it was no use and I gave up hope. They were now giving me till the end of the month — ten days away — to accept their offer. The time expired and I wrote a note of regret to Dr. Symonds. Then Jessica and I consoled each other as best we could. Our hopes of early marriage receded and I began once more to look into the advertisements for 'partners wanted'.

Then one day I ran into Maurice Price Jones, one of my year in Hospital. He was exuding confidence as usual and told me he was about to become a partner in a practice in Devon.

'I didn't know you were a capitalist,' I said. 'What did you do when they asked for the purchase price?'

'Told them I would pay it when I was satisfied with the practice.'

I gasped. 'What are you doing for money?'

'I've got plans,' he said.

After several beers, mostly at my expense, I got from him the information that the Medical Sickness Society had started making loans for the purpose of buying practices. It was they who had to be 'satisfied with the practice'! Within an hour I was in their London office where I discovered that under certain conditions they would make a loan of a hundred percent of the amount required. From despair I reached the highest pitch of elation. That evening I telephoned John Symonds with my news. I had a fair prospect of raising the whole two thousand pounds.

Instead of congratulating me his voice was flat. 'Your time was up,' he said, 'and I assumed you couldn't raise the money. We are negotiating with another man now.'

My spirits plummeted, but I finally discovered that nothing definite had yet been settled. I might still be in the running. As soon as the Medical Sickness Society was definite about the loan I was to be interviewed again and a final choice made between the two of us. This time the other man and his wife were to be seen one weekend and Jessica and I the next.

Anxious weeks passed in which the Medical Sickness Society investigated me, my health, my career prospects and of course the practice. In October nineteen twenty nine the decisive weekend arrived. It was going to be a nerve wracking business but Jessica took the prospect calmly in her stride. I was bound to be chosen, she said, because I was so much cleverer than anyone else . . .

It was twenty years later that John Symonds' wife, Barbara, told me what happened. 'I shall never forget Jessica that day,' she said. 'She was wearing a beautifully cut speckled suit and a very becoming soft hat trimmed with green. She was a picture.' She told me it had been a difficult choice between the other man and me. 'It was Jessica's hat that decided me,' she said, and I honestly believe she meant it. She had a strong influence on John Symonds.

It was agreed that on December the sixth, nineteen twenty nine, I was to begin work in the practice in Somerset.

With the prospect of a good partnership we could at last plan the date of our marriage. No house was available in Melbrook and I had to save some money so we still had to wait till the following summer. But this was clearly the last lap, the end of the difficult part of life. From now life was going to be wonder-ful — years and years and years of utter happiness.

I finished my house jobs at Guy's, and Jessica and I took a weekend off before I went down to Somerset. I had a brand new car, a blue Morris Minor and a joy to behold. It smelt new, it shone with fresh glory and — subject to a hire purchase agreement — it was mine.

We drove up the A 5 out of London on a crisp clear morning. The open road and all heaven lay before us. We sang. We told each other that paradise was just round the corner. It was impossible to be happier. An hour later we missed death by a hair's breadth.

Cautiously I tried out the speed. She was just run in and fifty was permissible. Presently we followed a lorry for a long way waiting for a safe place to overtake. I was running no risks. At last on a long straight bit of road some seventeen miles from Stafford I overtook it. When you pass, pass quickly, I said to myself. As I drew level with the lorry it suddenly, without any warning, turned to the right to enter a gateway I hadn't seen. We were doing about fifty and I was forced to the right to avoid a collision. We shot down a bank, missed a telegraph post by a fraction of an inch, turned a complete somersault and ended up with the car on its side facing the way we had come.

We climbed out unhurt. This didn't surprise us in the least. We were immortal, why should we be hurt? But the lorry driver and one or two other people who appeared out of the blue came up to us in amazement, white faced and shaken.

Before we started that morning I had been telling Jessica that I couldn't find the tool box but it really didn't matter because the car was new and faultless. We saw the tools scattered on the ground and both exclaimed at once 'there they are'. Everyone obviously thought we were mad or badly concussed because we were led away like a couple of drunks flanked by several people on each side of us. A kind woman took us in to her house and gave us tea. A taxi took us to the station in Stafford and after several changes we reached our destination — the home of my future in-laws — by rail that evening.

So, it came about that I arrived at Melbrook by rail a week or two later. The Morris had gone back to the factory for repair, its frame was hopelessly damaged. It was the sixth of December and a wet dismal afternoon. I walked the mile to my new lodgings with two suitcases containing all my worldly goods.

I was told later that it was eleven years earlier to the day that my predecessor, Dr. Ballard, had come home from the war. The hero had been an examining medical officer at Taunton all through the war and the town band actually turned out to welcome him and lead him back to his home. Evidently Melbrook had a high regard for its doctors. The procession over the same route made a nice contrast to the young fellow trudging with two heavy suitcases through the drizzling rain. Dr. Ballard's reputation had been high. Mine was yet to be made.

2

I acted as locum for the retiring Dr. Ballard from December the seventh till the end of the month and became a partner on the first of January nineteen thirty.

We had a combined surgery, Wyburn and I, with Hannah Woodruff as our secretary dispenser. Miss Woodruff had a high colour and her face was patterned with corrugations that seemed clear evidence of past rages. Her hair was done in what can only be described as an aggressively virtuous style that never varied. She was given to mumbling her complaints between her teeth but on occasion would give full rein to her grievances. It was better then to take refuge if you could. She had been a great favourite with Dr. Ballard who had engaged her when she was young many years before. I regarded her as approaching the extreme limit of old age. She was probably in her middle fifties or perhaps younger.

She showed pretty clearly from the start that the change from Ballard to me was not altogether welcome. All the same we were lucky to have her.

For historical reasons, ours was the central surgery of the firm. Doctors Flower, Boodle, and Waugh had practiced from there in the last century. I had never heard of Alec and Evelyn Waugh at that time but our Dr. Alexander Waugh was their grandfather. It was said of him that he always kept a half crown on his bedroom windowsill. When there was a night call he didn't feel like accepting, he would throw the coin out of the window to the waiting messenger and say, 'Take that to Dr. Worger. He'll come.' Dr. Worger was Dr. Symonds' predecessor whose large family absorbed every penny he could earn.

John Symonds worked from his own house in Radwell two miles to the east of us, and Bill Beverley from his house near the grounds of the school and Abbey two miles to the south. Both of them did their own dispensing but their methods were characteristically different. John Symonds was careful to the point of fussiness. His mixtures were made up by Ferris's, the Bristol drug firm and diluted by the doctor with absolute precision. Bill Beverley, always full of beans and benevolence, gave his drugs — simple and harmless as they were — with a generous hand. He would pour half a pound of bismuth (very expensive even in those days) into a bottle and throw in the other ingredients like an experienced cook who never bothers to weigh anything. The result usually looked and tasted terrible but it was harmless and dispensed by his own hand conveyed the most powerful therapeutic properties.

Naturally enough I worked closely with Tom Wyburn and met the others only occasionally. The geography of the practice dictated much of the running. There being two of us in the Melbrook surgery, one of us had to do the locum work for the others when they were away. When we did we had a sharp reminder of our own advantages.

The weeks before Christmas are usually quiet in general practice and during that first week or two I sat day after day in my room seeing virtually no one. My predecessor had retired at seventy-two and the change to a young looking twenty-three year old was too much of a shock for many of the patients. Occasionally a man who had decided not to wait for Wyburn would risk coming in to see me. When this happened I would shake him warmly by the hand and then apparently reduce him to stunned silence by calling him 'mister'.

One cold winter morning I had no patients in the surgery and went from my room to the dispensary, which meant passing through the waiting room. As usual it was full of patients for Tom Wyburn but the main window had been thrown wide open and they were murmuring together about the icy draught.

I looked round and said, 'Do you want the window open as wide as this?'

No one answered but glances were exchanged and directed

towards Miss Woodruff in the dispensary. She had evidently come out from her den and flung the window open herself. I was puzzled at first till I noticed the glances in the direction of one of the patients. Then I understood. A farm labourer was smelling strongly of the farmyard. Which was better, I wondered, cow dung or an icy draught? As a compromise I half closed the window.

In the dispensary I told Hannah Woodruff what I had done. 'Please yourself,' she said, and muttered something about a dirty stinking someone or other.

'Perhaps he'll come in and see me,' I said. 'What's his name?'

'Banks,' she answered.

'Mr. Banks,' I called out, 'would you like to come in and see me as Dr. Wyburn is busy?'

'Oi godder wait ver Darc. Wyburn,' was the only response.

This caused a ripple of amusement. I looked round. 'Anyone else in a hurry?' I asked.

A young woman got up, hesitated, then came towards me. 'Is it alright for me to see you?' she asked.

'Yes, of course,' I said. 'Come in.'

I don't remember what was the matter with her but we had a pleasant chat. When she left another patient came in to see me and then another. All had been Ballard's patients and strictly speaking were my responsibility. So it came about that I began to come into my heritage through the aid of a pair of farm corduroys plastered with cow dung.

Miss Woodruff was amused by my success that morning. 'It takes a load of farmyard manure to drive them in to you,' she said with just that little spice of malice that she couldn't resist.

Brian Hobsley was one of my first patients. Having sat down and looked me over he gave me a long account of his skills as a first aider. It appeared he had won all the medals and competitions in the district during the past few years. When at last he came to the point he told me that he was applying for the job of ambulance driver at the Isolation Hospital. As Dr. Ballard, whose favourite patient he had been for many years, had left would I recommend him? (It spoke well of Dr. Ballard that so many of his patients felt they had been his favourites) I explained that as I didn't know him very well it might be better if he asked one of the other partners but this wouldn't do at all. He had always been a Ballard man and now intended — other things being equal — to become a Lane man.

'Perhaps,' I said, 'Dr. Ballard would still recommend you. He doesn't live far away and you could ask him.'

The idea didn't appeal to him and he then handed me his formal application to the hospital committee. The list of first aid successes occupied most of the page then, under the heading of driving experience, he had written that he was 'quite capable of driving the ambulance provided it was a horse drawn vehicle'.

I could hardly believe my eyes. The man must have been living in the last century. When later I spoke of the conversation to other people they frankly did not believe me, but the explanation lay in the character of Brian Hobsley. He was naive, innocent, utterly dedicated to first aid which was his life. He was the sort of man who would accost the President of the Royal College of Surgeons who happened to be helping at a street accident and tell him to move aside because he was a first aid man. All the same you couldn't help liking him. He was a man of single purpose, an enthusiast and generally he radiated happiness.

In due course I managed to make him understand that in this year of grace nineteen twenty nine ambulances were propelled by the internal combustion engine. His disappointment lasted only a matter of seconds but I found myself being very gentle, almost apologetic with him. I am not sure how I got him out of the surgery but he took no offence because I treated him for many years afterwards.

Tom Wyburn was helpful and encouraging, but I was not at ease with him for a long time. He was very reserved and it was often impossible to hazard a guess at what he was thinking. His high degree of competence and absolute integrity were qualities that only revealed themselves gradually.

Our immediate opposition firm consisted of Dr. Blaythwaite who was courteous, gentle and friendly and his assistant who no doubt had many other good qualities but not these. His name was Paul King.

I spent Christmas in my new lodgings but the Cottage

Hospital was a centre for Christmas activities and I first met Paul King there at a party on Boxing Day. He was unmarried, had an eye for the girls and was a splendid party man — the life and soul of every social gathering.

Somehow that evening he arranged for all the nurses to be lined up in two rows, then to show his gallantry and affection he proposed to kiss them one after another. To make this more respectable he called on me to do the same saying it was traditional for the two younger members of the staff to have this privilege. Tom Wyburn murmured to me that last year it was only the youngest and I felt I was being made a fool of. I found the challenge embarrassing. Either I had to look a dumb spoil sport, or make an ass of myself pretending to a heartiness it was all too obvious I didn't feel. Finally I did the kissing with a face like a beetroot. Alas, the affair removed any natural liking I might have had for Paul King. Not a good start.

After Christmas we fixed the date of our wedding. It was to be July the third — one hundred and eighty days away. My mind was divided between thinking of the glory ahead and coping with the competition of Paul King who was my natural rival.

In the days before the National Health Service, competition was always keen because the loss of a patient meant not only loss of income but loss of capital. A doctor's capital was largely invested in his practice and when he retired the sale of the good will was the main source of his livelihood. So it came about that each patient had a capital value. At two years purchase for instance each panel patient was worth one pound.

I knew of one doctor in the west country who spent his time buying run down practices, building them up and selling them again making a useful capital gain each time. It was like buying old houses, doing them up and reselling them.

It must have been in February that year that I was first called to the Duke's Head to see a boy with a broken leg. I was not in when the message arrived and Paul King was sent for in emergency. He went at once, gave treatment and got the boy as comfortable as possible. The normal procedure, of course, would have been to telephone me, let me know what had happened and ask me to carry on. We treated our own frac-

24

tures and it would be necessary to admit him to the Cottage Hospital and reduce the fracture under general anaesthesia.

When I arrived at the house the mother told me that Dr. King had called and would carry on with the case.

'I thought you sent for me first,' I said.

'We did Doctor, but you were out on your round.'

'You were patients of Dr. Ballard's before I took over?'

'Oh yes, for years.'

'Then I don't understand. Why is Dr. King going on with the treatment?'

'He said he would.'

'But you didn't ask him to?'

'Well, not exactly.'

'But you agreed with his going on with the case?'

'Yes, Doctor.'

The family were good private patients of our firm and it is hard for anyone in these days of too many patients to realise the fury the small event produced in me. I was hopping mad but quite powerless because the family had agreed that King should take over. I talked to Tom Wyburn about it but he only laughed.

'I shall phone him and tell him what I think of him,' I said.

'Do you think that will do any good?'

'It will do me good.'

He gave a deep sigh and abandoned the subject, leaving me with no idea what he was thinking. I couldn't take such glaringly unethical behaviour lying down and telephoned King.

'You saw a patient of mine today while I was out,' I said. 'The boy at the Duke's Head. Thankyou for seeing him.'

'Oh yes. That's alright. As a matter of fact he isn't your patient any longer.'

'What do you mean?'

'They asked me to carry on. Sorry old chap but they were very definite. I couldn't very well refuse.'

'So you intend to carry on treating my patient because you happened to see him in emergency?'

'There was really nothing else I could do.'

'There's a strict ethical code that you seem to take no notice of.'

'You weren't actually treating the boy. You had never seen him in fact. They intended to transfer to me when Ballard left but hadn't got round to doing it. That was why you got the message. I'm not doing anything unethical.'

'I see.' I rang off, angry, frustrated — and defeated.

Then came the appointment of medical officer to the Isolation Hospital — a job that had been done by the retiring partner of our firm and that I hoped would come to me. Tom Wyburn had deputised for Dr. Ballard until March when the new appointment was due to be made. Ballard came out of retirement to give me his backing and did his best for me. Among other things he told me that I must be prepared to blow my own trumpet. 'It's no use being shy with these people,' he said. 'You've got to make them understand you are the best man for the job.' But I was not good at blowing my own trumpet. At the interview I was able to tell the committee of the considerable experience I had had at the Metropolitan Fever Hospital in North East London as well as my house jobs at Guy's Hospital. I was in fact far better qualified than Paul King for the job and thought this would be obvious to the members of the committee. But I reckoned without the machinations of the enemy.

It turned out that only three of the committee were patients of our firm while five or more were attended by various opposition doctors in and around the town. I discovered later that my rival had canvassed each one of their votes, pointing out his longer experience in practice which was of course undeniable. What was more he was a man of much confidence and very popular. He acted as M.C. at many of the local dances and was especially admired by mothers of unmarried daughters. Everyone remarked what a good sport he was.

In due course Dr. King was appointed medical officer to the Isolation Hospital.

I was bitterly disappointed. I had let the firm down and been defeated by someone I honestly believed was less fit for the job than I was. Envy and resentment began to simmer . . .

It was later that spring that our most embarrassing conflict sent us both scurrying for cover. A new family had come to live at the Grange and they had hardly settled in when the wife col-

26

lapsed quite suddenly one Sunday morning. She was a woman of fifty, of previous good health, and her sudden fall into unconsciousness naturally alarmed the family. They had not yet decided which doctor to have and, as sometimes happens in emergencies, several doctors were sent for at the same time. I was doing a Sunday morning surgery — we took turns for this duty in those days. The message was clearly urgent and I set out at once — not displeased at the prospect of a new family of patients.

The Grange was on the right of the road as I approached it and I had to wait for a car coming from the opposite direction before I could turn in to the drive. The other car turned in too and being on that side of the road had right of way before me. It was Paul King. I cursed inwardly but followed close behind him. We parked simultaneously in the drive. 'Hullo,' he beamed, 'have you been sent for too?' His good humour indicated a degree of confidence that added to my discomfort.

Like Tweedle-dum and Tweedle-dee we walked up to the front door together. It was already being held open by a teenage girl. What should we do now? Who was to give way? We were of course both asking ourselves the same question and there was no answer. We walked together into the sick room.

The husband was sitting by a couch supporting his wife's head. King strode across the room in front of me, took the woman's wrist and said, 'May I?' I stood on the opposite side and could only use my eyes and wait. King made a cursory examination and then got out an ophthalmoscope and examined the eyes. I could only observe that the woman was deadly pale, that her breathing was shallow and she was sweating.

Then King got some sort of history. How had she been lately? A little irritable but otherwise well. Had she seen a doctor recently? Not for some months. Had she ever fainted? Not for some years. Yes, she had been to Church that morning and had not started her breakfast.

'What is it, Doctor?' The husband looked at King and then at me. King was anxious to speak first and hold the initiative. 'It looks like a stroke I think don't you Doctor?' For a split second I had a chance to speak and be listened to so I seized it.

'I think we should check a few points first. Could I have her stockings off?' All the reflexes were normal. By now I had the advantage of being on the right side of the patient and in a convenient position to go on with the examination. With help I got her undressed enough to examine her fairly carefully and by this time she was moving restlessly with an occasional sigh. I was beginning to enjoy myself. I asked whether she was having any medical treatment, tablets, injections. None. Then I saw her swallow and move her head from side to side.

'Could we have some sugar and water and a little brandy?' I asked.

Paul King couldn't contain himself any longer. We had to give the impression that we were giving the benefit of our combined knowledge and not competing with each other. 'Is brandy wise?' he said rather more loudly than was necessary.

I looked straight at the husband. 'I think your wife is suffering from a lack of sugar in the blood. We must find out why later. Meanwhile if we can get her to swallow a little sugar in water and brandy she may improve quickly.' King suddenly saw the light. 'I agree,' he said. 'Just two teaspoonfuls of sugar and two of brandy with about an ounce of water.'

I was so involved in the affair that I still didn't see how absurd our behaviour was. I was then by the patient's side and unless I was forcibly ejected I intended to stay there. I raised her head and shoulders and fed her a little of the mixture as soon as it arrived. In a few minutes she was much better.

Paul King was just as determined as I was to remain in the limelight. 'Well done,' he said to the patient standing directly in front of her. Quite naturally she spoke to him as she recovered consciousness. I counterattacked by taking the husband on one side. I had only seen one case of this sort before and was pleased with my diagnosis. I wanted it to be understood that it was my diagnosis we were acting on. 'I think she will need some further investigation,' I said. 'This attack was alarming but not necessarily serious. She certainly hasn't had a stroke. If you can get her to take light food for the rest of the day we could arrange the follow up examinations tomorrow. I think we shall need to consult a physician.'

Meanwhile Paul King had been listening to every word I said and he joined us at the window. 'I suggest Dr. Carey Coombs of Bristol for a consultation — today if possible,' he said. 'The sugar has cured her for the moment but I think we should get another opinion as soon as possible. If you agree I will telephone him straight away. I know him very well and I think he will come out at once if I ask him.'

So there it was. King had been altogether too smart for me. If left alone he would probably have made a fool of himself by diagnosing a stroke and it would never have occurred to him to give sugar. On the other hand if she had recovered spontaneously he would have taken the credit saying it was a blessing he had been on the spot in good time. He had cleverly taken my diagnosis to his own credit and by sheer effrontery taken the patient from under my eyes. An urgent call to a consultant made him absolutely safe and put him in charge of the case.

I felt so sore at my latest defeat that I went over to talk to John Symonds that evening. I gave him a full account of every detail of the encounter and he received it with a characteristic smile that I came to enjoy when I knew him better.

'You've got to remember King's point of view,' he said. 'Blaythwaite's practice is a one man affair. To have any hope of a partnership King has got to get a lot of new patients. He'll be given two years, three at most, and if he hasn't built up the practice very considerably he will have to leave and start again somewhere else. He has no capital I gather. Now in your case you have a solid practice to start with. You can be quite content to look after the patients you have taken on. So don't be in a hurry to get more.'

'But the blighter had no idea what the diagnosis was,' I said.

'Pathological hypoglycaemia like that is very rare. You had seen a case before?'

'Yes,' I said proudly.

'You were lucky, weren't you?' He spoke gently with a rather quizzical smile and I suddenly realised that I had not been brilliantly clever, only lucky.

'What would you have done under the circumstances?' I asked.

'I should have handed responsibility over to King without

going in to the house.' He thought for a moment. 'Then I think I should have telephoned a polite enquiry later saying I had responded to the call but found a doctor already in attendance so had not wanted to intrude. Then of course if they had not been satisfied with the doctor in attendance they would have known where to send.' He chuckled to himself.

'Of course,' I said, 'he would have got the diagnosis wrong and as likely as not made a fool of himself.'

'No, he would have got help if he needed it. He is not a bad chap. With you two breathing down each other's necks the patient did well to recover.' Another chuckle.

I had been gently put in my place. But I was learning.

Tom Wyburn took my defeats philosophically. He had such a large practice himself that my failures would make little difference to the firm's income. He didn't worry unduly about my injured pride. There is however a postscript to my tale of woe.

One evening later that spring I was sent for to see a woman in her early twenties with acute abdominal pain. She was tall blonde and very shapely. I asked a few questions and made my examination. It became fairly apparent that she was not an acute appendix but that she needed a second examination a few hours later. As I prepared to leave the mother said, 'Is Dr. King not at home then, Doctor?'

'Dr. King?' I must have gasped.

'We sent for him. I wondered whether you were doing his work.'

I explained that I had been asked for by name and was sorry. There had been a mistake. Someone must have misunderstood the message. Sometimes when a neighbour is asked to send for 'the doctor' they will send for their own doctor instead of the patient's. It looked as though I was going to stumble over Paul King at every turn. I said I would telephone him and ask him to look in later that evening.

Then matters became difficult. The girl said firmly, 'I don't want to see Dr. King. I'd rather have you Doctor.'

'But aren't you on Dr. King's panel list?'

'Yes but I'd rather transfer to yours. I can do that can't I?'

If you have ever been a young doctor struggling to establish himself, heavily defeated by an opposition colleague three times in a few weeks, and faced by an attractive young woman begging to become your patient you will understand the temptation I was under. After wrestling with the devil for what seemed like an hour or so, but must only have been a few seconds, I compromised by saying that I was bound to inform her doctor and ask him to continue treatment of her present condition. If, when she was better, she decided to transfer to my list there was nothing to prevent her doing so.

A week or two later she brought her panel card to me and did in fact become my patient. Afterwards I wondered whether the family at the Duke's Head had just as frankly asked for King to attend them. In that case I had nothing to complain of.

I met him shortly afterwards and he said, 'I hear we've done a swap. You've taken my beauty queen and I've got your fat boy with the broken leg.' His laugh was high pitched. 'I think you've got the best of the bargain.'

Not quite, I thought, that will be forty-fifteen in the first game.

31

3

'You haven't bought a pig in a poke,' Dr. Ballard said to me when I paid my courtesy visit to him. He had retired to a town a few miles away. 'There's plenty of good will there. A few guinea visits, but most of the work is in the four or five shilling range. Four shillings for visit and medicine. That's the backbone of the work.'

Some of old Ballard's ways were so much a part of the practice that it would have taken a revolution to change them quickly. He kept three large bottles of aspirins coloured green, pink, and yellow. These formed an important part of the dispensing. He also prescribed a mixture the dispenser called Mist Explo. It was a clear yellow liquid made from a few bright yellow crystals dissolved in water. The crystals were apt to ignite if left to dry in the sunlight, hence the name Mist Explosive. I don't remember the exact chemistry of this wonder drug but it was a derivative of picric acid and quite harmless when well diluted and used as a bitter tonic. About one old pennyworth was dissolved in one hundred and fifty ounces of water to form a concentrate which was dispensed as two ounces in eight ounces of water.

I tackled Tom Wyburn about this one day. I couldn't believe he would countenance the continued use of this extraordinary substance. 'This Mist Explo,' I said to him. 'What do you think of it?'

'It's harmless,' he smiled, 'and what a blessing that is. Quite quite harmless.' His voice was always quiet, almost caressing. I later came to believe that if he could have been more openly aggressive at times he would not have been such a martyr to migraine.

'Do you know how much profit we make on it?' I asked. 'I worked it out that at half a crown a bottle we make two hundred and twenty thousand percent profit on it.'

I thought he would have been amused but he looked at me as though I were a child of about six. 'But you see it's not the medicine we charge for. It's the advice. That surely is worth half a crown.'

'Do you think the stuff is any good?'

'Pharmacologically none at all.'

'Then why not give the advice without the medicine?'

'Oh that would never do. People need something to take home. They may not have understood a word we said so they can't take our words home. The medicine gives them a sense of value for money. It's quite valueless in itself. In fact the only treatment of any real value is surgical. Medicines are at best palliative and at worst dangerous.'

'What about digitalis for hearts?'

'It may prolong life a little.'

I laughed. 'I wonder what you are doing in general practice.'

'A little surgery. And for the rest, reassurance and sympathy as long as I have the patience.'

'Spelt with a 'c' or a 't'? Patience or patients?' He laughed somewhat artificially at my mild dig. (I gave up pulling his leg as I got to know him better). 'Seriously though, what about belladonna and alkalies for duodenal ulcer?'

'If I had a duodenal ulcer I should want to have it cut out surgically.'

'You'd rather have a major operation that might not be successful than a long course of drugs with a fifty fifty chance of a cure?'

'I question that.'

'If you have no faith in the medicines you give they won't do so much good. You'll miss the psychological effect.'

'Oh no doubt the bottle of coloured water is as valuable as the charms of a witch doctor, which I understand are often very effective.'

It wasn't often he would talk or argue like this and I wanted to keep it going as long as I could. 'What do you think of the quack doctors, the herbalists and what not?'

33

'Like Pennybacker, the herbalist, you mean?' He was interested now because he had a caustic story to tell. We all get an occasional kick at hearing of the failures of other people and Tom Wyburn was very partial to this particular pleasure. 'Do you know,' he went on, 'I once had a patient that that man had treated for two years, first with homoepathic remedies, and then by manipulation — manipulation if you please. And do you know what the diagnosis was when I had him Xrayed?'

I was prepared for anything from foot-drop to apoplexy.

'He had an advanced tuberculosis of the spine.' He never raised his voice but on occasion he spoke with an emphasis that was more effective than a shout.

I was suitably impressed and when he had repeated the diagnosis several times we ended the conversation.

He was often very silent when we were together and I gradually learnt not to talk too much. Sometimes he would give the impression of being struck by the splendour of a sudden thought. I would wait expectantly. But he would remain silent.

He was at his best in the operating theatre or at the piano — places where his brain worked through his hands. He was a loner of course and a very good pianist. His other hobby was learning strange languages. I remember his learning Welsh for many months and later Russian. He didn't appear to need the support or company of other people, most of whom he criticised — often it must be admitted with good reason!

He was a fine surgeon and possessed a dexterity that many operators would envy. Quite unflappable — outwardly at any rate. The most violent expression I ever heard him utter when under severe pressure was 'This case gives me mental perspiration'. Each syllable came out slowly, like the plucked strings of a harp.

Even Matron Pang at the Cottage Hospital was forced to give him grudging admiration. She would have found fault if she could because she was very much biased in favour of the two opposition firms of Dr. Blaythwaite of Melbrook and Dr. Furlong of Peterdon. They were all Bristol trained men and each one of our firm came from Guy's. Perhaps we allowed our obvious superiority to show too much!

Wyburn was very keen on physical fitness. He would walk every day, do press-ups each morning and bought a rowing machine to develop his shoulder muscles. All this was very successful. He was a fine physical specimen. My own conclusion was that he needed a wife — someone stimulating, feminine, merry and able to stand up to him.

He took two weeks holiday in April that year and left me in charge of his patients. We had no locums in those days. One patient I remember very clearly was a Mrs. Summers — an elderly soul with congestive heart failure and gross swelling of the legs. She was the Dutch doll type and had been something of a beauty in her time. She still had a good complexion and golden hair. Her medication was digitalis washed down by a quarter bottle of champagne three times a day. This maintained the status quo and kept her fairly cheerful although she could only just hobble across the room. Her husband seemed to enjoy life less than she did. Having just retired he was chamber maid, lady's maid, companion and part time cook.

Now it is a widely recognised fact that young doctors recently out of hospital are often regarded as the possessors of a store of ultra-modern knowledge denied to older men. Mr. Summers cornered me after my first visit to his wife and asked anxiously whether there was any new treatment available for these cases. There was not of course. Modern diuretics were thirty years away. Doing my best to respond to the challenge however I gave her a remedy named Guy's Pill. It was probably the best diuretic available at the time but had only a slight advantage over plain digitalis. By some amazing chance she responded like magic to this treatment. Enormous quantities of fluid were excreted each day and in ten days her legs were slim and elegant. The husband was delighted and my stock rose to unimagined heights. The only thing that bothered me a little was how Tom Wyburn would take it. It is not exactly a part of the Hippocratic Oath but an unwritten rule that no locum must ever give better treatment than the principal he is acting for. I feared my partner would not take my intervention kindly. He didn't.

I spoke casually when I handed over to him saying his

patient seemed a bit better for a change of treatment though she would probably have improved in any case. No modesty on my part however could affect the enthusiasm of Mr. Summers and when Tom Wyburn called and found his patient walking in her garden the inevitable resentment must have set in. He never mentioned the matter to me again and a certain coolness invaded the atmosphere.

Inevitably a degree of tension arose and was not long in showing itself in practical terms. I was inexperienced in midwifery. I had done my quota of some thirty deliveries on 'the district' at Guy's, but there the Resident Obstetrician was always available if we were in trouble. Things had gone pretty well for me and I had never had to use the classic alarm signal. This was the patient's hospital card with her name and address on it smeared with her blood. Sent by fast messenger to the Front Surgery, this was guaranteed to bring the R.O. at top speed on his bicycle. Once in practice I dreaded the day when I might have to put on forceps in front of my partner for the first time. One night between two and three in the early hours the moment arrived.

It was my first delivery in the practice and I was sent for by the district nurses because the patient — a Mrs. Dunster — was tiring and making no progress. Knowing the value of leaving things alone if possible I watched the pains come and go for half an hour.

Our two district nurses — we called them Martha and Mary — always worked together. 'Martha' was of course practical, strong and somewhat domineering. The other was very efficient but quiet and gentle — 'Mary'. They watched me as I watched the patient, Mary sitting on the opposite side of the bed and Martha standing behind me, alert and ready for action. The little room was lighted by several oil lamps and the illumination was fairly good. The bed was low enough to produce a bad backache in anyone in attendance for very long. Instruments and swabs were laid out on a towel nearby.

Seconds seemed like minutes and minutes like hours as we watched. At that time of night our little group seemed isolated from the rest of mankind, encapsulated in a globe of light in a dark, silent and sleeping world. There would be a deep stillness between the pains and then a wave of restlessness like a gust of wind before a storm — a grunt, and the powerful straining young muscles would be working again . . . I feel the patient's pulse, listen through her abdomen to the baby's heart and decide the moment for action is not yet. There is no advance as the clock moves slowly on, the nurses are anxious, the patient begs for help and I am all too well aware that to them I am an unknown quantity, hopefully to be trusted but very young. It is not easy to wait patiently when you are twenty four and longing to have your first delivery safely over.

As I watch between the pains I make my plans. I must send for Dr. Wyburn to give the anaesthetic. Then I must get the forceps ready. In my mind I go through every movement of the forceps delivery, admitting to no one that never before in my life have I delivered a woman by forceps. If only Tom Wyburn were not nursing a resentment against me at this critical moment. I can imagine his quiet satisfaction if I go wrong and he has to take over from me. Could I not manage the job on my own, quietly and slowly, with no critical eye to watch me? It has often been done before. I could give the anaesthetic myself and then hand it over to Martha while I apply the forceps and deliver the infant.

In a flash my mind is made up. I know exactly what to do and I will do it alone. I tell the nurses my decision. They know nothing of my experience or capability and assume that I have so much confidence I have no need of help from another doctor . . .

So it came about that I gave Mrs. Dunster a light anaesthetic of chloroform and ether — the standard mixture of the time — then handed the bottle over to Martha. I washed again and proceeded. I suppose my pulse was about two hundred and no doubt my hands shook but the gods of midwifery were with me that night and the forceps slid into position. From time to time I told Martha to give a few more drops of anaesthetic and I slowly delivered the head. I felt the patient's body tense powerfully as the head came through but took no notice and a moment later the job was done.

Without a moment's hesitation the mother raised her hand

and quite deliberately took the mask from her face. 'What is it?' she asked.

'I thought you were asleep,' I said.

'I felt it all,' she panted, 'but I didn't mind. What is it?'

My excessive caution had led to her being far less than adequately anaesthetised. This of course was better than putting her too deeply under but a difficult patient might have caused me to rush the delivery and damage the baby. Fortunately she was a splendid woman and — no thanks to me — all was well.

A little later, sweating but triumphant I examined the baby. He had bilateral club feet. My conscience must even then have been troubling me because in a moment of panic I thought 'God, I've crippled the baby.' The panic passed and the mother was intelligent enough to understand it was not my fault.

A few days later I had occasion to be driven to the hospital by Tom Wyburn. He was unduly silent and after humming a few bars of music — a sign that he wanted to deliver himself of something weighty — he said quietly, 'You shouldn't have delivered that woman by yourself, you know.'

'I know.'

'I wouldn't do it again if I were you.'

'I won't.'

He was a good chap really, Tom Wyburn.

4

We did our surgeries from nine to ten in the morning and from four to five in the afternoon — each of us having one afternoon off a week. We never took weekends off except by special arrangement which meant we worked six and a half days a week and were on call every night.

I seemed to get on well with the patients, but there were two women in my life who gave me no end of trouble. They were Hannah Woodruff our secretary dispenser, and Matron Pang of the Cottage Hospital. They seemed to vie with each other to make my life as difficult as possible. Hannah Woodruff was an employee and had to behave with some degree of circumspection but Matron Pang was mistress of her own domain and had all the senior doctors eating out of her hand to such a degree that she could afford to treat me with scant respect. I frequently found myself a victim of her machinations.

As to Miss Woodruff, the best example of my running battle with her was the affair of Mrs. Peak.

It was, I suppose, natural that most of the private patients should be attended that first year by Tom Wyburn, whereas I had most of the 'parish' and the less important panel patients. There were four distinct classes of patient — private, panel, club and parish — in a peck order as rigid as the social groups of the eighteenth century.

Beginning at the lower end of the scale, anyone in real poverty could obtain a note from the relieving officer — a dispenser of public funds — which entitled him to treatment from the 'parish' doctor. In our practice we were paid about sixty pounds a year to look after between two and three hundred patients.

The clubs represented a brave attempt by the many ill paid workers to buy medical attention as cheaply as possible. There were a number of working men's clubs which made contracts with doctors for the treatment of wives and children. For a year's attendance and medicine we were paid six shillings (thirty pence) for each woman and three shillings for each child. It was an Alice in Wonderland arrangement because although children are usually smaller than their mothers they need about twice as much medical care. Needless to say this was a half charitable scheme but it was better for the doctors than the alternative which was free treatment.

The third group was the panel patients. The capitation fee was nine and sixpence a year (forty five pence) and this covered all workers earning less than four hundred pounds a year.

The last group comprised the private patients and this provided more than half the income in our own practice.

Hannah Woodruff never allowed anyone to forget which class they belonged to. The private patients had their medicines wrapped in strong white paper and sealed. They were addressed with respect. The panel, club, and parish patients had no wrapping for their medicines and had to provide the bottle or pay tuppence for it. Mean as this sounds it was almost universal practice. As a further distinction between panel and parish patients she would hand the latter their bottles of medicine at arm's length with her head turned away as though she was afraid of catching something. At first this made me laugh then it began to irritate me.

Working in my own consulting room it was a long time before I began to realise that my patients were being kept waiting much longer than Wyburn's for their medicines to be dispensed. Several times when I had finished my surgery I came out into the waiting room to find that patients I had seen half an hour before were still waiting for their medicines. I was annoyed but it seemed a small matter to make a fuss about. Then one morning, when I had been particularly busy, I saw two of the patients I had seen at the beginning of the surgery still waiting for their medicine. I asked Miss Woodruff the reason for the delay. She bridled at once.

'I'm doing them as fast as I can,' she said and I left it at that.

Then one afternoon Mrs. Peak came to see me. She was a parish patient, the mother of five and grossly anaemic. It was not uncommon to find a mother in this state, ill fed, over worked and losing far too much blood every month. A blood strength of forty or even thirty percent of normal was likely. We talked of the possibility of getting more rest but this was out of the question. Her husband was demoralised by unemployment and no help to her. The children were ill-disciplined and she hadn't the strength to control them. She had given up trying and lived from day to weary day in an endless struggle to survive when even the will to survive was flagging.

One's heart bled for these poor souls but if they could be persuaded to take iron regularly for a long time they improved dramatically. I ordered her iron medicine and told her to see me in a week.

At the end of my surgery I went out into the waiting room and found her still sitting on the hard form looking a picture of wretchedness, still holding her bottle and prescription in her hand. She must have been waiting at least an hour. I walked up to her and asked if she was feeling alright. Would she like to lie down?

A woman next to her spoke up for her in no uncertain terms. 'It's Miss Woodruff, Doctor. Mrs. Peak has been waiting all this time for her medicine and she won't serve her. She keeps seeing the other patients first, Dr. Wyburn's patients, and her turn never comes.'

Perhaps that day my temper was not at its smoothest but I suddenly became furious. One couldn't have an open row in front of the patients and what was said in the dispensary could easily be overheard in the waiting room but I longed to give Miss Woodruff a piece of my mind. I took Mrs. Peak's bottle to the dispensary and said she had been waiting an hour and was not in a fit state to wait at all. 'Will you make her medicine up now please.'

Miss Woodruff looked venom. 'I've got to finish what I'm doing' she said.

'You haven't been seeing the patients in their turn, have you? This woman's turn must have been ages ago.'

She used her favourite weapon of silence and went placidly

41

on with what she was doing. I waited. She took as long as possible to wrap up the medicine of one of Wyburn's private patients then handed it with an unctuous word to a well dressed woman in the waiting room. I presented her with Mrs. Peak's bottle and prescription and waited.

'I can do it without being supervised,' she said.

'We'll talk about it later,' I said and left her.

Ten minutes later I went back to check that all was well. Mrs. Peak's bottle was standing half filled and she was dealing with another of Wyburn's patients. I had had enough.

'This woman is ill and has waited far too long,' I said. I took a box from the shelf, filled it with some special and expensive iron tablets, wrote on it and poured the contents of the half dispensed bottle into the sink. Then I took the empty bottle and the tablets to the patient and explained that she was to take these instead of the medicine.

Of course I had given Hannah Woodruff ammunition to attack me with and it would have been wiser to be patient and talk to her later but Mrs. Peak's haggard face haunted me and I was very angry.

When I had seen my last patient there were still several waiting for Wyburn and it was still impossible to talk to Miss Woodruff plainly. I went to the dispensary to say I would like to see her before she left but she forestalled me. She had already made a complaint to Tom Wyburn. 'Dr. Wyburn wants to see you as soon as you've finished your surgery.'

'Is he free now?'

'No, he's got a patient in.'

I looked at my watch. 'I'll come back in twenty minutes and see him and you too.' Then I went off in my car pretending I was busy and hoping to cool off.

When I came back I told Miss Woodruff to let me know when Dr. Wyburn was free and retired to my room. I hadn't long to wait and I was still angry. I think Wyburn saw by my looks that he had better be gentle with me.

'You wanted to see me,' I said.

'You have been having trouble with Miss Woodruff?'

'I have. I intend to speak to her as soon as the surgery is empty.'

'She kept a patient of yours waiting?'

'She keeps my patients waiting regularly while she sees to yours. This woman was kept waiting for over an hour. She should not have come to the surgery at all. Her haemoglobin is thirty five and she was made to sit there while one after another of your patients was attended to.'

'There's nothing wrong with giving the private patients a little priority in the ordinary way.'

'That's what it is! The private patients. I never thought of that. I disagree entirely. They should all take their proper turn. They come in to see us in turn according to when they arrive, so why not take proper turns at the dispensary? In this case the woman was really ill and should have had priority if Miss Woodruff had had a grain of sense.'

He was silent for a moment. 'Miss Woodruff seems to have been very upset. What did you do? Take the bottle from her and throw its contents down the sink?'

I told him what I had done. 'Miss Woodruff is so enchanted by the importance of private patients that her treatment of parish patients is little short of disgusting.'

'Very well then we must leave it at that.'

'We can't leave it at that. Don't you agree that medicines should be dispensed in proper turn with no queue jumping?'

'Shall we talk about it later. I have some more patients to see.'

I left him and decided to postpone my talk with Miss Woodruff till the next day. If Tom Wyburn agreed to my suggestion, which I was determined he should, we could put things right. My anger by this time had spent itself but Hannah Woodruff was evidently becoming as angry as I had been. She came to the dispensary door and said, 'I shall go over and talk to Dr. Symonds.'

'We are going to decide in what order you do the dispensing. Dr. Wyburn will let you know in a day or two.'

Whether or not she went over to report the matter to John Symonds I didn't know at the time, but Wyburn agreed that the dispensing should be done in the proper order and this was arranged. When we talked about it the second time I asked him whose idea it had been to give the private patients priority. He said he hadn't realised she was doing it.

'So it was Miss Woodruff's idea,' I said. 'No one else would think of it of course.'

The atmosphere settled down in the surgery and there was no more trouble for a time. Looking back it is amazing how maddened some things can make you. It is injustice, or what we see as injustice that really angers most of us.

It was some months later, after we were married, when we were playing bridge with John and Barbara Symonds, that I learnt that Miss Woodruff had in fact appealed to John Symonds over the Peak affair.

He said, 'You had a bit of friction with Miss Woodruff some time ago. Are things alright now?'

'You heard about it then?'

'She came over to see me in something of a state. Threatening to give notice and so on. It sounded at first as though you had been a bit rough with her but in the end I decided there was no point in my interfering.'

'It's all settled now. It was a matter of who should have priority in the surgery over the dispensing of medicines. It turned out that she was keeping panel and parish patients waiting until all the private patients had been served out of turn.'

'That doesn't sound very outrageous to me. The people who pay should have the advantage.'

I told him about Mrs. Peak and he agreed it was wrong to keep someone in that state waiting a long time. Then he asked me what had actually happened over the half dispensed bottle of medicine. I told him. The affair was still fresh in my mind and I became vehement again as I spoke of it.

'You've got to remember that Ballard was a stickler for the rights of private patients,' he said. 'He would have insisted on their having priority however long the others were kept waiting. You can't blame Miss Woodruff for still following his instructions.'

'I see that. All the same her manner to parish patients is still inexcusable. They are human beings and shouldn't be treated like dirt.'

'Is it really as bad as that?'

'It was. It's better now because Wyburn and I have agreed that patients who come to the surgery must wait their turn to see us and then wait their proper turn for their medicine. The problem doesn't arise in your surgery because you do your own dispensing and deal entirely with each patient as they come in to see you.'

'That's true. Yes, I think you are being reasonable.'

'I'm afraid I'm not prepared to work in any other way Dr. Symonds.'

'Alright,' he nodded, 'but you must make allowances for Miss Woodruff's previous training. The change from Ballard to you can't be easy for her. You must remember too that she is a very fine secretary. Her accounts are perfectly kept. Only last year the accountants told me they were a model of what they should be. She is an old and valuable servant and she has given us the best years of her life.'

I felt for the first time the toughness beneath John Symonds' benign manner. He was reasonable, but would brook no nonsense. Wyburn was easier to deal with because he was more detached from everyday affairs. His head was in the air, Symonds was down to earth. It would have been easier to work in close proximity with Symonds. He was incisive and practical. I decided I had been hasty in my condemnation of Miss Woodruff and I resolved to be more understanding in future. So I was, until she infuriated me again.

'Now,' said Symonds, 'what about this game of bridge? Shall we play families or split up?'

Life wasn't all work and tension by a long way. There were other people around besides Hannah Woodruff and Matron Pang. For one thing our wedding was approaching — desperately slowly but quite surely — and there was all the fun of collecting things for the home. When I had a free evening I would go with my landlady's husband on expeditions into the county to buy antique furniture — mostly at Mr. Pattimore's in Somerton. They were splendid evenings. We would browse round the shop, find a table, a chair or a cabinet and then repair to the village pub with old Mr. Pattimore. I suppose he was about forty five. In due

45

course a price would be mentioned, drunk over and amended, then finally agreed for a job lot of several pieces. I have no doubt Mr. Pattimore knew very well what he was doing but the end result was that we all felt satisfied we had made a good bargain. Any leisure time in the next few days would be spent applying linseed oil, cleaning, polishing, and in due course another piece of the home-to-be would be ready.

My companion on these trips was the schoolmaster, Joe Poynor. I hope his sons will forgive me for using his real name. Tough, small and splendid company, he was one of the few who had fought through the whole of the first world war in the trenches in France. I believe he enjoyed our outings as much as I did though I am not sure why I feel such nostalgia for them. I suppose it is because the world was fresh and young and all my married life and all my years in practice lay ahead of me, full of promise and variety.

There was some sparring between Paul King and myself from time to time but on the whole the ten of us on the staff of the Cottage Hospital got on well together. There were stories of old skirmishes such as when Dr. Furlong came to the district twenty years before and offered to attend confinements for half a guinea. This was a threat to the general livelihood and at last Dr. Ballard managed to persuade him to charge the 'full guinea' and peace was restored.

Once, on a Sunday afternoon, we had a meeting of all the doctors at Dr. Furlong's house. We discussed the problem of whether or not we should persuade the clubs to pay us seven shillings a year for each woman and three and sixpence for each child. The decision was passed unanimously after some hours of talk over endless cups of tea and later endless glasses of beer. The clubs of course refused and the status quo was maintained. There was no inflation in those days.

The variety of our work was astounding. We were general and orthopaedic surgeons, physicians, obstetricians, gynae-cologists and pathologists. We did our own blood transfusions with the antique method of tube and funnel, our own post mortems in primitive conditions and all our maternity in the homes of our patients.

There is a vivid image in my memory of one of my first post

mortems. The story concerns Police Constable Bailey.

One of the few disadvantages of being a young man is that youthful self-assertiveness sometimes interferes with the business of understanding people. This was how it was between me and P.C. Bailey. I first met him over a case of sudden death in March 1930. The patient was a man of middle age who had been eating his Sunday lunch and collapsed without warning over the table.

Fifty years ago of course there was never any serious argument as to whether you were alive or dead. No one ever asked for evidence of the cessation of brain activity. You were either alive, or dead, and any intelligent observer could say which. However then, as now, no one could be actually pronounced dead until a doctor had made the necessary statement.

The police force in Melbrook consisted of Sergeant Sperring and P.C. Bailey. The sergeant was a Somerset man, strong in a gentle sort of way, quite unflappable and looking down at most people with mild blue eyes placed over six feet above ground level. P.C. Bailey was a foreigner from South Wales. I am not sure how accurate my memory is, but I seem to recollect dark brown eyes and a suspicious expression. He was a man determined, I guessed, to get on, the sort of man who would report the most law abiding citizen who travelled at thirty one miles an hour in a built up area.

I arrived a minute or so before the policeman but when he reached the house he became professional straight away. 'You didn't move anything, did you Doctor?' he said.

'Only the patient,' I answered.

He looked at me with disfavour and I explained that I had had to decide whether or not he was dead and he was lying face down across the table when I arrived.

'Will you put the body in the exact position you found it in please.'

'Don't you want to know whether he was alive or dead when I got here?'

More disfavour. P.C. Bailey frowned. 'I take it the man is deceased,' he said.

'Yes, only a short time though.'

47

'Then will you put the body back in the position you found it in.'

I didn't like sudden death. I had been involved in no wars at that time and the fact saddened and sickened me. In a few minutes a man who had been enjoying his meal had become 'it'.

I put the body in the half prone sitting position with the head on the table and told myself the policeman was hard boiled and callous.

P.C. Bailey was now in his element and began to busy himself with an inventory of all the surrounding objects. Evidently this was a case of murder until proved otherwise. 'No vomit,' he muttered, 'no external violence to the head, no stains on lips or mouth.'

'I imagine you can safely leave the state of the body to me Constable. There will have to be a medical report and presumably the coroner will order a post mortem.'

'Undoubtedly a case for post mortem but my duty is to observe every detail. We take nothing for granted in the force. Have you interviewed the deceased's wife?'

'I'll have a word with her while you go on looking at the body if that's what you want.'

Bailey frowned again. He didn't seem to like me although I thought I was being very polite to him. 'I shall need a statement from her,' he said.

'She's going to be pretty badly shaken,' I told him. 'You'd better leave your questions till I've had a little time with her.'

'You are new to general practice, Doctor, aren't you?'

The brilliant repartee — if there was one — didn't occur to me and I said, 'Not exactly. I've been here four months.'

By his expression you would have thought he suspected the new widow and me of being accomplices in murder with malice aforethought. I left him with the body and did my best to console the poor woman whose life had been suddenly shattered. When I left the house P.C. Bailey was still busy with his investigations. 'You'll know where to find me,' I said to him.

'We'd like a statement from you, Doctor. The time you were called and time you arrived, whether death had occurred and when. And your opinion if any of the cause of death.'

I confess the man irritated me. I was to meet him again over the post mortem.

In those days the coroner usually instructed the notifying doctor in a case of this sort to do the post mortem himself. The examinations were done in a wooden shed about twelve feet by eight. It was at the end of what the modern generation call Excelsior Terrace — Gas Lane to the oldies. There was no heating of any sort and the only compromise with hygiene was a cold water tap over a sink. An old examination couch covered with a red mackintosh stood in the centre of the shed. It had no central drainage and any accumulation of fluid from the body simply ran over the sides.

It was an icy cold March day. Anyone who wants to discover the limits of sheer discomfort if not absolute human endurance should do a post mortem under those conditions. The hands become numbed and the whole body aches with the cold. Every movement becomes an effort. I took off my coat and put on an enormous rubber apron and a pair of Wellingtons a size too small for me. In half an hour I was shivering uncontrollably and I had an hour and a half more of this ahead of me.

Examination of the abdominal viscera produced no surprises, the lungs were normal and the heart though enlarged revealed no clear cause of death. Bailey did a little sponging and provided a bucket of ice cold water now and again but we proceeded in silence. We were too cold to be chatty or even to quarrel. If I could find some clear cause of death there would be no need to embark on the terrible job of opening up the skull but there was nothing. With increasing gloom and discomfort I set about the wearisome business of removing the skull cap. After what seemed like hours of sawing it came off and in a few minutes, to my enormous relief, I found a massive cerebral haemorrhage. Thank God I should now be able to shut up the body and get out of this charnel house. My hands and feet were completely numbed, my nose ran and I was so miserable that I clean forgot the presence of P.C. Bailey.

As I began the suturing there was a strange noise as though someone had emptied a sack of potatoes through the window. I turned and saw Bailey sprawled on the floor. I stood and stared

49

wondering what to do. Perhaps my brain was numbed too. It must have been an extraordinary scene — a half frozen G.P. with a mutilated cadaver on the table and a seemingly dead policeman on the floor.

It could only have been for a second or two that I stood like a statue, but the scene is imprinted on my memory. What brought me back to life and action was a thin trickle of blood and water that ran slowly off the table on to poor Bailey's trouser leg. I stripped off my gloves and bent over him. He had fainted of course.

At that moment the hut door opened and Sergeant Sperring came in. 'What the . . . What have you done to him Doctor?' He grinned and his cheery expression did me more good than a hot toddy.

We soon revived him and the sergeant got him out into the fresh air. There were no cars for their rank of the police force and in a few minutes they both trundled off on their bicycles. Ten minutes later the sergeant came back to see that all was well with me. 'I ought to have warned you,' he said 'A sensitive lad is Bailey. He only tries to pretend he's tough.'

I called at Bailey's house that evening. He was a little shame-faced. 'It was when you sawed away at his skull,' he said. 'That was what finished me.'

'I ought to have kept an eye on you,' I said, 'but I was a bit preoccupied.'

'It wouldn't have mattered if the sergeant hadn't come in.'

I became good friends with Bailey after that. He was a human being after all — sensitive, suffering, trying to justify himself, to become significant like all the rest of us. He got promotion in due course and left the district. Sergeant Sperring became our firm's debt collector after he retired and a real artist at the job — but that's another story.

5

'How do you get on with Matron Pang?' Tom Wyburn asked me one day.

'Not very well,' I said.

'She's not an easy woman to deal with.'

'I'd call that an understatement.' I wasn't sure what he wanted to say, and with him one always had to wait patiently. This must have been May or June, and I knew him well enough to realise that he had something on his mind but didn't know how to put it.

'She was very attached to Basildon you know, before he left a year or two ago. Very attached.'

I didn't know how to interpret this information. Basildon had been a G.P. in the district for some years. 'You mean she had an affair with him?' I asked.

He sounded shocked. 'Oh dear me, no. Nothing so definite as that.' I waited again. 'Since Ballard left,' he went on, 'she has been rather off hand with me. Not very co-operative.'

'She was affable enough to me for about a week when I first came. Then for no apparent reason she decided to make me public enemy number one. I can never get a patient into the hospital without a long argument. Whenever I want to borrow anything — the other day I needed an oxygen cylinder urgently — she hasn't got it to spare. When I do a round she is always busy and sends the most junior nurse available who knows nothing about the patients. Unco-operative is an understatement.'

'I wonder,' he said slowly, 'whether it makes a difference that you are engaged. Some days she is all honey and sweetness

51

to me and on others I can do nothing right and she becomes obstructive.'

'Perhaps she regards any unattached male as fair game and expects you to make advances to her.'

'That wouldn't explain her antagonism.'

'Yes it would. That's how she would behave if you didn't come up to her expectations — socially.'

'She does give me the impression that she expects something more of me than she gets.'

'There you are then. She wants you to replace Basildon. You are not interested in her that way, are you?'

'No, definitely not. She's not my type at all.' He sounded uncharacteristically emphatic. 'I confess I'm not an expert at understanding women. You may be right. I shall have to be careful.' The thought of Wyburn being careful not to get involved with Matron Pang was somehow rather amusing.

Until then I had thought of her as a dragon rather than a woman. She was, though, well educated, had a good figure and was not at all bad looking. She was about his age too. The conversation set me thinking. Perhaps, because my own mind was at that time obsessed with the prospect of my marriage, I felt that poor old Wyburn was missing out badly. I began to wonder what sort of woman would do for him. Someone vivacious. Someone with an excellent sense of humour. Someone who could tease him. Someone very feminine. If such a woman could fall in love with him it might do him a power of good. It was just what he needed.

I thought again of Matron Pang. Was I sure she wouldn't do? She was rather solemn of course and hadn't much sparkle. And evidently he felt this too. Then it suddenly struck me, he must be on the look out for a wife, feeling the need of one. I would observe Matron Pang, think of her as a woman. The choice in the country was not very wide as far as I knew. For the thousandth time I thanked God for Jessica and soon forgot about Tom Wyburn.

It must have been soon after this revealing talk that I had a night call. Certainly the two events are connected in my mind. As usual I was sleeping like a log when there was a squeak and a clang of the gate, followed by hurried footsteps and the ringing of the front door bell. The sounds penetrated the deeps of sleep and I began the struggle, against superhuman odds, to extricate something vaguely called self from infinite blackness. The sounds stayed at the heart of things then turned to a small point of light that grew and grew until quite suddenly I was awake, leaning out of the window and talking to a patient at the door.

'It's Simon, Doctor.'

'What's happened to him?'

'He fell down the stairs and I think he's broken his arm.'

By this time I was properly awake and a few minutes later I was driving through the silent empty High Street towards the Bunch's house. Simon was about twelve at the time. His arm was broken above the wrist but he seemed unnaturally distressed even for someone with a fractured arm. The shock of a fall down the stairs when he got out of bed, half asleep, had sent him to the verge of hysterics. I put him in a splint and sling, gave him a dose of pain reliever and waited for a while. It was three o'clock anyway and the night's sleep could be virtually written off. Then I left him with the promise of an Xray later in the morning. I resigned myself to the usual day one had after a bad night. Everyone would be that much more demanding or obstructive, or irritating. And so they were . . .

In those days we did our own Xrays in the Cottage Hospital. An ancient machine purchased some years before by voluntary subscription from the community still did good service — once you had mastered its idiosyncracies. Matron sometimes did the Xrays for us. It depended how she felt and how busy she was. I remembered my resolution to take a fresh look at her and telephoned from the surgery to say I had a very nervous boy who had to be Xrayed that morning.

She was too busy to do it herself, she said. Very well then I must do it.

'The electricity is variable. You may have trouble getting the right exposure,' she said.

'Then I must go on taking pictures until I get a good one.'

'We are rather short of films too,' she added and this began to irritate me.

I spoke, I think, with quiet dignity. 'I'll bring him to the hospital at eleven-thirty. He may need an anaesthetic later. I'll arrange that when I have seen the Xray.'

'We haven't got a bed.'

'I don't want a bed,' I snapped with rather less dignity.'I want an Xray and probably an anaesthetic in the theatre this afternoon.'

'Dr. Blaythwaite will be using the theatre.'

'All the afternoon and all the evening?' The sarcasm was meant to be heavy.

'I hope not.'

'So do I.' I rang off thinking how strange it was that on the very day I intended to make a character analysis of her she should be so difficult.

I took Simon to the hospital at eleven thirty. Few patients had cars then and of course there was no ambulance service except for emergencies.

The Xray room — you couldn't call it a department — was just inside the main entrance. In later years it was turned into a surgeons' lavatory — it was just about the right size for this. I took the boy into the Xray room and told him to sit down while I got the machine going. A film in its casette had been left out for me and as I was adjusting the tube the Matron came in.

'Is this the boy?' she asked.

'This is Simon Bunch.' I put the injured arm in position over the casette and Matron adjusted the tube. If she was prepared to take the Xray I was happy to let her.

She moved the injured forearm putting a sandbag to support the fingers but Simon was not co-operative and moved to a more comfortable position. 'No, not like that.' And this time she was a little firmer in her placing. He moved again and she was firmer still. Simon began to cry.

'Don't be a baby.' Miss Pang was contemptuous.

I put the arm gently in the right position and held it there. It would have been easy to take the picture at once but she proceeded to turn the hand into a more supine position. Simon howled and Matron raised her voice. The situation was becoming ridiculous but I waited patiently holding the hand in position. 'That should be alright,' I said. 'Take that position will you?'

'Not if you want a good picture,' she said.

'I want this view. Take it please.'

'I can't spare films for wrong views,' and she moved the hand again. Simon howled louder than ever and I had had enough. He was still very nervous and the last thing he needed was rough handling. 'Leave it to me will you Matron.' But she stood glaring.

'If you will kindly leave the boy to me I will take the Xray and develop it later.' I glared at her and, breathing heavily, she walked out. I wondered what I had done to deserve such a woman but Simon was crying and I had to get the job done. With a little coaxing this was not difficult. I replaced the splint and sling and led him out to his waiting mother.

There was now the problem of developing the film. I had only been in the practice a month or two and hadn't had to do this before. I had watched my partner do it once and had played with photography as a boy, but I wasn't very sure of the procedure. Having turned Matron out it was most important not to make a mess of things. In the small adjoining dark room there was no sign of any developer fluid and after several minutes fruitless search I gave up.

Much as I disliked the idea I had to find Matron and ask where the stuff was. She was of course closeted with one of the sisters. I knocked on her door and was greeted with an imperious 'wait please'. A full minute later I knocked again and opened the door. 'I'm sorry to interrupt,' I said, 'but where is the developer?'

She stared at me. 'The Xray developer,' I repeated.

Her voice became honeyed. 'I'm rather busy Doctor. Could you wait a minute?'

I waited, went off to see some inpatients, and came back quarter of an hour later. Matron had gone to lunch.

The patient and his mother were waiting patiently. I apologised for the delay. What was I to do now?

I could telephone to the nurses' quarters and ask for a reply to my question or I could request her to come over to the Xray room. But would she come? I decided to take the patient home and get in touch with him again when I had developed the film. Then I telephoned the hospital and asked for an appointment with the Matron that afternoon. Eventually I saw her in her office at — I think two thirty.

I was young and angry. 'May I sit down?' I asked.

'Certainly Doctor.' So far so good.

'Matron, I had a patient here this morning with a fractured radius. After pointing out all the difficulties in the way of getting him Xrayed you finally made it impossible for me to develop the film.'

'But the developer is there, Doctor — in the cupboard, for anyone to see.'

'It wasn't there this morning. I want to know why you deliberately set out to waste my time.'

'Whatever do you mean? I was there to do it myself and you told me to leave you alone.'

'You know very well why that was. You were having a pitched battle with the patient.'

'I was doing my best to get a good picture.'

'Now Matron let's stop beating about the bush. Would you have gone off to lunch knowing a doctor was waiting for the developer and the patient waiting for treatment — would you have done that with any other doctor?'

'I'm sorry. I forgot you couldn't find the developer.' She smiled ingratiatingly and I found the new manner more irritating than the antagonism.

'You forgot?' I asked with impressive irony.

'Yes, I'm sorry.' She smiled again, like a patient mother with a refractory adolescent.

'Will you kindly show me where the developer is or ask one of the nurses to show me?'

She sent for a nurse who took me to the Xray room. In the cupboard was a winchester full of developer. It hadn't been there in the morning. Surely Matron wouldn't have played a schoolgirl trick on me.

'Is there any possibility that someone might have removed this during the morning?' I asked the nurse.

'Only to fill it, Doctor. I filled it myself this morning.'

Much as I would have liked to, I couldn't very well cross question the girl and ask when she had been told to remove and fill it. But I was sure Matron had arranged this on purpose.

I developed the film successfully and met Matron on the way out. 'Nurse had taken the bottle away for filling,' I said, trying to read her mind. 'That was why I couldn't find it.'

We parted on superficially friendly terms — a state of armed neutrality you might say. I had no further trouble with her. No doubt she would say she had no further trouble with me. We both had to take special care to behave correctly and this didn't lead to easy co-operation.

Looking back next day I told myself that my suspicions had been absurd, that my judgement had been upset by lack of sleep. There was no doubt she had been unco-operative, but in a normally cheerful mood I would have laughed it off. As it turned out she treated me with great respect after that. As to my character analysis, I struck her firmly off the list of possibles for Tom Wyburn.

I told him about the episode, adding a certain amount of free criticism of Miss Pang's character.

'A strange woman,' he said. 'She has changed lately.'

'Hell knows no fury like a woman scorned,' I said. 'Perhaps she fancied her chances with you and is now disappointed.'

'Not a pleasant thought,' he said and that was all.

Somehow or other although I liked and admired Wyburn I never seemed to get close to him. All that year we ran on parallel lines and never really met. I was convinced now that only the right woman — exactly the right woman — could shake his rigidity and really loosen him up. Perhaps I was imagining it but it seemed possible that he was thinking that way himself.

6

We were married on July the third nineteen thirty and from that day onward my life was cheered by Jessica's radiant enthusiasm for all the things in life that matter.

We made our first home at 'The Cedars, Melbrook' which sounds impressive but was in fact a two hundred year old stone cottage with one cedar tree in its small garden. It suited us to perfection.

The formal round of polite calls started at once. J. had been instructed by Mrs. Ballard — who appeared to make a special return visit to Melbrook for the purpose — as to precisely whom she must make contact with. Naturally enough she listened politely and took no notice. She would walk out in the afternoons to leave two of my visiting cards and one of her own on each of those who had called on her.

'Why two of mine?' I asked her.

She thought for a moment and then said, 'I have no idea but that's what you do.' Never having looked the matter up in a book of etiquette I still don't know. Sometimes on my round I would see her walking briskly along, I would wave and wonder how many hours it would be before I should be home for the evening.

She looked so absurdly young that one day when a patient called at the house he looked her up and down and said, 'Is your Dad at home?' I heard her say, 'I'm the Doctor's wife. Come in and I'll fetch him for you.' What the patient thought when 'Dad' turned up I don't know but the problem was solved by a few years in general practice.

There was one intractable problem — one that lasted for years — what should be done about calling on newcomers to the district. Her instinct was to call on anyone who was new or lonely but on the other hand she didn't want to give the impression she was cadging patients for me. It had been Mrs. Ballard's habit to call on newcomers at once — provided of course they belonged to the right stratum of society. It would be outrageous to call on the wrong people.

Money in our household was in short supply. My share of the firm's income was to be a thousand a year nett, but in the first year I was not entitled to book debts which meant that my earnings for the year would be about seven hundred pounds. The Medical Sickness Society, which had lent me the whole of the purchase price of the share in the practice, quite naturally insisted on a complete modernisation of the firm's agreement. This cost me £140 in solicitors' fees and in addition I had to pay £150 off the loan. I paid about £90 in the year for the hire purchase of the Morris Minor, £80 for some essentials of furniture and £40 to the Kent Education Committee in payment of part of the loan on my education. This meant we had about £100 to live on in the first six months of our married life. In October that year we engaged a maid — an essential in a doctor's house at that time — and paid her twelve and sixpence a week. Without going into any precise calculations it is pretty clear that by the last quarter of the year there was precious little left. All the same my wife managed the housekeeping on a pound a week and the lack of money meant very little to us.

We decided to decorate the whole of the house ourselves, so I bought paint and brushes and one Saturday afternoon we started work on the hall. Decorating materials were less well adapted to the amateur in those days and after a couple of hours we were making very heavy weather of it. Both of us were dressed in old clothes with white paint all over us when the front door bell rang and in walked Bill Beverley. His first reaction was to stand back and roar with laughter.

'What on earth are you two children doing? Washing down the rabbit hutch or having a fight?'

'We are painting the walls' I said with dignity.

'You haven't done the ceiling yet.' Then looking up at our patchy ceiling he added, 'Or have you?' More laughter.

In a few seconds his coat was off and his sleeves rolled up. 'You go and organise a cup of tea, young Jessica, while I take over. You haven't got another ladder and a board? Never mind, I can manage.' And he was at work on the ceiling with a rush and flurry that made me expect a cascade of drops and splashes. But there were none. Bill was an expert.

We had tea a little later when Bill of course did most of the talking. I remember him telling us about his youngest daughter who was three. During a hot spell in the summer she had dispensed with the superfluity of clothes and wandered off through the Abbey gardens adjoining his house. She was later brought back by a tall monk in black who walked sedately hand in hand with the small naked nymph. It must have made a memorable picture.

Presently I walked back into the hall to admire his handiwork. He had left the pot of paint in the middle of the floor and looking upwards I knocked it over. Bill seemed to have been expecting something of the sort and after a brief explosion he rushed into action.

'Alright,' he said. 'All hands now before it runs under the skirting. Load your brushes and put it straight on the walls.'

We worked feverishly and in a few minutes the floor of old flagstones was left with a mere white patch on it while most of the walls were painted. Somehow or other after this Bill and I retired down to our cellar, probably because I had related the story of our first barrel of cider. I had had difficulty in knocking the bung out with the tap and had resorted to a hammer and chisel. Naturally enough before I could get the tap in place a good deal of cider was awash on the floor. The story naturally intrigued Bill Beverley and he insisted on inspecting the site of the tragedy. Anyway the upshot was that we added a mug or two of cider to the cups of tea we had consumed. I don't remember the conversation but I seemed to get to know Bill that Saturday afternoon. There was very soon a feeling of compatibility, a sense of warmth and agreement that was to last over forty years. It is often when talk is trivial that real communication is established.

The friendly contact with Bill Beverley somehow lent the final element to the deep satisfaction we both felt in our new life. That evening we sat in the small dining room. The drawing room on the other side of the hall was still unfurnished but the dining room was so packed with furniture it was hard to move. The gateleg dining table, the carved sideboard and ladder back chairs from Mr. Pattimore's were my earliest proud possessions. We sat one on each side of the fireplace in our only two armchairs and, apart from a powerful smell of paint, life was good.

I don't know quite how it came about but we both became gradually obsessed with a sense of obligation — a feeling that we ought to try and do something for someone. I had talked a lot about the poverty in the district and the idea occurred to one or other of us that we might give some anonymous presents to some of the hardest hit families at Christmas.

The trouble was that we literally hadn't a penny to spare, so we decided to write letters to various people away from Melbrook — mostly family — to beg for money for the purpose. We did and the money rolled in. Evidently there were plenty of other people suffering from the same sense of obligation. I made a list of fifteen or twenty families who were really below the poverty line and the whole plan seemed splendid.

Compared with our own good fortune the lives of many of my patients were bleak. North East Somerset was a mining area at that time and the mines had not recovered from the nineteen twenty six general strike. Work was short and the pay poor. The most senior and responsible men on the coal face earned about two pounds for a six day week. Most face workers were paid six shillings a shift. Many worked only three shifts a week and were entitled to three days dole which brought in a weekly pay packet of twenty eight shillings. Worst off were the men who worked four shifts a week because they were entitled to no dole and had to manage on twenty four shillings a week.

So poverty was rife. The average miner's dinner was a plate of potatoes. Sometimes it would have a tiny rasher of bacon or an egg on top of it. These men had no ounce of fat on them but as long as they kept free from pneumoconiosis they were fit and tough. Paying five or six shillings a week in rent and bringing up two or three children on less than thirty shillings a

61

week, they made our own income and prospects seem like riches. Children still developed rickets and their resistance to infection was dismal.

Our parcels only contained a few shillings worth of goods each, but it was something. The next problem was how to deliver them without looking like Lord and Lady Bountiful. They must be given anonymously, but how? The solution came when a French girl friend of Jessica's came to stay for Christmas. We drove her round late on Christmas Eve and she delivered the parcels on our instructions. It was dark, wet and cold, and we hoped our car would not be much in evidence. I remember hearing her say something about 'le Père Noel' in each house, and this I thought would leave people sufficiently puzzled. Anyway the giving helped to assuage our sense of obligation, and no doubt the parcels were acceptable.

It was early in January that the repercussions began. First there came a softening up bombardment from Hannah Woodruff. She came to my room one day with a self-satisfied expression that warned me an attack was imminent.

'You are getting yourselves talked about — you and Mrs. Lane.'

'What do you mean? What have we done?'

'Aha.' A self-congratulatory smirk and a head shake left me wondering what was coming. When she could bear to part with the pleasure of anticipation, she went on, 'Talked about, yes. Some of Dr. King's patients too.'

'What on earth are you trying to say?'

'Those Christmas parcels. It was risky giving them to anyone but when you gave them to some of the opposition patients — well.'

'Well, what?'

'Bribery, that's what they are saying. Mrs. King, Doctor's mother, is very upset.'

I stared at her in puzzled disbelief. She was obviously enjoying herself as she goaded me to the point of explosion. 'Go on,' I said with heavy calm.

'You gave presents to some of Dr. King's patients. People are saying you are trying to get them on to your list.'

'By bribing them. Is that what you are saying?'

'It's not me, it's other people.'

I was still virtually speechless and instead of letting out a stream of blistering invective I went on the defensive. 'As far as I know we didn't give anything to any of Dr. King's patients. If we had, the last thing I wanted to do was to bribe them. Which of his patients are we supposed to have given parcels to?'

She mentioned two names and addresses and beamed with pleasure.

'Do you mean to tell me that in Somerset no one is allowed to give people living on a starvation wage a small parcel at Christmas?' I was warming up now with righteous indignation.

'If you think they are on a starvation wage you had better tell Sir Nathan.'

'I don't know Sir Nathan or any of the other colliery owners or I certainly would. The men in the mines are near starvation.'

'I shouldn't say that if I were you. He is one of Dr. Symonds most important private patients. And the miners have only got themselves to blame. Sir Nathan was nearly ruined by the 1926 strike.'

I knew enough about Sir Nathan's way of life to know this was nonsense but I wasn't going to be sidetracked. 'You say Dr. King has complained that I have tried to bribe his patients to transfer to my list. Have you heard him say this?'

'People are talking, that's all.' And I could get no more out of her.

Needless to say I was thoroughly irritated. We talked about it at home and Jessica dismissed the whole story as nonsense. What she meant was that it was an old maid's bitchiness but she couldn't quite bring herself to use the words. I fumed for days on and off. The suggestion that the miners were underpaid through their own fault infuriated me too. I suppose what annoyed me most was the thought that I had been unethical in giving parcels to some of the opposition patients. Had I? Was I an idealistic fool, not ready to face the realities of life?'

Jessica laughed me out of it all and gradually I forgot about it. Then Paul King came to see me.

He wasted no time in pointing out the error of my ways. We had been engaged in fair competition up to now, he said, but this affair was quite another matter. It transpired that in two of the families who had been given parcels the man had been my patient but the wife and children were King's. That was how the trouble began.

'You remember the Widowson family when you complained that I had asked the wife and children to come on my list because I treated the man?'

'I remember very well,' I said. I knew he had broken the rules on that occasion.

'Well of course I hadn't done anything of the sort. They asked to come under me. I did nothing to persuade them. And now you have actually given presents to two of my families. What's the obvious inference?'

'The obvious inference is nothing. I gave some small presents to two of my own patients who had been on the sick list and were even more hard up than they were before.'

'The parcels were handed to the wives and were clearly intended for them. Some mince pies and small toys. That's hardly what you'd give a miner.' He laughed loudly as though he had produced a trump card.

'For God's sake be sensible,' I said. 'Naturally the best present for a man at Christmas is something he can pass on to his family.'

'To my patients you mean.'

'In those cases yes.'

'Then there's nothing more to be said.' He got up to go, pulled on his gloves and added, 'You'll be hearing from the Ethical Committee of the B.M.A. in due course. I can't let this pass.'

We parted in anger, each equally sure of his own rectitude.

The whole thing was quite idiotic, a storm in a teacup but I was bothered and couldn't sleep. As I lay awake I thought Jessica was asleep but she suddenly spoke in a wide awake voice. 'What are you worrying about?'

'I don't want to be hauled up before an ethical committee and charged with trying to bribe the opposition's patients.'

'You won't be. Don't you see he was just giving himself a nice dramatic exit?'

After which piece of feminine wisdom I no doubt presently went to sleep.

7

I heard no more from Paul King about the Christmas parcels and next time I met him he greeted me as a long lost friend. I was surprised. There was obviously little point in taking too much notice of what people said in anger or when they were trying to make a prestige point. Probably more than half of all human behaviour is dictated by the state of the liver.

Work increased enough during my second winter in the practice to increase my confidence but Tom Wyburn still did the bulk of the work. He had a large practice and did all the firm's surgery and this made me anxious to pull my full weight. Accordingly I used to count up the number of private patients I saw each month. At the end of March I told him proudly that I had done over two hundred private visits in the month. He said rather disdainfully, 'What energy.' Then added, 'How long did that take?'

'How do you mean?' I said.

'To count them all up,' he answered. I felt deflated.

Things however were to change gradually. So long as patients had something physically wrong with them Wyburn would treat them with care and consideration but woe betide the 'neurotics' who 'wasted' his time or those who called on the family doctor for a reassuring chat.

A famous teacher of medicine once said that some people, instead of going to the pub for a chat with the landlord and a drink of beer, would come to the surgery for a chat with the doctor and a drink of medicine. If there is any truth in this statement it didn't work with Tom Wyburn.

Nervous patients who were either rich or who belonged to the upper classes were of course different. He would rationalise by giving a physical cause to the various nervous ailments — an arrangement that suited them well. Most people would rather be told they were suffering from 'a virus infection' or 'chronic fibrositis' than be diagnosed as nervous or emotionally ill.

It came about that the 'neurotics', the emotionally ill, those with psychosomatic illnesses began to come to me and at an early stage I began to wonder how much they really suffered. The more I talked to them the more I realised that they were often every bit as ill as those who suffered from so-called organic disease and sometimes much worse. Family quarrels and tensions could be the cause of intense misery and a good deal of real illness. I tried to develop a technique of listening to people without making any emotional response to what they said, of trying to find out what lay behind their behaviour, their aggressions and their complaints. I was beginning to congratulate myself on a more scientific approach to the neurotics when what I regarded as my praiseworthy attitude was one day tried to its limit.

A miner named Charlie Chiswick developed what was popularly called a pin knee — an inflammation below the patella region due to kneeling for long periods at work — and came to see me in the surgery. Previously he had seemed a sensible quiet fellow but that day he was thoroughly truculant.

'Enough to gie anyone a pin knee where Oi der work,' he said. 'No air, no room. Ought to be shut down.'

'The colliery you mean?'

'Where Oi der work, yes.' He began to shout. 'They don't care whether you der live nor die. Oi der want un cut.'

'It's too early for that,' I told him.

'Oi don't want to be kept about till it der suit you. Oi want un done now.' He could probably be heard not only in the waiting room but down the road.

I soothed him as best I could, told him to go home and rest and I would call on him in two days.

'What on earth did you do to make him so angry?' Miss Woodruff asked. 'Dr. Ballard would have run him out of the surgery. Disgraceful behaviour. I don't know what patients are coming to.' Panel and parish patients seemed to be her natural enemies unless they were quiet, respectful, grateful and uncritical.

The moment I entered his house a couple of days later Charlie Chiswick became abusive again.

He lived with a good looking wife and two children in one of a row of miners' cottages. The house was spotlessly clean and fresh. There was the usual smart front room — little used except at Christmas and on special occasions — and the back kitchen and living room with its fire at the range always burning — thanks to free coal — summer and winter. Like the other miners Charlie would come home from work each day black and grimed with coal dust and take his bath in front of the kitchen fire. His wife's prime duty was to scrub his back. Few 'working class' families were as clean as the miners because the man would usually insist on the rest of the family bathing as regularly as he did. The Chiswicks were a solid reliable people and Charlie though usually quiet was a pleasant enough chap to deal with.

'Why is it so long getting better?' he asked.

'It's early days,' I said.

'It's costing me good money this, you know. Half pay comp. is no good to I.'

'It shouldn't be too long. Ten days to a fortnight.'

'And how am I supposed to live for a fortnight on eighteen bob a week?'

This was difficult to answer but as I didn't feel any direct responsibility for the state of the economy I must have made a gesture to this effect. By this time I was trying to act as the professional observer unaffected by needling or abuse.

'It's no use you saying you don't care. It's your job to get 'un right, and quick.'

'Keep on with the poultices,' I said. 'I'll look in again at the end of the week.'

'End of the week.' His voice rose. 'That's no good. I want that knee put right.'

It was on the tip of my tongue to say he needed a magician not a doctor but he was obviously distressed so I held my peace.

Three days later I saw him again. He was very quiet at first and I supposed he was resigned to the facts of the situation. Then just before I left he said, 'I've reported this to the police, you know.'

'What have they got to do with it?'

'I were reading in the paper. Where is it Mother? There you are.' He handed me a copy of a daily paper with a minor headline 'Doctor held negligent'. I forget the nature of the case but it was quite irrelevant.

'What do you expect me to do for you?' I asked.

'Cure it. That's what.' He was becoming aggressive again.

'Would you like me to get another doctor to see you?'

'No I 'ouldn't. You'm only trying to get out of it. I want that put right.'

'I'm afraid it's coming up to a head,' I said. 'We may have to lance it.'

'I don't care what you do but get on with it. Cut it now. Go on.'

'It's not ready yet. If we cut it now we shall only get blood out of it. You've got to wait patiently. There's nothing else to be done.'

'I b'aint going to wait. I want that done now. Come on.'

I had had enough. As far as I was concerned there were limits to scientific observation of people's behaviour. 'Listen to me Chiswick,' I said. 'There's nothing more to be done than what I've told you. Poultices, rest, and wait. I shall open it when it's ready and not before. You can either take my word for it or get another doctor.'

He stared at me as though he would attack me but for his injured leg. Then his wife put her arm round him and spoke some soothing words. 'He's all upset, Doctor. He doesn't mean to be rude.'.

Suddenly Charlie began to weep and I felt ashamed of myself. Tears rolled down his face and he said nothing more. I was puzzled and spoke gently to him, promising to come in again next day.

At the next visit he spoke not a word and two days later I got him into hospital for incision and a day or two's rest and after treatment.

We did our own minor surgery and I didn't trouble Tom

Wyburn over this. The usual procedure was to ask anyone of the medical staff who happened to be in the hospital to give gas when it was needed. Bill Beverley gave the gas while I did the incision of the abscess. Afterwards Bill went off chatting to the Matron and I prepared to leave too.

Suddenly pandemonium broke out and everyone seemed to be shouting at once. I went into the men's ward where I had just left Charlie lying quietly in bed. He was out of bed and shouting at the top of his voice. 'Clear out o' here. Go on all on yer. Out o' my bedroom.' And he began to lay about him, tearing bedclothes off the other beds and even trying to rip someone's bandage off. I grabbed him from behind and tried to push him back towards his bed but he was too strong for me. At last I realised the significance of his strange behaviour during the past week. He was literally raving mad.

His recently incised knee gave him pain so automatically he tore at the bandage and managed to remove the drainage tubing. Blood flowed freely and with every second that passed the place looked more like a slaughter house.

'The straight jacket,' I called out, 'and get hold of anyone, doctors, porters, anyone.' But before help arrived Charlie had got hold of a Balkan beam — a heavy six foot bar of iron that was attached to a bed frame for cases of fracture of the leg. With this lethal weapon he began a systematic attack on me sweeping it over a wide arc and so far missing me by inches. I was fairly strong but he was stronger and had no inhibitions about doing grievously bodily harm to anyone in his way. None of the male patients were in a condition to help and there followed an undignified struggle. A sturdy nurse helped to push him back towards his bed but he brushed us both off and took another swing with the iron bar. Then catching him off balance I wrestled with him again.

After what seemed a long time but was probably only a period of about a minute Bill Beverley arrived on the scene. We got poor Charlie on the floor and very soon had the straight jacket on him and lifted him into bed.

Matron Pang's naturally ruddy complexion turned a deeper red as she stood looking on without a hair out of place. 'You'll get him away Doctor, won't you? We've got no one here to manage a man like that.' She seemed to suggest that I was very much to blame for admitting such a case.

When I had straightened my clothes and run a hand through my ruffled hair I retired to the out patient department to remove the blood stains mixed with pus that had dispersed themselves thoroughly on my coat and trousers. As we cleaned ourselves up I said to Bill, 'That was a nice tackle.'

'Not often you get a chance like that,' he laughed and I was glad the patient's relatives were not within hearing. They might not have understood.

I got Charlie into the Mental Hospital the same evening. He must have had some sort of toxic psychosis because he recovered completely in a few days. Afterwards he was as quiet and docile as you could wish. He remembered nothing of the escapade but was told in no uncertain terms by someone or other that he might have murdered his doctor and ended up in Broadmoor. He was never very easy with me after this and eventually changed over to Tom Wyburn.

If your knee is inflamed you are a pleasant ordinary patient but if your brain is inflamed you are possessed by a devil. I felt really sorry for Charlie Chiswick.

I learnt that in observing the strange behaviour of patients — and other people too — the rare and unexpected is all too often lurking in the background. With more experience I might have recognised the sudden character change and the violent alterations of mood as something more than an emotional disturbance.

When I went back to the surgery after my battle with Charlie that afternoon Miss Woodruff had already heard about it. How gossip travelled so fast in her direction I never discovered.

At first she sounded concerned for my welfare. 'Are you alright?' she said, laughing cheerfully. 'You aren't used to fighting are you? Pity Dr. Wyburn wasn't there. He's so strong he'd have got him under control straight away. Or Dr. Ballard, he'd have knocked him down with one hand tied behind his back.'

What a strange woman she was. Anyone who gave trouble had to be knocked down, or thrashed, or hanged or otherwise forced to bow to authority. Had she been a German' one would have expected her to be a founder member of the Nazi party.

I ground my teeth but managed to say 'Poor chap' as I gained the tranquillity of my own room.

8

One of our problems for the first year or two was that of language. When a patient comes to you and says 'Wen oider boiden glutch derpenoi crool' you wonder for a moment or perhaps longer whether he is talking English or some foreign language from Eastern Europe. Wireless sets were a rarity and speech was little influenced by the accents of radio announcers.

I came of course to love the warm west country sounds in time and when, during the war, I met in North Africa some men from a unit of engineers who came from Frome in Somerset, I almost wept for joy. I was working in a hospital tent when I heard them outside. The soft rounded vowel sounds seemed to caress my ear drums and in a moment I was outside talking to them.

Some time in the spring of nineteen thirty one I was called to see a man I regarded as old — he must have been in his fifties — who spoke the old language. He lived alone in an old stone cottage. The district had been misnamed 'Belle Vue' and consisted of miners' cottages built in the last century. Georgie Grindle's cottage was at the most derelict end and was something of a museum piece. You entered by what had once been the parlour but was now like a dark walled prison cell. A tiny fireplace acted as a receptacle for a few old tins otherwise the room was bare. The floor was stone, those flag stones coveted now as ideal for terraces in large houses.

The living room at the back had in it a table and chair, a heap of coal in one corner and a fire in the kitchen range which was kept going winter and summer. At the back of the table against the wall were a saucepan or two and various articles of food, some bread, cheese, a few rashers of bacon and some unpeeled potatoes. In the chair by the fire sat Georgie with his ragged beard, long grey hair and piercing eyes that shone through his heavy eyebrows.

One thing more I always remember is the sticky area of floor round the fire. The reason for this became abvious when he coughed and spat inaccurately in the direction of the flames. He stared at me, coughed and spat.

'What is it Georgie?' I said.

'You'm darctor. You tell oi.'

'It sounds as though you've got bronchitis,' I hazarded.

Slowly he undid the top button of some sort of clothing he had on that encased his chest and neck. It exposed about four or five square inches of skin to allow examination.

'I need a bit more clothes off,' I said.

'Want oi to ketch me death loikely,' he said and began to cough again.

When I had dodged the resulting secretions on their way to the fireplace I undid as much of his clothing as I could without actually engaging in fisticuffs with him. He was feverish and had a fairly severe bronchitis but in all probability a pretty good heart. He needed fresh air and reasonable nursing — as well as a good blanket bath — and this was impossible where he was. The only available hospital bed would be in the poor law institution four miles away and this would have to be arranged through Mr. Swallow the relieving officer, a man whose duty it was to apply public funds to those in dire need.

'I think we'll have to get you into hospital Georgie. You've got bronchitis.'

'Wod if oi arve? Oi bent gwine to no arspital.'

'I can't do much to help you here.'

'Yew give oi zum vusick loike Doc. Ballard useter. Brown and strong wi' plenty o' garlic.' He coughed again. I side-stepped.

I did my best to persuade him but it was a losing battle. The Union, as the poor law institution was called, was according to popular opinion no place to get better in. You went there to die not to get better.

'Is there anyone to come in and get you some hot drinks?'

'Don't want no wummin yere. Yew give oi the vusick. Thic be arl oi der need.'

'How will you get your medicine?' I asked.

'Yew write un deown. Oi'll get 'e.'

I did and left feeling as useless as I had ever done in my life.

I have always disliked fleas and was bound to have one or two after contact with Georgie so I went straight home and called on Jessica for help. She knew the routine very well. I stripped in the bathroom handing her each article of clothing which she examined and shook over the bath. When a flea fell into the white bath she pounced on it with her bar of soap, dug the flea out of the soap and washed it down the hand basin. When I was stripped she examined my body carefully and pronounced me all clear. I dressed and was ready to go out again. This time only two fleas had emerged. The whole process only took about ten minutes.

I asked Martha and Mary to look in and see Georgie later in the day. A neighbour moved a bed downstairs and got him into it with plenty of pillows. The bedclothes couldn't be said to reach an acceptable level of hygiene but things were a bit better. Martha and Mary did their best to give him a blanket bath but I gathered this was quite a story in itself. We could do no more on day one.

Days two three and four were pretty much a repeat of day one. Then I met Martha over another case and she told me that Georgie's daughter had arrived from Canada.

'No one can have sent for her surely?' I said.

'It's just coincidence. She's home on holiday. She hasn't been home for five years.'

'What does she think of the old man?'

Martha laughed. 'I think she blames us for most things.'

'How does she work that out?'

'She says he ought to be in hospital.'

'So he should but he won't go.'

'She's coming to see you.'

I had been warned.

The daughter — Mrs. Beasley — arrived at the surgery and was the first to come in to see me. She explained who she was in an exaggerated Canadian accent and said she was absolutely disgusted at her father's plight.

'You mustn't blame him too much.'

'Blame him,' she broke in, 'of course I don't blame *him*. No proper care when he's seriously ill. It's not his fault.'

'Whose fault do you suggest it is?' I asked.

'Them as are responsible for his health of course.' She glared at me. 'What do you reckon to do about him?'

'I can't force him into hospital against his will and he is determined to stay where he is.'

'But he can't stay there. The place is worse nor a pigsty.' The accent was half Canadian and half Somerset now.

'I couldn't agree more.'

'And tis no use saying he won't go to hospital. I'll see that he do go if proper arrangements be made.'

'Then I'll ask Mr. Swallow to see him and arrange his admission to Clutton at once.'

'Clutton! That's the workhouse.'

'It's the only place there is a bed for him. The Cottage Hospital is reserved for surgical cases.'

'I never heard such rubbish in my life. Why in Canada he'd 've been in hospital from the start and better by now as like as not.'

'He's not in Canada. And if you will undertake to persuade him to go to Clutton I will make the arrangements.'

Perhaps I looked a little smug. I was looking forward to the contest between father and daughter.

She glared at me again and got up to go. Then in the heat of the moment the Canadian accent disappeared altogether. 'I der feel upsat and ashamed. My Vather.'

'Don't worry,' I said. 'He's much better than he was a day or two ago.'

'No thanks to no one yere if er be.' And she marched out.

Mr. Swallow the 'relieving officer' was a smallish man with what you might call a first degree Somerset accent. He could be gentle but could be as tough as old boots when necessary.

'Well George,' he said, 'I hear you are needing a little help.'

George stared at him, coughed, spat and missed him by inches.

'A bad chest,' Mr. Swallow went on. 'The doctor tells me you need to be in hospital for a day or two.'

'Oi be stayin' yere. 'Arspital!'

'Not if the doctor says you can't, Father.'

'Vather!' the old man mocked. 'Twere allus Dard till you went out yarnder.'

'He'll go Mr. Swallow.'

'Yew go back where 'ee come vram gal. Oi be stayin' yere.'

'The doctor is afraid you'll get worse if you stay here, George,' said Mr. Swallow. 'Best come in for a day or two.' He began to write on an admission form.

'Will er be vatched tonight?' asked Mrs. Beasley.

Mr. Swallow looked at his watch. 'I think that's best. I'll send an ambulance in say an hour and a half.'

George was silent.

'I shall be glard to know 'e'm bein' prarperly looked arfter.' Mrs. Beasley gave me a sidelong glance.

'I shall telephone the doctor in the hospital and tell him all about you, George,' I said. 'You'll be home again in a few days.'

'An Oi'll come an' see 'ee every day, Vather.' Mrs. Beasley's accent was now approaching her father's in richness as her confidence grew.

'Right,' said Mr. Swallow. 'We'll say eight o'clock then.'

It all seemed too easy but George had only been saving his breath and his energy. Slowly he got out of bed and shuffled to the door.

'Not yet Dard, they'll come an' fetch 'ee presently.'

We had all of course underestimated George Grindle. There followed a blistering attack on all and sundry in language that Merlin the Wizard might have understood but I certainly didn't — except for a word here and there which gave me the gist of his meaning. 'Out all on yer — 'cept in a box — blarst 'ee — vetch policeman Sperring — ' Then he began to cough and presently I helped him back to his chair.

Lamely I uttered the obvious understatement, 'I'm afraid he won't go.' And Mrs. Beasley went out into the yard at the back silently admitting defeat.

Mr. Swallow and I looked at each other. He knew when to give in. 'We could only move him if he became non-volitional,' he said quietly and began to pack away his papers.

'Which in his case means unconscious,' I added. 'I'm sorry to have got you out for nothing. We'll manage him here. It was his daughter who was so keen to move him.'

To tell the truth I was quite pleased at the way things had turned out. I should have been sorry to have pushed George into hospital against his will and he was not seriously ill. I had enjoyed seeing him deal with his daughter too.

When I was alone with Georgie again he slowly regained his composure. 'That bloody gel,' he spluttered, 'wot do 'er want comin yere upzatin volks? Oi were doin voin wi' 'em nusses till 'er did come.'

But Mrs. Beasley was not beaten yet. Next day I had a telephone call from a physician in the city. He had been asked to come out and see a Mr. George Grindle. For a moment I thought I ought to warn him off then on the spur of the moment I changed my mind. Let the woman pay a consultant's fee. It would relieve her feelings of guilt towards her father which were probably the cause of her aggressiveness.

Dr. McNeil came out late that evening, met me at my house and I warned him what he must expect. To give him his due he made a good show of the consultation. He made a careful examination and found a normal temperature, a recovering bronchitis, a normal heart and a mouthful of carious teeth. He ordered the teeth to be extracted after the convalescence and then proceeded to tell the daughter what she must do to clean up the house. The thought of getting George to the dentist was pure comedy but the advice made a nice tidy package.

'My fee would normally be ten guineas,' he went on. 'I shall accept half of that and you will spend the other five guineas in cleaning the house — unless you decide to do it yourself. The coal must of course be removed and this floor scrubbed. With reasonable nursing he will soon recover.'

Mrs. Beasley was flabbergasted. She had expected an ally who would place the blame for her father's bad habits and general condition on my shoulders. She had met her master.

'On second thoughts,' said Dr. McNeil, 'I will have the full fee and give five guineas to Dr. Lane who will spend it as he thinks fit for the benefit of the house.' The suggestion that

Mrs. Beasley was not to be trusted with the spending of the money was lost on her.

Presently he counted out the notes and coins of his fee with great care, handed half to me and swept out of the room.

When I said goodnight to him outside I asked whether he had a good routine for catching fleas. 'I have my boy, I have. I was in general practice myself once.'

In case there should be any complaint of fee splitting I handed the five guineas to Mrs. Beasley saying she would know how best to spend it on her father's house. She was quite unabashed. 'Thank God I live in Canada,' she said. 'This country is goin' from bad to worse. Of course darctors always stick together, everyone do know that. I shall report this whole case to the papers.'

I let her babble on for a few minutes. It seemed to do her good. I didn't see her again after that evening. I saw her husband a few years later but that is another story.

Georgie soon recovered. 'Trouble wi' yew young darctors,' he said, 'is yer wunt du nuthin on yer own. Speshalust!' he spat the word out. 'Arl oi needed were prarper vusick. Your'n weren't as powful as Darctor Ballard's. Nothin' loike.'

'Never mind Georgie. You're better anyway.'

'Oi shud uv bin arlroight any road. Speshalust.'

I fancied his eyes were not as piercing as they were at first. Not a bad old chap.

9

When the twentieth century becomes part of history the insanity of two world wars will be set against the advances in medicine and the incredible conclusion will be reached that in terms of human life the balance is about even. In nineteen thirty one however, the discovery of chemotherapeutic agents was five years in the future.

A young couple came briefly into my life in the spring of that year. The young man was a giant with huge chest and powerful arms, the girl by contrast was almost fairylike, quick, dark, vivid and pretty. I was reminded of John Ridd and Lorna Doone. They were on their honeymoon, travelling west by horsedrawn caravan. Intending to stay only one night in our district, they parked the caravan in a field in what was then the outskirts of the town. The field has long since been turned into the tidy gardens of a housing estate but at the time it was bordered by thorn hedges and lush with grass dappled by clusters of cowslips.

I was sent for that evening because the man had a violent shivering attack followed by pain in the chest. Pneumonia. The warning signs were nearly as foreboding to us then as those of cancer. The churchyards of the world record the deaths of countless young men and women over the centuries many of whom died of pneumonia. That evening you could feel the leathery pleural rub and even hear it faintly without a stethoscope. Kaolin poultice to the chest with some aspirin compound to relieve the pain were all I had to offer.

The caravan was spotlessly clean and airy — as well kept inside as a millionaire's yacht. The dark wood gleamed and a whole lot of brass fittings shone in the evening sun.

Next day the pneumonia was well developed and the inevitable eight days of anxiety, pain and weary struggle to breathe and to live stretched ahead like a long nightmare.

My first reaction was that it was impossible to treat the man where he was. I suggested that he should be admitted to the hospital in the city twelve miles away but the wife's response was almost violent. She could, she must, nurse him herself she said. She was strong and young and had some nursing experience. To let him go into strange hands in a large impersonal hospital was unthinkable.

'It would be safer for him to be in hospital,' I told her, 'where he can be kept in the best position for his breathing, where oxygen can be given constantly and where he can be watched night and day.'

'I can watch him night and day,' she said, 'and can't you get oxygen for him here?'

I admitted I could but was doubtful whether she could nurse him alone for so long even with the help of the district nurses. After a while she began to hesitate and asked whether there was a 'village hospital'. When I said there was she agreed to let him go there if it were absolutely necessary because she would be able to stay close to him and sit with him much of the time. I understood her distress very well. I felt sure my own wife with her nursing experience would react in the same way if I had been the patient. At the same time our Cottage Hospital admitted only surgical cases and I knew it might prove impossible to get him in, but as this was a life and death affair I agreed to try.

I tackled Tom Wyburn first, telling him the facts of the case and pointing out that good nursing and oxygen were our only weapons against pneumonia. 'Surely,' I said, 'the nursing facilities at the hospital couldn't be put to better use.'

He hesitated for a bit and then after appearing to give the matter careful thought he said, 'It would be the thin end of the wedge. Once we admitted a medical case we should be inundated with them. There would be no room even for acute surgery. You see, Lane, medical cases take so long to get better — if they ever do.'

I didn't want to be side-tracked on to the old argument. 'It would be easy enough,' I said, 'to have a small subcommittee to decide which cases were absolutely essential. This case for instance where there is only a caravan to house the man and only an inexperienced young wife to nurse him is the sort of case that couldn't be refused.'

'There's really nothing that can be done in hospital that couldn't be done outside. Do you suggest that four-hourly temperature taking and an occasional blanket bath would make all that difference?'

'A hospital bed where you could keep him well propped up all the time and where the oxygen can be properly controlled would certainly make a difference. It could well make the difference between life and death. This man's bed is against the side of the caravan. It takes a superhuman effort just to keep him upright for instance and bedpanning with his weight is virtually impossible.'

'I wouldn't object to having him in as a special case in the side room but I don't think the other members of the staff would like it. Would you like to ask Matron? If you can get her on your side it would help.'

I was getting to know Tom Wyburn by this time. He had rigid ideas about the priority of surgical cases but he was far from unsympathetic towards suffering of any sort. He merely felt that medical diseases were a sort of act of God that man was virtually powerless to alleviate. His resistance to my suggestion was slackening to some extent.

I went to see Matron Pang and her first reaction was to say she hadn't enough staff for such a heavy case.

'It's no heavier than nursing an empyema,' I pointed out. 'Why admit a case of pneumonia only when it has become necessary to use a knife on the complication of pus in the chest? Why not admit the case in time to prevent the complication altogether?'

She evaded my beautiful logic. 'You'd have to get the hospital committee to agree Doctor. I couldn't admit this man without their instructions.'

I then called on one of the senior members of the committee. He was very sympathetic but adamant that such an old-standing rule couldn't be changed overnight for my benefit. I

81

began to feel angry and frustrated. If this man dies, I said to myself, I shall raise all hell.

I was still fuming over the hard boiled rigidity of the stuffed shirts who ran the hospital when I ran into Paul King in the little hospital car park. I blurted out my story as I would have done to anyone at that moment and to my surprise he was not only sympathetic but ready, he said, to back me to the hilt. The fact that his influence was practically nil didn't occur to me at that time but he too wanted to have the right to treat medical cases in the hospital.

'This crazy rule,' I said, 'will result in murder one day.'

'Exactly. Blaythwaite is on the committee. Have you spoken to him? He might help. Try him.'

We were in agreement and it was pleasant to have him on my side for a change. The two junior and powerless members of the staff were in favour of revolution.

I telephoned Blaythwaite early after lunch but he was out. I rang again at four o'clock but he was busy in his surgery. Finally I got hold of him in the late evening. I told him my story with all the force at my command adding that Paul King agreed with me.

'What will you have to drink?' he said. 'Whisky or a glass of port?'

'Oh a little whisky and water, thankyou,' I said.

He prepared it with all the care he would have lavished on the prime minister or the Archbishop of Canterbury. 'Now then,' he said at last, 'you have a case of pneumonia and you think he would be better off in the Cottage Hospital.'

'Yes, I think good nursing in the hospital might well save his life.'

'You may be quite right,' he said, 'but the difficulty is changing the rules.'

'But surely when a life is at stake the rules must be broken.'

'And suppose your man took the last bed and we couldn't admit a serious pit accident?'

'The accident case would have to go to the City Hospital.'

'Yes, I'm sure they would help us but why shouldn't your man go there?'

And here of course was the weak spot in my argument. 'I

couldn't persuade the wife to let him,' I said. 'She has only been married a few weeks and is determined to nurse him herself unless she can be with him all the time as she thinks she might in the Cottage Hospital.'

'But you see if we were going to change our policy and admit medical cases as well as surgical we should not only have to persuade the committee but the public at large. Every penny of our funds comes from the pockets of the local people. They have asked for a hospital for mining accidents and surgical cases. We should have to launch a campaign to get them to change their minds. Then the committee could act but you can't do that over night.'

I realised at last that I had asked for the impossible. Very well then, we must nurse the man in his caravan.

The prospect was gloomy enough but a complication appeared straight away in the person of Farmer Hookham. John — I must call him that because I remember him by no other name — had not felt well when they arrived and had parked the caravan in his field without permission. Not unnaturally the farmer was incensed. It would soon be haymaking time and a caravan in his field with trafficking to and fro was the last thing he wanted. The actual loss of grass was not very great but the attitude of a small farmer who felt the world in the shape of small boys and caravans was against him anyway was easy to understand. What was more the tethered horse was busy eating the grass that should have been his hay crop.

Before my visit the second morning Farmer Hookham appeared and demanded immediate removal. The girl was frightened by his manner and begged him to let her stay at least until the doctor arrived. He could hardly help agreeing and the problem was placed firmly on my inexperienced shoulders.

I went to see Farmer Hookham, explained the serious nature of the illness and asked if he would be generous enough to allow the caravan to remain where it was. They would pay whatever rent he asked.

He was a short square man with red face and bulging blue eyes. And he was very angry. 'I'm not going to rent my field to anyone. If I start that every bloody gypsy in Somerset will be setting up there. They've got to get out.'

'He ought not to be moved. He's very ill. And they are not gypsies.'

'What about the hospital? Don't I pay good money every year to keep that going? What's it for if not for people like that with no home to go to?'

I tried to explain that the hospital only admitted surgical cases but as I still regarded this rule as quite idiotic I was probably not very convincing.

When Farmer Hookham began to rave about the hospital and the injustice of life in general I thought I was winning. Perhaps if I got him to let off enough steam he would go away and leave us alone. This is exactly what he did but as I discovered later it was no thanks to me.

It was next day that I realised we had a staunch ally in the farmer's wife. This marvellous woman arrived at the caravan while I was there and after a whispered exchange it turned out that she had agreed to undertake sewage disposal and to provide water, milk and eggs. She brought a bucket of clean water and went off with another bucket containing the waste products of the previous twenty four hours. How the young woman I must call 'Lorna' had won her heart I didn't know. Somehow Mrs. Hookham kept her husband at bay for several days but we had not heard the last of him by any means.

Three times a day I called and then four. The district nurses — Martha and Mary — went in three times a day. Their sleeves rolled up and purposeful looks gave a fine impression of confidence.

For two nights the patient had no sleep. If he failed to get rest on the third night the outlook was bleak. Morphia was our only weapon and this could depress the respiration enough to put an intolerable strain on the heart. This was the old dilemma faced by physicians for centuries. I gave him a small dose of morphia hoping it would give him at least a few hours sleep. He had practically none and next day his pulse rate rose still further. I brought oxygen from the hospital ready for the first deterioration in colour and from time to time gave him small doses of brandy. The struggle went on through the fourth, fifth, and sixth days, and still there were two more before the crisis. By this time he was only half conscious and slightly cyanosed whenever the oxygen was stopped. His pulse hammered on at a hundred and twenty to the minute. The girl seemed to have grown smaller, her eyes red and her face lined.

It is not easy to encourage relatives when the case looks hopeless. 'It won't be long now,' I said. 'If he can hold out another two days he could get better quite suddenly.'

'Two days,' she wailed and it seemed an eternity.

By about the eighth day the heart had been strained to the limit and the body's defences were at the same time raised to their highest pitch against the invading organism — usually the pneumococcus. One of two things could happen very quickly. The defences might quite suddenly turn the tide and overwhelm the bacteria. Then the thick exudate in the lungs would loosen so that the resulting debris could be coughed up. The relief would be immediate and the straining heart could relax. On the other hand the defences might not reach the necessary level quickly enough and the heart would fail. In cases of pneumonia everyone knew that in the last few hours the result could go either way. It was as dramatic as the efforts to drag a man back from an imminent fall over a thousand foot cliff. The result was an all or nothing, life or death decision.

Doctor and nurses were always deeply involved in these cases and relatives could think of nothing else as minutes and hours passed with desperate slowness. However strong the patient there was no knowing how long the thrashing straining heart could hold out against such an onslaught. In this case the heart was young and here was the hope and tragedy of the whole situation.

In the final days I was in and out of the caravan many times a day. It was difficult to keep away or to concentrate on other patients. The eighth day came at last and on the same day Farmer Hookham turned up again, this time with Police Constable Bailey. They must have armed themselves with a court order to have us moved and just at the critical time.

'Now then,' said Farmer Hookham, 'listen to what the law's got to say.'

To do him justice P.C. Bailey was uneasy. 'The owner of this caravan is trespassing,' he said, 'and causing damage to private property.'

I knew Bailey fairly well by this time. If he had had any threatening documents he would have flourished them. In any case they would move the patient over my dead body if at all. I glared at them.

'The caravan will have to be moved forthwith,' said Bailey.

'The man is too ill to move.'

'I'd like to see him please.'

We admitted him and one glance at the flushed face, the oxygen cylinder and the sound of the grunting breathing shook his confidence and I seized the opportunity. 'If we move him now,' I said, 'there will be a charge of manslaughter and it won't be against me.'

There was silence for a moment then some angry muttering and the two of them went off, Farmer Hookham threatening dire retribution. So that was that. But we still had to face the crisis.

Late that evening I walked along the now familiar path. I can still remember the scene. My pulse rose as I approached the door. Usually I could hear the rapid breathing from several yards away but there was absolute silence. It could only, I thought, be the silence of death.

Seconds later I was by the bed. He was sweating profusely, breathing quietly and bubbling gently in the chest. His pulse was weak but slower and he spoke coherently for the first time in days. 'What time is it?' he said. 'Time I was up.'

I turned to see the tears streaming down the girl's face.

It usually took three months for a young adult to recover from lobar pneumonia but John must have been as strong as an ox. In a week he was walking quite well and expanding his enormous lungs by deep breaths of good country air. A few days later they demanded my bill which was for six or seven pounds. They thanked me profusely for all the world as though I had saved his life, and next day the exact money was given me wrapped up in a crisp white five pound note. I think Farmer Hookham must have been paid generously for his field because he became very friendly after this.

I sat with them once or twice in their caravan.

'How did you manage to get Mrs. Hookham on your side?' I asked the girl.

86

'I expect it was one farmer's wife to another,' she said. 'She's been a farmer's wife for twenty years and I for only a month but we seemed to understand each other.'

John was a farmer from Devonshire and they had planned this rather novel form of honeymoon months before. Through Dorset and Hampshire they had travelled without a care in the world until the evening I first met them.

'Did anyone ever tell you you reminded them of John Ridd and Lorna Doone?' I asked one day.

'Oh, yes,' he laughed. 'Pity my name's not Ridd.'

And I still can't remember what it was. After such a gruelling episode it seemed only fair to indulge in a little romance over his ancestry.

They moved off some time later and the last I saw of them the great horse was drawing them at a sedate trot along the high road over the Mendips towards Wells.

10

The telephone exchange in Melbrook was manually operated by Mr. Brown. This simple statement covers a multitude of that gentleman's activities. He was a friendly man, always helpful and in the dark hours of the early morning his warm west country accent could be curiously reassuring. If you had a long conversation on the phone during the night you could usually hear his heavy breathing as he waited for you to finish. Sometimes he actually snored. Of course we used carefully veiled language about patients, otherwise every vestige of confidence would be breached. Apart from this no one minded his hearing of our activities.

I remember on one occasion being called to a neighbouring village to see a sick child during the night. While I was there another patient in the same village telephoned for me. When the second caller asked for my number at the exchange Mr. Brown spoke to him. 'You want the doctor?' he said. 'Well he's over your way now. Down at Martin's at Shell House. You'll catch him there if you do go along. Save him coming all the way home and out again.'

The conversation was reported to me by the second caller who was waiting for me by my car when I left the first house. This was one of the blessings of personal service and I mention it because it has a bearing on my recollections.

One summer night — it was a few weeks after our first baby was born, probably in July nineteen thirty one — Mr. Brown played a more active part in our affairs than usual. John Symonds was away and our usual threesome in the operating theatre was one short. What was more for that one night Bill Beverley was in London. As junior partner I was generally called on to 'wash up' and act as assistant to Tom Wybrun. In the absence of John Symonds I became anaesthetist and one of the hospital sisters would act as assistant. The routine surgery was done on Tuesday afternoons and emergencies of course at any time — often during the night. There was never any question of leaving things till the morning because, apart from the patient's welfare, the three of us could spare the time better during the night than during the day. On the whole they were pleasant affairs — an extra camaraderie develops on a night job when the rest of the world is asleep. On this July night however things didn't go according to plan and I was faced with a painful conflict of loyalties.

Soon after midnight the anguished voice of a friend of mine roused me from the clinging vapours of sleep. 'Something awful has happened' he said 'could you come round at once?'

'What is it?' I asked hoping for time to wake up.

'I can't tell you on the phone but please come quickly.'

His urgent voice made me hurry. I expected disaster and found it.

Edward Philpotts met me at the door of his house, a jersey over his pyjamas and hair on end. 'Beatrice has killed herself,' he said shaking uncontrollably. This was such a contrast to his usual suave manner that I was rather shaken myself.

'How?' I asked as we went up the stairs two at a time. 'What happened?'

'She took a whole box of sleeping tablets.'

'What tablets were they?'

'You gave them to her in the surgery the other day.'

'That was only phenobarbitone. How many did she take?'

'She's emptied the bottle.'

'How long ago?'

'Not more than three quarters of an hour.'

'She couldn't be dead in that time,' I reassured him.

By this time I was by her bed. Beatrice Philpotts lay completely relaxed, black hair spread over her pillow and an ashen pallor over her regular features. I pulled up an eyelid. Her pupils were half dilated and her eyes moved a little but her breathing was so shallow as to seem absent at first glance. I couldn't feel a pulse and slid a hand under her left breast. In my hurry I couldn't feel a heart beat either but with a stethoscope the heart beat was audible. I ran a hand over her abdomen but there was nothing there — no obvious pregnancy and no distension.

Edward was fingering the empty bottle of tablets. In those days they were not labelled but I had given Beatrice fifty half grain tablets of phenobarbitone when she had consulted me with a complaint of unexplained attacks of nervous tension. They were to be taken when necessary. If she had taken the whole fifty tablets at once it was just possible they could be fatal but very unlikely. Fatal doses were usually much larger.

'Stomach wash-out,' I said. 'We'd better do it here. Get a lot of newspapers, a jug of warm water and a bucket or a big bowl.'

She was an attractive woman, generally happy and vivacious, and I found it hard to believe she would make a serious attempt at suicide. I got her on her left side with her head well back and slid my stomach tube down her oesophagus. There was some retching which reassured me but not enough to give me any real confidence.

A stomach wash-out is no picnic under any circumstances, but in her state of stupor she wouldn't feel much of it. We poured a pint of warm water into the funnel and syphoned it back into the bucket. No tablets returned so a good deal of what she had taken must have been absorbed. It was just possible that she had a lethal dose of the stuff in her system. I repeated the wash-out, then, as I withdrew the tube, there was more retching and I fancied the breathing was a little deeper. I sat feeling her pulse. It was still weak but easily palpable now.

'Get some strong coffee,' I said, 'and as soon as she can swallow we'll give her some.'

'Is she going to be alright?' Edward was looking in need of resuscitation himself.

'The smallest amount that could be fatal would be something like forty or fifty tablets and if it's less than an hour since she took them we shall have got some of the barbiturate out of her. She should be alright. Why did she do it?'

Edward groaned. 'It's my fault. It's all my fault. She accused me of flirting with one of my secretaries and I got furious. We had a hell of a row and I actually hit her. Then she ran upstairs and I was alone for a bit, calming down. I went up to see her at about half past eleven and she told me to go away. I don't think she had taken any then. She was lively enough anyway. I tried to apologise but she was so furious that I gave up the effort and came down stairs again. I don't know what came over her. She's never been like this before. Just before I rang you up I got ready for bed. I was going to sleep in another room. I went in to see her and I thought she was dead. The empty bottle was by her bed.'

'You get the coffee. She'll be alright.' Her eyes were moving from side to side and her breathing was definitely deeper. I talked to her and thought she responded a little but when the coffee arrived it was impossible to get her to take any.

She got no better and I began to worry. Some people were much more sensitive than others to phenobarbitone and we had no effective antidote. There was nothing to be done now except to wait and give stimulants when she could swallow. After about half an hour her breathing was still very shallow and I said, 'I think we ought to get an ambulance and send her in to the City Hospital.'

'Must we? We shall never live this down if everyone gets to hear about it.'

'There's no need for anyone to know.'

'There are some who'd make it their business to find out. What can they do in hospital that you can't do?'

'Not a lot.' I didn't add that the main value of the hospital in this case was to shift the responsibility on to someone else.

'We'll wait half an hour and see if she improves. We've done the most important thing — washing out the stomach.'

Then the telephone rang.

'Who the hell's that?' Edward muttered.

It was Tom Wyburn for me. Fortunately or unfortunately I had written down the name Philpotts on a piece of paper by my bed as I took the message and so my wife knew where I was.

'I'm afraid I need your help,' he said. 'A perforation, already five or six hours old and we'll have to get on with it. As you know Symonds is away so will you come and give the anaesthetic?'

91

'I can't leave here at the moment,' I said.

'How long will you be?'

'An hour or more.'

'That's too long.' His voice became edgy. 'What have you got there?'

'I can't explain over the phone. I'm sorry but I really can't leave for a while. Can you get someone else?'

There was silence then 'No, I'm not prepared to ask anyone else. It's a matter of priorities. Which is more important, your case or my emergency.'

'Exactly,' I said. 'And for the moment mine has priority so far as I'm concerned. Could you come round here so that we can discuss it?' This seemed to be asking a good deal from a senior but there was nothing else I could do.

His voice became curt. 'Very well' and the line became very dead. I heard a little grunt from Mr. Brown before he cut off my end of the line.

When Wyburn arrived we solemnly retired to a separate room. 'What have you got?' he asked 'An acute heart failure?'

'No, an attempted suicide. Barbiturate poisoning. She's still deep nearly an hour after wash-out.'

'Then there's not much more you can do in the next hour. Why not come back when we've done the perforation?'

I was in a real dilemma. To leave an unconscious patient with no nurse at hand seemed very risky. If she vomited for instance while half conscious the result might be catastrophic. If she died I should never be forgiven. On the other hand I couldn't believe a perforation was all that urgent. Anyway Wyburn should get another anaesthetist. I dug my toes in. I mentioned Paul King's name but this was received with icy silence.

'Well, if you must stay,' he said at last, 'I'll wait an hour. Meet me in an hour at the hospital.'

'I'll either be there or phone you,' I promised.

We were back to the old problem of the priority, in Tom Wyburn's mind, of all surgical cases and this was nonsense here. Perhaps this was a good time to be absolutely firm and demonstrate the importance of a medical case. Not very sensibly I stoked up the fires of my obstinacy.

It may seem strange nowadays that we didn't telephone the nearest major hospital twelve miles away and ask them to admit the perforation. The answer is that such an idea would never occur to us. We had an operating theatre, a hospital bed, we did our own surgery and that was that.

For a while the dilemma tormented me. I could of course have insisted on sending Beatrice Philpotts to the City Hospital but I sympathised with Edward's feelings. All being well his other friends would never know about the attempted suicide. This, in a small town, would never be forgotten. As it was, the incident could be called a bad stomach upset from which one hoped she would soon recover. Sometimes a marriage could be cemented after a night of acute anxiety. Why should I send her in? There was nothing they could do in hospital that we couldn't do here.

At one moment I was convinced that my place was here, and the next the danger of delay in an acute perforation stared me in the face. This was much more dangerous in the days before penicillin. What was I to do if my patient had not recovered consciousness when the hour was up? The problem of priorities was new to me and so was the degree of tension that seemed to be growing between Wyburn and me.

I waited anxiously, trying stimulation of various sorts from time to time. Just before I was due to leave for the hospital I tried more vigorous efforts — cold towels, light slapping and lifting the head and shoulders. I thought she was improving but as I still couldn't get her to respond I didn't dare to leave her. Another half an hour might have seen a difference but I had promised to phone Wyburn in an hour and my time was up.

I decided I couldn't leave and the perforation would have to wait unless another anaesthetist could be found. I telephoned the hospital to say so. 'I'm sorry but I still can't leave,' I told Wyburn.

'Do you mind telling me why?'

'For fear of her vomiting and getting an inhalation pneumonia'

'Why can't you get the district nurses in?'

'That would make this whole business public. I've promised to keep it quiet.'

'Do you really mean that keeping things quiet,' the words were spoken with scathing intensity, 'is more important than a perforation being kept waiting? The risk to this man's life is increasing with every minute.'

I was almost defeated and on the point of giving in against my better judgement when another voice came on the line. It was Mr. Brown. 'Excuse me sir, but I couldn't help hearing what you were saying about the urgent case in the hospital. I happen to know there is a specialist staying with Dr. Blaythwaite — a specialist from London' the words were spoken with reverence. 'Perhaps he might be able to help. Only my suggestion of course.'

The voice not only brought a ray of hope but broke the tension that had been growing between us. Each thought the other was being unreasonable. There was a moment's silence then Wyburn spoke in his most measured tones. 'Thankyou Mr. Brown. It's most kind of you to offer the suggestion. We are in a little difficulty while Dr. Symonds is away. I'll telephone Dr. Blaythwaite.'

Mr. Brown's intervention had probably saved us from an open quarrel. Wyburn was to ring back if the visitor was unable to help.

I went up to see Beatrice Philpotts again and she was at last showing signs of responding to stimuli. I felt I had got away from the verge of a precipice just in time. With Bill Beverley or even John Symonds a brisk argument, even involving harsh words, would have been got over without much difficulty because my relationship with them both was easier. Tom Wyburn was different. He would have refused to talk about it and resorted to a cold politeness that kept you at a distance. He had probably been right in his assessment of the priorities in our two cases, and I had been obstinate, but this wouldn't have helped if we couldn't talk about it.

Beatrice was able to cough and swallow now and most of the danger had passed. A moment later Tom Wyburn was on the phone again. He sounded different.

'Any good?' I said.

'The specialist was a well known expert in tropical diseases.

Not, I fear, a useful anaesthetist.' He was almost laughing.

The atmosphere, previously charged with hostility, was now suddenly dissipated. I was able to say my patient had improved and I could leave her almost immediately. Mr. Brown's good intention had worked wonders.

When we had put the perforation patient back to bed I went to see Beatrice Philpotts again. Edward met me and was still worried. 'She's sleeping all the time,' he said.

'Well after all it is four o'clock in the morning,' I told him. 'She's bound to sleep heavily after that dose.'

I roused her once more and got a few words out of her. 'Why did you do it?' I asked her.

'Do what?' she said. And as she dozed off again I had my first laugh of the night.

So I left her and she made a complete recovery.

Next morning when Hannah Woodruff came to my room to hand over my morning messages she was in her 'I know something you don't' mood. This produced a degree of cheerfulness and exclamations like 'Things have been happening, haven't they?' or 'Who'd have thought it.'

It seemed a pity to rob her of her pleasure, and I gave her mild encouragement as I wrote out my visiting list. 'Who'd have thought what?' I asked.

'You had a busy night,' she countered.

'Yes, not much sleep last night.'

'I hear Mr. Brown at the telephone exchange was very helpful.'

'Yes, he did his best, bless him.'

'A specialist in tropical diseases.' The words were spoken with something between a chuckle, a gasp and a laugh. She was not quite at ease with me and was evidently forcing herself to this degree of amiability for some reason of her own. I guessed she was curious about something.

'Dr. Wyburn told you about his efforts to help, did he?'

'He told me himself. Very funny I thought.'

'H'm.' I went on preparing my visiting list but she seemed reluctant to go. You needed to concentrate on your visiting list so as to take the best route from patient to patient whilst at the same time attending the urgent cases first. She was distracting me and I looked up at her.

'Very funny,' she said again, 'and you had a queer case before the hospital one.'

'Why queer?' I asked. If she had got wind of what had happened at the Philpotts' house they had little hope of secrecy. She claimed to be very strict over confidential matters but if she had learnt something from an outside source she would certainly not keep it to herself. She had an insatiable thirst for knowledge about patients in any case. Wyburn was like a clam and she couldn't have got any information from him. Mr. Brown had been talking to her and I tried to remember what we had said on the phone. Had our heated disagreement made us indiscreet?'

'Quite a party there, I heard,' she said.

'What sort of party?'

'Oh yes, quite a party.'

Damn the woman, what was she getting at? 'I wish you'd tell me what you are talking about,' I said. She obviously knew something about the suicide attempt but who had told her? I looked at her and waited. Perhaps now she had gained my full attention she would come out with it.

'You must know more than I do,' she said.

'Apparently I don't. What happened?'

At last it came out. 'Mrs. Mount their neighbour told me they had a terrible row, Mr. and Mrs. Philpotts. Shouting their heads off. She thought they came to blows and then you were sent for.'

So she didn't know about the overdose of phenobarbitone and was curious to know why I had been there so long. 'They had a quarrel, did they. They had got over that when I was there, thank heaven. I don't like getting involved in family quarrels.

'No, I should think not.' And at last she left me. I must have disappointed her over and over again by not gossiping with her. Perhaps she was trustworthy but I was never sure.

As to Beatrice Philpotts one would delve nowadays into her state of mind. All I did was to tell her that she had nearly succeeded in killing herself for no good reason and ought to be thoroughly ashamed of herself.

They had three children after that and a long and successful marriage.

11

Hinton Mendip is an attractive village lying in a hollow of the Mendips about six miles from Melbrook. It is dominated by a great estate, has a church tower in tune with others in the district, several fine farms and neatness enough to satisfy the fastidious. We held a branch surgery there twice a week. I attended this on Tuesdays and Tom Wyburn on Fridays. The arrangement probably dated from the last century when the doctors of our firm did their rounds on horseback. Now that transport was so much easier it was not really necessary but the old practice of seeing patients in a rented room of one of the cottages still held. By the summer of nineteen thirty one — my second summer in the practice — I was collecting a mildly encouraging number of new patients in Hinton. It occurred to me that if Wyburn would leave that end of the practice to me I might be able to pull my weight a bit better. When old Mrs. Tadcaster — a reliable seven and sixpenny visit — appeared to be growing attached to me the outlook was distinctly promising. Mrs. Tadcaster was a woman of influence in the village, a widow of character, one whose advice was heeded. If I satisfied her it was likely that others would follow her lead.

I reported my hopes and prospects at home but my wife was not in the least surprised. Of course everyone in Hinton would fall over each other in the rush to consult me. I expect I purred gently and my confidence grew. Perhaps I could get Wyburn to leave that whole area in my hands.

Then one evening after surgery — it must have been in September — Wyburn came in to my room with the look of a man who has just replanned the world to his complete satisfaction. He leaned back against the couch while I sat back at my desk prepared to listen.

'I've been thinking,' he said slowly. 'I've been wondering whether it is necessary or even economically wise for both of us to go over to Hinton every week to the surgery there. It occurred to me that we should save a good deal of time if one of us undertook that end altogether and the other concentrated more on the home area, as it were, round Melbrook.'

'I couldn't agree more,' I said. 'I had been thinking of suggesting the same thing myself. As things are we might both of us spend a whole morning going over there to do one visit each instead of one of us doing them both.'

'Exactly. I'm glad you agree. How nice that we feel the same about it. So you would agree that I should take on that area altogether leaving you to concentrate on the villages closer to Melbrook.'

I was jolted into silence.

I had of course been expecting him to suggest retiring from that area and leaving it to me. After all he already had far more to do than I had as well as all the surgery. 'Oh,' I said when I had partially recovered but he didn't seem to notice my change of manner.

'You see,' he went on, 'I have looked after several of the big houses there since I took them over from Ballard and it is really no trouble to me to do the lot. They're a pretty healthy crowd out there anyway. Well, shall we say I will take on both the surgeries after next week? You do Tuesday as usual and I will do Friday and carry on from there.'

'I've got quite a number of new patients there,' I said. 'Mrs. Tadcaster for one and she seems to be quite an influence in the place. I was thinking I might pick up quite a few more through her.'

'Oh that old body. Yes, I haven't attended her. Well if you like to carry on with her do by all means but if you don't go over on Tuesdays to the surgery most of the people will come to me. I should be most happy with that arrangement.'

I made one more effort but it was a rearguard action. 'Don't you think you're taking on too much,' I said. 'After all I'm supposed to be trying to relieve your burden as much as possible.

This is going in the wrong direction.' It was really very difficult to understand why he was prepared to take on more patients when this was just where I could have given him some real relief.

We talked round the subject for some time in ever widening circles. I could of course have refused to give up my Tuesday surgeries there, but I didn't. He seemed blissfully unaware that I was unhappy with his plan. I did say several times that I wanted to take on more work so as to relieve the pressure on him, but he thought I was just being polite.

'Oh you mustn't feel like that in the least' he said. 'You are doing very well in Melbrook. I see your panel list has been growing steadily this year. Oh no, you are pulling your weight very well. Leave Hinton to me and concentrate on the other villages.'

I gave in. Perhaps I was being weak but he was ten years my senior and was being complimentary about my prospects. I could hardly make a direct confrontation over the affair.

When I told Jessica about it she seemed pleased. 'You won't have to waste time doing those surgeries every week,' she said, 'and people will send for you just the same when they want you.' She always managed to put my failures and weaknesses into perspective against the background of the important things of life, like us and our baby.

It was a week or two later that I wanted Wyburn's help — probably a surgical opinion over some case. I was passing his house and dropped in.

Annie Gentle, his housekeeper, opened her eyes very wide as she always did at the slightest provocation. 'Doctor's out, Doctor,' she said. 'Over at Hinton I believe.'

'I rather wanted to get hold of him,' I said. 'You don't know which patient he's seeing? Perhaps I could telephone him.'

'No I don't Doctor, I'm sorry.'

Annie Gentle suited her name to perfection. She was quiet, slow moving, a good plain cook, utterly loyal and discreet and very fond of 'the doctor'. There was of course only one member of the medical profession.

Some time later the same thing happened again. I wanted Wyburn to give an anaesthetic for a maternity case and phoned his house.

'Doctor's out, Doctor. Over at Hinton I believe. Very busy he seems to be over there lately.'

This time I had to get Bill Beverley to give the anaesthetic. I explained my predicament and he said. 'Right. I'll be there in fifteen, let me see, seventeen minutes. Just polish off the school surgery.' He boasted that he kept his appointments to the nearest half minute. He certainly drove his car like a maniac and no one was anxious to buy his cast-off vehicles.

I don't remember the midder case in question but no doubt he talked incessantly while he put the patient under, the hypnotic effect of his voice potentiating the effect of the chloroform.

This time Wyburn telephoned me later that evening sounding full of the joy of life. He apologised profusely for not being available.

'Your practice in Hinton is growing pretty fast,' I said. 'Are you sure you don't want any help there?'

'No, I'm managing very well thankyou. Very well indeed.'

As I rang off I said to Jessica, 'I shall never understand that chap in a thousand years.'

It was not long after the rearrangement at Hinton that a case cropped up that was laden with the possibilities of friction. It concerned a farmer's family, Henry and Kate Norval.

It is always May in my memory when I think of the journey out to that farm. The lane is always a ribbon laced on each side with cow's parsley — Queen Anne's lace. The rich Somerset pasture would be ready for hay making in a week or two and the cattle in the other fields would be shining with health and contentment. The Norvals had one of those small neat farm-houses with a small neat garden and small neat fields all round it. They kept a herd of fine red polls which always seem to me good looking cattle, chunky and solid with small unostentatious horns that are every bit as capable of doing their job as the long curved spikes of Jerseys or Ayrshires.

It must have been about October nineteen thirty one that the journey out to the farm began to pall. I had to drive there daily for some time and I went there with increasing anxiety.

Henry Norval was a young farmer who had been obliged to

take over from his father before I joined the practice. He was married to Kate who looked the picture of a farmer's wife and was a most pleasant girl into the bargain. They had lost their first baby two years before and Kate was pregnant again.

I had taken over the Norvals earlier in the year from Tom Wyburn. I had suffered a fair amount of humiliation in my first year by losing several patients to the opposition. Then there was the appointment of medical officer to the Isolation Hospital which I had hoped to take over from my predecessor but which I also lost to Paul King. I was delighted with the small evidence of success that the Norvals brought me.

Naturally there was no financial gain or loss when a patient changed from one partner to another, and as far as capital investment was concerned it made no difference either. When you retired the remaining partners bought your share which was valued at a fixed percentage of the firm's total income. All the same, competition was so keen throughout general practice that it had some effect even between partners. None of us could resist the mild flattery of being chosen in preference to a colleague. I wasn't surprised that Tom Wyburn had been a little annoyed at my taking the Norvals from him.

Kate had had her first baby easily enough and had no worries about her second confinement but she was terrified that something would go wrong with the baby. I attended the birth and watched with almost obsessional care over the early days of young Martin's life. For a couple of weeks all went well then he began to worry us. He didn't 'do'. He cried a lot, fed ferociously and vomited freely. Kate began to worry and there was the usual argument about whether the breast milk was suiting him. I was loath to change the feeding but parental pressure mounted and at last I agreed to a change of food. We gave one of the proprietary brands of food and a week later changed to another but there was no improvement.

At a month I began to suspect a congenital hypertrophy of pyloric muscle — a fairly common condition which acts as an obstruction preventing the food from passing from the stomach to the intestine. This meant looking for considerable periods at the baby's abdomen after a feed in the hope of finding confirmation of the diagnosis. I didn't want to alarm the mother so I didn't tell her what I was looking for.

I tried to radiate confidence but probably failed dismally as I was far from confident myself. It may seem strange that I didn't get the opinion of a paediatrician but we were so independent in those days that we only asked for help when we were really in trouble. The first thing to do was to get the help of my partners.

As the family had transferred their allegiance from Wyburn to me it would be embarrassing to ask him in so I asked John Symonds. He was very experienced and I had a lot of confidence in his opinion. He suggested that the infant was feeding too ravenously and would benefit from a small dose of sedative before each feed. We tried this but it didn't help.

My conviction that surgery was indicated was growing and at last I had to overcome my embarrassment and call in Tom Wyburn. He came over to the farm, made a careful examination and disagreed with my diagnosis.

'If you don't agree, what do you think is wrong?' I asked.

'Babies do have feeding troubles from time to time,' he said. 'He'll be alright.' I had half expected him to be resentful or at least embarrassed with the Norvals, but he was most friendly and charming.

'The child's five weeks old at the moment,' I said. 'Perhaps we had better review things in a week's time.'

'By all means,' he beamed, 'keep him under observation.'

The consultation had gone off very well but I was no nearer a solution to my problem.

When Wyburn had gone I had to deal with Kate and Henry. They were becoming very worried and neither of my partners had been of any help. I took refuge in absolute frankness and explained my uncertainties and my fear that an operation would be necessary. The effect on Kate was astounding. Placid and sensible as she generally was, she burst into tears.

'I knew it would be an operation case,' she said, 'since before he was born. I was dreading it.'

'But why?'

Kate looked at Henry who took over the story while she tried to compose herself. 'She has a friend, Doctor,' he said, 'and her baby was operated on at six weeks for something or other and died after the operation.'

'That was probably something quite different,' I told him. 'What may have to be done here is a very simple operation with very little risk at all.'

'That's what they told my friend,' said Kate and the tears flowed again.

'I might try and find out what it was, that operation. Who was the surgeon?'

'Dr. Wyburn,' said Henry.

'But Dr. Wyburn doesn't think there is any need to operate does he?' Kate sobbed.

'No, he thinks the baby may settle down without it but to be quite honest, I don't. We'll watch him carefully for a few days and decide then.'

I left them both very unhappy.

It wasn't often that a six week child gave signs of needing an operation and it was quite likely the other child had suffered from the same condition as Martin. I began to wonder whether the history of this previous case was the reason why Wyburn was hesitating about surgery now. And I began to wonder whether it was the reason why they had asked me to attend them in the first place. The whole affair was becoming complicated.

I watched the baby's progress, or lack of it, for several more days then made up my mind. If I sent the child to Bristol in opposition to Wyburn's opinion there would be an open rift between us. He was ten years my senior and a good surgeon. On the other hand I had had some experience in paediatrics in London and I felt sure this child needed surgery. I called him in again.

He was rather a stickler for classical signs and symptoms and was still not convinced. 'There's no projectile vomiting,' he said.

'But there's visible peristalsis.'

'Only slight constipation.'

'Enough for the diagnosis.'

'Have you tried belladonna?'

'No good. It would be months before it did him any good and in the meantime anything could happen.'

'I would like more evidence before I operate.'

Surgical treatment of this condition was of course not as simple then as it is now. It meant a general anaesthetic of ether on an open mask and there was no easy way of giving intravenous fluids beforehand. 'It's safer to operate now than to wait until he is dehydrated,' I said.

I couldn't persuade him.

As usual when I was worried I went over to see John Symonds and put the whole case to him.

I had my usual warm welcome and he insisted on my taking a glass of whisky before he would listen to a word I had to say.

When we were settled and relaxed and had exchanged generalities about work, epidemics and patients I said, 'You remember seeing a baby named Norval a week or so ago? Well I am convinced that baby needs surgery. Congenital pyloric stenosis. I got Wyburn to see him and he disagreed. I watched him for another week and became still more sure of the diagnosis so I sent for him again. He still doesn't agree. Now two questions are worrying me. This family transferred from Wyburn to me some time ago. Is it possible he might be unconsciously influenced by this? And secondly I gather that a friend of Mrs. Norval had her baby operated on by Wyburn a year or so ago and the baby died. Could this make him over cautious about operating on these cases?'

He thought for a moment and sipped his drink. 'No,' he said, 'neither of those things would influence him. No one likes losing a patient, even to a partner, but this wouldn't affect his judgement. You can rule that out. As to the other case I remember it of course. The child was very frail and died of bronchopneumonia a few days after the operation. It certainly wasn't his fault. So I should say if he said surgery is not indicated that is his unbiassed opinion. I saw that child with you didn't I? And I didn't even consider pyloric stenosis. Are you sure of the diagnosis?'

'Is one ever sure of anything?' I said. 'But I'm pretty confident here.'

'Then it's quite clear what you have to do. You are responsible. If you need a surgeon you must get one. If Wyburn is not willing to operate you must get someone else. There are good men in Bath and Bristol.'

'I had thought of that, but would Wyburn ever forgive me? He's pretty rigid — authoritative in his ways.'

'That's not the point.' He waited. 'Is it?'

'No, I suppose not.'

'Tell him first what you propose to do.'

I agreed of course, but I didn't look forward to the interview. I decided to go straight on to Wyburn's house and get it over. It was latish in the evening by then. I imagined the exchange between us. I would tell him of my conviction of the need for surgery and he would probably react by saying that he, an F.R.C.S. and experienced surgeon knew better than I did. I would say I felt we couldn't leave the child any longer without surgery and would he be prepared to do it. If he said no I had to tell him that I had made up my mind to ask a surgeon from Bristol to see the child. This was the tricky bit. He would blandly say 'go ahead' being convinced that another surgeon would agree with him. At the same time I knew he was very sensitive in spite of his apparent confidence and he would be very hurt at my not trusting him. Then, if the other surgeon operated, Wyburn would be put in the wrong and he wouldn't like that either.

It couldn't be helped, and I had Symonds behind me anyway.

Wyburn was a good pianist and when I arrived at his house he was playing the piano. It was usually Bach but on this occasion it was Chopin. He beamed with pleasure at me as he struck the last chord.

I heartily disliked having to bring matters to a head. I plunged straight in,

'I've come to ask you to operate on the Norval baby. I'm sure of the diagnosis. Will you?'

It took an appreciable time to bring his mind back from Chopin to surgery. Half a minute later he said, 'Have you thought of asking someone from Bath or Bristol?'

For a second I wondered whether he was psychic. Then I said, 'I have more confidence in you than anyone else in the district.'

'Very well, if you are confident and will give the anaesthetic I will agree.' He beamed again and I was amazed. It was all too easy. I must have misjudged him all these months. He was the acme of cooperation and friendliness, even when things were difficult. I wondered afterwards whether Symonds had telephoned to warn him of my plan and make it easier for me. Why otherwise had he asked me whether I had thought of asking the opinion of a surgeon from Bath or Bristol?

Once an operation was agreed between us, I had to get the approval of the parents and Kate was going to be very unhappy at the prospect. This was the biggest test I had had in general practice and I felt very much alone. It would have been much easier to have a visiting surgeon to the house who could put the case for the operation clearly and confidently. As it was, I had to do all that part myself. When I had expressed full confidence in surgery and in Tom Wyburn in particular and had pointed out the risk of doing nothing, they agreed. The atmosphere however was tense. They had lost one baby and I seemed to be pushing them into the risk of losing another.

After that I had only myself to deal with. I had virtually blackmailed Wyburn into operating and had agreed to give the anaesthetic myself. The whole responsibility was on my shoulders. Why, I wondered, had Wyburn asked me to give the anaesthetic and not Symonds as usual? It might have been because he knew I had given a good many anaesthetics to babies when I was an H.P. at Guy's. On the other hand if the other child had died of bronchopneumonia he might have blamed the anaesthetic given by John Symonds. The complexities of partnership relationships were beginning to dawn on me.

If the operation went well all three partners would feel added confidence in each other. If it didn't, there would be a good deal of open or silent mistrust. In all probability the whole thing would be quietly and unhappily buried. And so I thought would the baby. The very idea was a nightmare.

I didn't sleep very well that night.

Forty eight hours later, after careful preparation, I gave a light anaesthetic of open ether and Tom Wyburn found a hypertrophied pylorus, treated it by simple incision and in a very few minutes the job was done.

Martin never looked back.

We didn't analyse the case afterwards. Wyburn was always reserved but he seemed remarkably friendly and bore me no ill will for forcing his hand or, more important, for being right.

Wyburn remained easy going, cheerful and friendly and one day I went in to his room after surgery. He was whistling Shepherd's Hay and dancing round the room. What was more he was not in the least embarrassed when I caught him unawares. I was astounded. If I had seen the Archbishop of Canterbury doing a series of head-over-heels down the aisle of his cathedral I couldn't have been more surprised.

It was a few weeks later that the odd events of the past month or two fell into place. He came to me one evening and said 'I have some news for you. I am engaged.'

I gasped. 'Engaged to be married?'

'Yes.'

'Congratulations! Who to?'

'Helen Martindale. Have you met her?'

I hadn't. 'Is she a Melbrook girl?'

'No,' he said. 'She lives in Hinton Mendip.'

12

I met Bill Beverley at the hospital one morning. 'Have you met Tom Wyburn's future intended?' he asked.

'Not yet,' I said, 'but I made a precise blue print of what was needed some time ago.'

'Tell me,' he laughed. 'I'd visualised a sturdy women's hockey captain with regular features and blonde hair.'

'No, that wouldn't do. She needs to be slim, vivacious, merry with a good sense of humour — and probably a brunette.'

The formal introduction followed a week or so later and I was delighted to find that Miss Martindale corresponded remarkably well to my prescription — for which of course I took no credit. I didn't get to know her very well until a year or so after they were married when I attended her with her first baby, but her influence on Tom Wyburn was just what I had hoped. He became more relaxed, more cheerful and even his attitude to patients began to change.

Previously he had put patients into three classes (my analysis not his). The first class contained the highly approved surgical patients who were cured by operation; the second class comprised those with serious medical diseases, most of whom steadily deteriorated and died; and the third and much disdained group were the 'neurotics' who were not really ill at all but existed for the sole purpose of paying fees which helped to earn his living. As his attitude changed we actually engaged in discussions about medical cases who now appeared to have developed a right to exist.

To say that in the nineteen thirties 'neurotic' patients were imperfectly understood is an understatement. Such people were of course a considerable source of income to the general practitioner. A few favourite prescriptions given week after week, year after year, for a few shillings a bottle produced a very steady financial reward. Equating half a crown in nineteen thirty with two pounds fifty in nineteen eighty, every neurotic patient under treatment was paying that sum to the doctor every week. As every practice had fifty or more 'neurotics' on its books it can easily be calculated how large their contribution was.

The system satisfied the patients because it gave them invalid status and symbolised their dependence on help from outside the family, which came to accept their inability to behave like the more fortunate healthy members of society. General practitioners had a vague understanding that the disability was in the mind but few had any conception of the underlying causes. The idea of giving neurotics insight into their own problems may have been explored by a few far sighted physicians but was certainly not contemplated by the vast majority of us.

Occasionally powerful suggestion produced a cure. A woman with obstinate constipation consulted Dr. Herbert French of Guy's Hospital. After careful examination he concluded that the cause was nervous. With all the force of his strong personality he told her that from henceforth her bowels would act at nine o'clock every morning. A few weeks later she wrote to him thanking him for his help and adding that nine o'clock was a little inconvenient could he make it eight?

Looking back at old practice day books it is clear that something like half the income was contributed by these patients and it is small wonder that the status quo was happily accepted.

Only now and again did something happen, fifty years ago, which, seen in retrospect, shouted evidence from the rooftops that we were all on the wrong track and behaving in a manner which, if not immoral, was reprehensible.

One such patient came under my care early in the new era of Wyburn's enlightenment. Her name was Mrs. Marian Martell. She had previously consulted Dr. Braythwaite and then Tom Wyburn and finally came to me. It is characteristic of some 'neurotic' patients that from time to time they will change from one adviser to another as though unconsciously searching for something — Mrs. Martell did just this.

She was in her late twenties, was comfortably off and had a husband who was too weak for her. No one in those days thought of questioning whether he was weak in bed, or insensitive, or selfish in that sphere of life, but he was probably all those things. She had come to me because she had tried everyone else and I was young and therefore 'up to date'. She suffered from a common mixture of symptoms — headache, pain in the back, poor sleep, indescribable feelings and so on. I examined her and found no sign of organic disease. I probably told her that her nerves were in a bad state and gave her the latest bit of fashionable nonsense, or perhaps a mixture I used for years of bromide and strychnine.

She came to me every week but failed to improve. As she had been to Tom Wyburn previously I talked to him about her.

'I'm doing her no good,' I said. 'She will soon be coming back to you.'

Instead of groaning he sounded interested. 'She seems to be in genuine trouble,' he said. 'I wonder what we mean when we tell people they are suffering from their nerves. Is it a mild form of shell shock like we saw in the war?'

'I suppose it could be. Due to shock or distress of some sort. She's genuine alright but if it's worry why should worry make your back ache?'

'Heaven knows'.

'Suppose you are worried, suppose you quarrel constantly with your wife or your husband, this would make you pretty miserable and when you are miserable any mild pain becomes worse. Is that it, I wonder?'

We agreed that marriage could cause elation when things went well and misery when things went badly but most people refused to talk about their marriages. I had tentatively broached the subject with Mrs. Martell and she had said her husband was wonderful and they were perfectly happy apart from her nerve trouble.

I was agreeably surprised that Wyburn was beginning to regard neurotics as genuine patients and even to regard them as subjects for intelligent investigation. Of course we got nowhere but it was something to be asking the right questions. It was so much easier to regard patients with these peculiar symptoms as fuss pots or malingerers and to treat them with lofty disdain while at the same time laughing with your colleagues at the more outrageous symptoms. From time to time during the next few years we both relapsed into the old attitudes but questions once asked kept recurring and long afterwards our eyes were opened.

After a few more weeks Mrs. Martell reported she had improved and she went away happily with her bottle of medicine. Then she arrived saying she was so much better that she would not need to see me again.

I was delighted of course but instead of asking myself why several bottles of relatively inert chemicals had done so much good I assumed that my reassurance as to her general health had been so effective as to change her life.

I saw nothing more of her for several weeks until one day I was sent for to see her husband. He was suffering from the early stages of rheumatoid arthritis which had lately become worse. Mr. Martell was a large flabby man with a gross abdomen and an offensive halitosis. Mrs. Martell was full of wifely attention. She had no children and I thought perhaps her husband's illness had given her an adequate sense of purpose and value.

I treated the husband as best I could but I had little to offer except aspirin and general advice. I think at that time iodine was a fashionable treatment — a few drops in milk several times a day. I must have given him this and visited him until the exacerbation of the chronic illness subsided a little. He had a flourishing business which was threatened by his illness and a month or so before I was called in, his nephew, a young man in his early twenties, had come to the rescue. The youth of course lived with the family.

Then one day Mrs. Martell came to see me again in the surgery. She told me she was pregnant.

I congratulated her. She had been married some years without prospect of children and this must surely complete the cure of her neurotic tendencies. Certainly there was no hint of neurosis now and a strong minded woman sat before me. 'I shall have to get rid of it,' she said.

I stared at her and said I didn't understand.

'You'll have to know,' she said. 'It's not my husband's. He hasn't been well enough for months and he was never very — well —'

The magnitude of the problem settled slowly on me like a heavy weight. The father of the child was the nephew who had been her lover almost since his arrival. The cure of her neurosis was due to him not to me.

Of one thing I was certain, I could take no part in arranging an abortion. In those days this was a crime liable to bring ruin more certainly than robbing a bank.

I examined her. She was two or three weeks late with her period but I couldn't by any means be certain of a pregnancy. I told her so.

'You haven't told your husband about your suspicions?'

'No, of course not.'

'If it should turn out to be a pregnancy you will have to tell him.'

'That's quite impossible.'

'Then is it possible to make him think it is his?'

'You know what that would mean. I don't think I could seduce him even if I wanted to and I don't think I could bring myself to anyway.' She gave me to understand by a series of grimaces that the act of seducing a fat man with bad halitosis was beyond her powers. 'I must get rid of it. It would kill my husband.'

'I'm sorry, I can't help in that way.'

'Other people have abortions, why shouldn't I?'

'I can't help you. I'm sorry. You must either tell your husband or let him think it is his. The best thing is to tell him.'

'You don't know him. He might even divorce me.' Gloves were pulled on with that curious threat of aggression that the activity sometimes conveys. 'You won't help me? Then I shall have to make my own arrangements.'

'I wouldn't advise any attempt at abortion. It's much too dangerous.'

I thought it more than likely that she would try various home

112

remedies for a 'delayed period' and then resort to some back street abortionist. I saw nothing of her for a couple of months and felt sure this must have happened. When Mr. Martell came to the surgery for treatment one day he seemed well pleased with life.

'We've got news for you, Doctor,' he beamed. 'The wife's going to have a baby. Never thought we should have one. Almost given up trying. Wonderful, isn't it? We both feel ten years younger — except for my hands and even they are a lot better. It happened while my rheumatism was at its height too. Amazing isn't it?'

Poor fool, I thought, but perhaps it was best this way.

The child was born in due course — a healthy boy. He was neither as early as Mrs. Martell had really expected nor as late as the official date we had worked out. Naturally I never discussed the boy's parentage with the family. I could do no other than help them live the lie Mrs. Martell had insisted on.

Wyburn and I discussed the affair at length. 'So what happened,' he said, 'was that this woman was unhappy, frustrated, probably disliked her husband and somehow this caused the symptoms.'

'Suppose so, but I don't understand how.'

'Then she had an affair with this young man and in the excitement of this her symptoms disappeared. Now she has the baby to occupy her and she keeps well.'

'Yes, but I still don't understand how distress can cause backache and headache. If I'm upset or worried I don't get a backache. There must be some other factor.'

And we could get no further.

A few months later the child who was giving great joy to both the Martells developed bronchopneumonia. He had become too fat and flabby and it was soon obvious that his chances were poor. When he was sitting up in his cot, his breathing rapid, his nostrils working and his colour poor I could have sworn he was the image of Mr. Martell. It would be strange if the husband were the father after all. I never knew of course.

The child died and in all the distress and wretchedness that followed Mr. Martell's rheumatism became worse for a time but Mrs. Martell had no physical symptoms whatever.

'What do you make of it?' I asked Wyburn.

'I make nothing of it at all.' he said. 'When their trouble is at its worst she has no symptoms. It's another medical condition that I simply don't understand.'

Neither did I. The triumph here was that Wyburn had called her neurotic state a medical condition. This was a step forward.

In restrospect several things become clearer. The distress that is usually called 'real' trouble — over her pregnancy and the death of her baby — caused no nervous symptoms. It seldom does. The distress that does cause symptoms is more internal to the mind and something we still need to know much more about before we can properly understand it. At the present time most doctors regard neurotic symptoms as distress signals — a half conscious scream for help.

It is not difficult to see the ideal treatment for her neurosis in the first place. Whether it would have succeeded or not is another matter. The modern G.P. would try to guide her into a state of mind when she could talk freely right at the start about her marriage and her frustrations and aggressions. Mr. Martell might have been able to talk about his own side of things — his wife's frigidity, her nagging and her criticisms. If each could achieve insight into their own behaviour it is just possible they might have been led to a moderately successful marriage. The man might even have avoided the stressful road that leads to rheumatoid arthritis. Psychotherapy had probably only a small chance of success in a case like this but such thinking was in any case twenty years ahead.

One thing is fairly certain. If such a case was presented to a family doctor today at the point where the woman became pregnant the outcome would have been abortion. Who can say how this would have affected their marriage or their lives? The new is not always better than the old.

114

13

Bill Beverley seldom went away during school term because he took his work there very seriously. During the winter of nineteen thirty two he was ill for a few days and I had to take on his work in the school as well as much of his practice. As junior partner one had to be prepared for sudden dislocations of routine and these became more arduous as your own practice grew. It wasn't the extra work that bothered me so much as the feeling of being a new boy all over again, the unwanted, the second best, as well as being regarded with just a shade of suspicion. You had to justify yourself with each new patient.

One morning I did the school surgery on a 'corps' day. This meant that some twenty or thirty boys would attend in the hope of a chit to be excused O.T.C. parade because of some minor disability. Matron of course knew them all well and told me beforehand who she thought was genuine and who was skrimshanking. One boy she was not sure about. He was complaining like half the others of pain in the back but also he said he didn't feel very well. Most of the boys trying to be excused corps were not feeling at all well so one tended to disregard this too. This boy could move his back quite well but said he had pain in a localised area near the spine over the ninth and tenth ribs.

'Any injury?' I asked.

'Not really,' he said and I began to take more notice. Most boys wanting a chit said they had sustained a really crippling blow at rugger or somewhere — although there was nothing to show for it.

So I examined Kirby carefully. His back was acutely tender over the site of the pain and when I listened with a stethoscope there was a large patch of airless lung. What was more this was board dull to percussion so I told him to wait until I had finished seeing the others when I would deal with him. 'No corps for him today anyway,' I told Matron.

When I came to look at him again I confirmed my findings. 'Temperature Matron?' I asked.

'Ninety eight point six,' she said which was neither here nor there.

'And you haven't had a knock there?' I asked the boy again.

'Well I did have a bit of a kick there at rugger the other day. Nothing unusual.'

We admitted him to the sick room for observation and I saw him again in the evening. There was no change and I concluded he had some basal lung damage and possibly some free fluid blood in the chest outside the lung. This would have to be treated because fluid blood in the chest could cause serious adhesions later if not removed. He would need to be Xrayed and probably have his chest aspirated.

While I was thinking about this and how it was to be done a message came from the headmaster. Would I go and see him in his room. I nodded and prepared to see the boy in the next bed when Matron drew me aside. 'Do you think you ought to go straight away, Doctor?'

'Is that what that message means?' I asked.

'Yes,' she whispered, 'I should go now.' So I went.

The headmaster at that time was a tall monk — six feet four or so in height — with a commanding presence and aquiline features which fitted remarkably well with his French sounding name. Thinking of him afterwards I seemed to see his Norman ancestors on powerful horses nine centuries ago chasing my Saxon forebears out of their heritage.

His room was oak panelled and austere, his desk immense. 'Oh yes Doctor. Tell me about this boy Kirby.'

I did.

'You are sure it is an injury?'

'Yes, pretty sure.'

'Pretty sure? What does that mean? How do you know it is not pneumonia?'

'His history doesn't fit pneumonia and his temperature is almost normal.'

'The onset of the pain was sudden and you say there is dullness on percussion in that area. I should have thought that sounded very like pneumonia. Why do you say it doesn't?'

'It's not in the least like it, Headmaster,' I said and suddenly the thought struck me that this imposing man must be a doctor of medicine as well as monk and headmaster.

'Then how does pneumonia begin? Doesn't it start with sudden pain in the chest?'

Thank God, he's not a doctor, I thought. 'It usually begins with a shivering attack then a high temperature and pain in the chest.'

'Always?' He sounded like an examiner again.

I hesitated. 'Yes.'

'I see.' Then quite suddenly he opened a large volume that had been lying on his desk. I couldn't see what it was but it looked remarkably like French's Differential Diagnosis. He opened it at a marked page and quietly set about reading it. In a moment he said, 'How do you know it is not kidney trouble? The kidney lies very near that area, doesn't it?'

'Yes, but he has no kidney symptoms.'

'Which are?'

'Frequency of passing water, abnormalities in the urine — blood and albumen.'

'What about a perinephric abscess? That would not cause symptoms like that, would it?'

I was appalled at this cross examination. Who did he think he was? My irritation must have shown. He looked coldly at me and I succumbed. 'A perinephric abscess would have a slow onset, be associated with deep tenderness in the loin and probably some swelling.' Anyone who has been cross examined on his own subject by a layman will understand how difficult it is to reply convincingly to questions of this sort. I would far rather be interrogated by an expert in my own profession who would be more penetrating yet would accept that there are certain things we take for granted.

'I understood this boy said he had no injury,' he went on.

'He admits to being kicked in the back two days ago in a match.'

'I understood differently.'

117

This time I waited. More cold looks. 'Well,' he said, 'what do you propose to do with him?'

'He will have to be Xrayed and probably the chest will have to be aspirated in case he had a haemothorax.' Layman's language was not indicated any longer.

He hadn't looked up haemothorax and I had a momentary advantage. 'When?' he asked.

'Tomorrow will do very well. I suggest he sees a physician in the City.'

His manner changed very slightly. 'Very well, Doctor. See me again tomorrow.

I rose to go. 'And Doctor,' he added, unable to resist a final thrust. 'When will Dr. Beverley be back?'

'The day after tomorrow,' I said and added with a trace of bitterness, 'I hope and trust'. And I left him with a cool good-night.

I felt as though I had been subjected to a prolonged viva in my finals and it was some time before my ruffled feelings settled down. A medical textbook used for cross examination! It struck me as outrageous. If he wanted to check my work he might at least have had the decency to read up the subject privately. Later I talked it over at home where my wife pointed out that he must be a very good headmaster to take such good care of the boys. This I couldn't deny.

The boy was duly investigated in the city. No free blood was found and the lung settled down in a week or two but another case of Beverley's took over the position of prime worrier the same day.

It was always more difficult to deal with seriously ill patients from a partner's practice. People expected their own doctor in those days and the burning question 'when will the doctor be back?' was always to the fore. The second case was far more serious — a child with bronchopneumonia — but there was no Spanish Inquisition here. On the other hand there was Granny Perkins.

In the days before penicillin and before any form of chemo-therapy was available, bronchopneumonia was one of the greatest scourges we had to deal with. We treated each case much as Hippocrates would have done two and a half

118

thousand years ago — by careful nursing, frequent changes of posture, care of the skin to keep the pores open, frequent fluids including weak tea to stimulate the kidneys, and small doses of alcohol when the heart was failing. In addition the air had to be kept fresh and steam kettles were used to soften hard obstructing mucus.

All this could be done at home and the hospitals had nothing magical to offer, so mothers invariably preferred to nurse their own children rather than leave them to strange hands in a hospital ward. The nursing had to be skilled and very patient and this meant a full time twenty-four hour a day occupation for many days. It only became possible with the help of neighbours, many of whom had had experience nursing their own children. The result was a valuable integration of families into groups who helped each other in time of trouble. In each district there would be at least one elderly woman who claimed a monopoly of wisdom and sometimes there would be fierce rivalry for the right to dictate methods of treatment. These Sary Gamps maintained a territory like an animal in the wild, and if this were invaded by another 'nurse' she would be attacked with a tongue sharp enough to give mortal injury. One of these women would be called on to supervise the nursing of any serious case.

Everyone knew that the risk from bronchopneumonia was high and often enough infants would die in large numbers during a winter of heavy infections. A child would become, for a few days, the centre of all the neighbours' attention. The doctor would visit three times a day and become, with the Sary Gamp, the central figure of the group. When a case terminated, whether well or badly, there was often a great bond of fellowship between all concerned. But not always. When temperaments clashed everyone suffered.

Granny Perkins was a stranger to me because she lived in High Compton, a village where most of the people were treated by Beverley. She was a character the like of whom one seldom sees. She was large of course — it is hard to imagine a thin woman being accepted as the mother superior of a group — she was possessed of enormous self confidence and an ability to forget the failures and remember only the

119

triumphs of home nursing. She had dark hair sitting tightly on her head as though she had used brylcream, and a rather red face. Being teetotal she could never be confused with the original Sary Gamp. A small girl who knew her well in childhood told me when she had grown up that she always thought teetotal meant someone like Granny Perkins who was totally devoted to tea. Certainly I never saw her without a cup of tea near at hand and a pot brewing to an impossible strength on the hob. Her brain power was minimal but one sometimes envied her confidence in the rightness of all her actions. She was an untrained midwife. The insistence on trained midwives for all confinements was not enforced till some years later. Her method of helping the woman in labour, as I discovered in the course of time, was to apply hot flannel to the lower spine every few minutes. She worked hard at this and firmly believed the outcome of every case depended on it. It was difficult to stop her doing it even when forceps were being applied.

It was during Bill Beverley's absence that her neighbour's child developed bronchopneumonia. The case being in the heart of Perkins territory meant that she had absolute precedence over her only rival who was Granny Hearne at the bottom of the village. Now Granny Perkins idolised Dr. Beverley and took it very hard that he was ill at the moment when her neighbour's child was struck down with bronchopneumonia. Not unnaturally her annoyance took the form of a powerful resentment at my presence. She was moreover determined to keep a sharp eye on my activities. It was impossible to see the sick child or her mother without the old lady being there because she would be at the cotside within seconds of seeing my car approach.

She was a great believer in warmth, no matter how stuffy the room became. On my second visit to the house there was a large fire burning in the kitchen where the child was being nursed and a primitive oil stove as well. The window was tightly shut. I opened the window wide and as it was a cold day said it could be nearly shut again in ten minutes. On my next visit the same evening the window was shut again and you could cut the air with a knife. The child was not a good colour but after the window had been open for a few minutes you could see the colour improving. I repeated my instructions but spoke to the mother instead of Granny Perkins. This was a tactical error as I realised afterwards.

'Baby's lungs are starved of oxygen,' I told the mother, 'and even cold air is better than stale air. The heart may fail if it doesn't get enough oxygen. So we must keep the window open some of the time. If you put the oil stove in front of the window it will warm the air as it comes in.'

Next morning the battle went on. The window was shut and the air was very bad indeed. A huge fire was burning in the kitchen range and the oil stove was full on as well. The child was being roasted between the two sources of heat. I waited till the air was fairly clear after opening the window then explained my reasoning once more with even greater emphasis, this time directed at Granny Perkins. I assumed she could understand plain English but the only reply I got was the old question 'When will Dr. Beverley be back?'

That afternoon the child had a convulsion. After the usual mustard bath and cool sponge to the back of the neck I fetched oxygen from the hospital and explained how it must be kept going. That evening I went to the house again only to find the oxygen cylinder empty, the window tight shut and the child cyanosed. It transpired that Granny Perkins had decided that if a little stream of oxygen would do good, a powerful stream would do even better. They had emptied a whole cylinder in an hour or so. I began to despair and at the same time was very annoyed. Why couldn't the woman do as she was told? This time I opened the window and watched the child's colour improve then fetched another cylinder of oxygen and repeated my instructions slowly and carefully twice over. I added that if the baby was not better in the morning I would have to send her into the City Hospital. There, I thought, at least the oxygen could be kept at a suitable level and Granny Perkins would be replaced by intelligent nursing. The mother began to cry and I felt very sorry for her. Poor girl she couldn't help what was happening. I reassured her that if she did exactly as she was told we could keep the baby at home. By this time Granny Perkins was looking murder at me. The air which was

121

clearer in one way became heavily charged.

Next morning I had an early call from Dr. Blaythwaite of the opposition. He was very sorry but he had been asked to take over a patient of mine in High Compton with broncho-pneumonia.

Granny Perkins had won.

It was several days before Bill Beverley came back to work and by that time the child had died.

According to Granny Perkins it was because of the cold air I had let into the room. This of course was nonsense but I was doubly distressed when I heard the news and the gossip.

Granny Perkins had published it abroad that I was responsible for the baby's death and no matter what anyone said she would believe this till her dying day. My first reaction was to blame her as a dangerous and stupid old woman. Then I talked to Bill Beverley.

I telephoned him and told him I was sorry the baby had died and sorry I had lost one of his families to the opposition.

'Don't worry about losing the family,' he said. 'They'll soon come back. You didn't get on very well with Granny Perkins I gathered.'

'That's an understatement.'

'What went wrong?'

I told him about the unventilated room, the child's cyanosis, the overheating and the wasted oxygen.

'I think I get the picture,' he said or words to that effect. 'Granny Perkins has to be handled rather carefully. You see it's no good giving her orders like you would a hospital sister. You've got to remember the material you are dealing with.'

'How do you persuade an old baggage like that to do as she is told?'

'Well it's like this. Her one and only joy in life is her reputation. Her husband died of drink and she has no children — right? Now if you start by questioning her value she will go on the defensive. She'll try to prove to the family that she is right. And if she is right you must be wrong.'

'O.K. But how do I persuade her to keep the window open?'

'Remember to safeguard her reputation in the eyes of the family, that's the first thing. So if you want the window open say something like this,' his voice changed to the tone he used for patients, '"as we both know, Mrs. Perkins, this child needs fresh air. I'm going to rely on your excellent nursing to hold the baby in your arms for ten minutes every hour while the window is opened and the room aired." Then you'd find she would eat out of your hand.'

Light began to dawn on me. 'I see what you mean.' The image of the child fighting for breath, nostrils working and face cyanosed flashed through my mind. Had my failure with Granny Perkins been the real cause of death? This added to my wretched interview with the headmaster was a severe setback to my tenderly growing confidence. 'I've made a bit of a mess of things,' I said.

'Granny Perkins is not easy,' Beverley said. 'And there's more in general practice than doling out medicines! To change the subject I hear you managed the headmaster very well.'

'Managed him! He tore me into small strips and threw me out of the window.'

'I didn't get that impression.'

'He actually cross-examined me with a medical textbook on his knee.' The memory of this first humiliation for which I wasn't to blame brought back my sense of outrage.

'Oh he does that to me too,' he laughed. 'He paid you a compliment though. He said he would be prepared to have you again as my deputy when necessary.'

'You call that a compliment?'

'It's high praise from the Head.'

I was left thoughtful. I was relieved about the headmaster's opinion. But Granny Perkins — Beverley was obviously right. I had mismanaged her. I began to learn that day that in general practice you have to make the best of whatever help you have — ignorant or skilled, irritating or cooperative. Granny Perkins liked Beverley because he understood her. He knew how to handle her so she gave him good service.

"Life is short. The art so long to learn." I wonder if Hippocrates uttered his famous aphorism after dealing with some Greek Granny Perkins twenty four centuries ago.

14

John Symonds kept a pretty sharp eye on the firm's finances. He was not mean by any stretch of the imagination — just correct. Tom Wyburn showed no interest in the accounts though I had the impression that he might have lost his indifference if anything happened to reduce his steady income. Bill Beverley had a more balanced outlook than either of the others, being concerned but not obsessed with money matters. Their differing attitudes were highlighted by the affair of our annual settlement in January nineteen thirty three.

Every year at about this time the accountants came out from Bristol to meet the whole firm in solemn conclave. The accounts were always sent to us a week beforehand so that we could study them and be ready for discussion. My own examination consisted of turning straight to page four where I could read my own balance for the year. In the two previous years the other three partners had received substantial cheques while I had been told that I had already drawn more than my total share and was in debt to the others. In January 1931 it turned out that I owed the partners just over £50 and a year later the debt had increased to £100 which was again carried on into the next year.

Naturally enough I awaited the 1932 accounts with some trepidation. It was impossible to estimate beforehand what one's share would be because of such imponderables as income tax and book debts. As near as I could guess I should be able to repay my debt. After this, I thought, I shall begin to save and establish myself in a secure financial position. I watched every morning for the postman to bring the large envelope from Bristol. Eventually it arrived during the last week of January, only ten days after I had begun to expect it. I opened the envelope and turned to page four where in the course of considerable research I found to my horror that I was another £50 in debt. I now owed the firm just under £150. I was badly shaken.

I sat at the breakfast table unable to eat. I looked at the amounts the other partners would receive and at the way the Melbrook end of the practice had increased. Apparently I had earned more but was to receive less.

Jessica's explanation was simple. 'They've made a mistake,' she said. 'Obviously. I shouldn't worry.'

'These blighters don't make mistakes,' I said bitterly. 'They are infallible. I'd have a better chance of robbing the Bank of England than getting them to admit they are wrong.'

I felt like a drowning man. I should never be able to repay the firm £150. In 1980 it would hardly pay a quarter's rates on a chicken house but then it was equivalent to about £3000 of today's money.

On calm appraisal later in the day I realised that two things had militated against me. During my first year I had only received three quarters of my expected income — about one quarter's book debts having gone to the retired Dr. Ballard. This I had been prepared for but, what was much worse, I found I was expected to pay income tax as though I had received the full £1000 share I had bought.

My protests at this outrage were easily brushed aside by the accountant. 'The firm is taxed as a whole,' he said, 'and each partner bears a share of the amount of tax in proportion to his share in the partnership.'

'But,' I had protested, 'this means Dr. Ballard has been paid £250 and is charged no income tax on it!'

'That's right,' said the accountant smiling to see that I was grasping the essential facts of accountancy, 'and when you retire you will have a similar benefit.' I wasn't unduly interested in my income forty years ahead, and this struck me as small compensation.

The second scandal as I then saw it was the matter of the firm agreement. The Medical Sickness society who lent me the purchase money for my share in the practice quite naturally insisted on the firm's antiquated agreement being brought up to date. Evidently it was possible to drive a coach and horses through the old agreement and they could not recommend a client of theirs to put his future in jeopardy by signing it. The account from Hempsons, the Society's London solicitors, amounted to £140 — nearly £3000 in today's money. I took this to John Symonds thinking that as the whole firm had benefited by the modernisation of the agreement the cost would be shared but he would have none of it.

'This is just routine, Lane,' he had said. 'You are responsible for your solicitors and we for ours.'

'But,' I said, 'the outdated firm agreement has been modernised entirely at my expense.'

'No. We have had to pay our people and you pay yours. The firm's solicitors were corresponding with Hempsons for months. And it wasn't at our request that the agreement was altered. We were quite happy as things were.'

I was left with a sense of injustice.

All this was ancient history by 1933 but it came back to me in force as I pondered the evils of the wicked world that January. It was no good talking to Tom Wyburn, but I tried. I couldn't very well bring up the old grievance about income tax on book debts, and solicitors fees, but I broached the subject of my debt to the firm. I hardly knew what I expected of him but I received little comfort.

With something of a yawn he said, 'Oh, don't bother about money. It will just be carried on into the next year and be straightened out in due course. Forget about it.'

But I couldn't forget about it. It seemed to me I was heading for ruin. My malaise smouldered for a day or two and then I went to see Bill Beverley.

I was always sure of a warm welcome at his home. His three children were brought up to be unfettered by strict rules and evidence of their way of life was usually strewn over every room. Gladys Beverley was (and is) a dear — one whose maternal instincts reveal themselves in every relationship. I was made to sit down and take a drink and soon felt as though my shoes would at any moment be removed and replaced by slippers. All this made it more difficult to talk of such sordid matters as money and I could easily have let myself be absorbed into the carefree family atmosphere but presently Bill said, 'If you want to talk shop we had better go into my study.'

We did so and he removed the genial schoolboy look from his face and put on his professional mask. The square jaw jutted, the mouth became firm and the grey eyes glared. This made it easier for me to take the plunge.

'It's about the firm accounts,' I said. 'I'm overdrawn £150 and I feel bad about it.'

'Why? I overdrew in my first year. It's these damn book debts and tax arrangements.'

'Yes, that stuck in my gullet, but this is the third year and I can't see how I'm going to repay the money. You see I pay £300 plus a year to the Medical Sickness Society in loan repayment and I'm still repaying the Kent Education Committee for a loan on my education. Then we've got bills for furniture. We spend very little. Jessica is still wearing her prewedding clothes and we have no holidays except to her parents which cost us nothing. We have to have a maid of course, otherwise she would never be able to leave the house.'

'Tell me exactly how you stand,' he said and took out a large impressive sheet of paper. 'What are your main expenses?'

We went through them and it was clear that with care and economy we could just about manage on our income but couldn't save anything.

'There's another thing,' I admitted. 'I've got an overdraft at the bank of £150. I had to borrow this to pay Hempsons' bill two years ago and haven't been able to get it down. You remember they battled away for months modernising the firm agreement.'

'I remember that. You did us a good turn there. Our costs were only some thirty or forty pounds between the three of us and yours were — what — a hundred or so?'

'Just over a hundred and forty.'

'Right. Let me have a think about your problem. I may come up with some suggestions. When are you due to increase your share in the firm?'

'In another two years. But then I shall have to pay two years purchase for it which means more borrowing. So it won't help for some time.'

'I see that.' And in his best heavy manner he drummed his fingers on the desk and looked the picture of the stern headmaster interviewing a prefect in trouble. I knew it would take very little to make him roar with laughter and break the solemn mask to pieces but I refrained. 'Right,' he added. 'Now another small noggin.'

After which the cares of the world receded for some time. At home I told Jessica that Bill Beverley was going to think about it and at least he had been sympathetic. She too had been doing some arithmetic. 'I'm going to do on less housekeeping money,' she said. 'I think I can manage on two pounds ten a week. That'll save twenty five pounds a year and I shall put it in a special account for paying off the overdraft.'

She always loved special accounts and little boxes where you kept small collections of money to pay this or that. I argued that if she could save anything it would be better to put it straight into the bank to reduce the overdraft because they charged interest on it. This seemed to spoil the pleasure of her plans and was likely to blunt her determination so we agreed to a 'special box'. She was always an expert housekeeper but it was not until the war when she was on her own that I recognised the skill with which she manipulated our financial affairs.

The firm meeting with the accountant was due shortly and I didn't look forward to it. I thought I had better have a word with John Symonds beforehand to explain my position to him as I had done with Bill Beverley.

He listened carefully then beamed at me as though a great concession was about to be announced. 'We haven't charged you interest on the amount you owe so far,' he said. 'I think we can waive that again this year. Then perhaps you will be able to wipe some of it off next year.'

I thanked him without much enthusiasm, I fear, but thinking about it afterwards this *was* a concession. If I had to borrow the money to pay them back it would not be interest free.

The annual meeting with the accountant took place in the small room above the Melbrook surgery which was normally

128

Hannah Woodruff's private sanctum. It was a bare place with white walls furnished with an old kitchen table, a hard leather armchair and several small ones and a corner cupboard used to keep crockery and other domestic necessities in. The usual greeting to the accountant was followed by the usual discussion of firm affairs. Everyone's receipts and expenses were looked at but no overt criticism was ever made — probably because the results were always satisfactory. I sat silent through it all. I had little to say and in any case felt rather too much like the prisoner at the bar.

At last John Symonds made out the cheques. Wyburn and Beverley received several hundred pounds each and pocketed the cheques with an indifference I envied. Symonds who had drawn very little during the year paid himself well over a thousand pounds. Then it was my turn.

Symonds cleared his throat. 'We've had a talk about your position, Lane,' he said. 'You owe us one hundred and forty nine pounds and some odd.' He blew his nose hard as he was apt to do when he had something important to say. I waited. Perhaps they would offer me a larger share as I was now earning it. He went on, 'We've decided to wipe that out and let you start again. This should help you to balance your budget in future.'

I was almost stunned by the good news. To wipe out a sum like that was more than generous and left me feeling deeply indebted. It made me determined to work harder than ever to pull my weight in the future. They shan't regret it, I said to myself, as my size seemed to increase with the seconds like Alice in Wonderland.

I thanked them as best I could and heard with profound relief the sound of Hannah Woodruff's heavy steps coming up the bare wooden stairs with tea and biscuits. How she always managed to time her entry so precisely at the moment our business was completed I never knew. I sometimes wondered whether she had a means of listening-in to our deliberations or whether John Symonds had some secret signal to let her know that the moment had arrived.

I remember leaving the surgery with a very red face, I don't quite know why, and I managed a word with Bill Beverley as

15

On April the twenty fifth and twenty sixth every year Melbrook Fair made chaos of the traffic through the centre of the town. Historically the fair began by right of some ancient charter as a market for horses, cattle and farm produce but by the beginning of the twentieth century only the fun fair remained. The roundabouts, the big wheel and the dodgems filled the centre of the square and for a hundred yards along two of the radiating roads were stalls and sideshows — coconut shies, rifle shooting, fortune tellers, the large lady, stalls for jimjaws, hot chestnuts and sweetmeats of all sorts. It was a paradise for children and an excuse for horseplay by the youth of north Somerset. Late at night, with two or three competing screaming and discordant tunes splitting the ear drums, things went on in the shadows behind the tents that you can well imagine.

The result of all this was an adventurous week or two in the practice a couple of months later when we found out which of the local girls had been too cooperative.

Hannah Woodruff came to life quite remarkably for this short period looking with practiced and appraising eye at every young woman who came to visit the doctors. 'That Reddy girl has been caught I'm certain,' she said to me one evening. 'I saw her going in with her mother to see Dr. Wyburn.'

I had finished my surgery and Tom Wyburn was seeing his last patient so the surgery was empty. The little dispensary in the old surgery occupied the corner between our two consulting rooms and Hannah would look out over the half door of her domain to chat when she felt like it and to scowl when she didn't. I was preparing to leave but she seemed to want to talk.

131

'Reddy at all times I call her,' she went on and laughed happily. She evidently found a vicarious pleasure in the girl's misdemeanours.

'You mean she enjoyed the fair?' I said.

'We always get a few damsels in distress at this time of the year and I expect she'll be one of them.'

'I saw one of them last year I remember,' I said.

'I wonder how many there'll be this year,' Hannah said. 'Nine was the most we've had. That was back in Dr. Ballard's time just after the war.' Her expression was saying 'those were the days'.

'Quite a party,' I said. Her pleasure was so real I hadn't the heart to dampen it.

'It's the girls' fault. They ask for it.' I pictured her creeping round the backs of the tents on April the twenty fifth gathering evidence for her moral assertions.

'The girl I saw last year said she couldn't get away. The boy held her so tight.'

'Don't you believe it. It's always the girl's fault,' she repeated.

Soon after this reminder that we had entered the season of reckoning a very attractive girl of eighteen came to see me with her mother. It is not very sensible to make a diagnosis on impulse but I fully expected what came next.

'I don't know how to begin, Doctor,' said Mrs. Gowland. She looked at the girl who was quite unperturbed. 'She's missed twice. She says it can't be anything but I do swear she's getting bigger.'

The anxious mother and truculent daughter combination was new to me in those days. After the second world war you could almost diagnose an unwanted pregnancy from the facial expressions of the two as they walked into your consulting room.

Dora's attitude was different. I knew she was engaged to a very decent young fellow in the town. They were to be married next year and she had already begun to collect items for her trousseau. She was neither truculent, guilty-looking nor unduly worried. Perhaps — the thought crossed my mind — she wanted to get married earlier and had purposely decided to

132

force things. But if she had she would hardly be so supremely unconcerned.

Two months amenorrhoea and an enlarging lower abdomen were evidence enough for the mother who was both angry and bewildered. While I waited for the girl to undress Mrs. Gowland went on unburdening herself. 'I can't understand it, Doctor. She's always been such a good girl.'

'What do you think, Dora?' I said to the girl behind the screen.

'It can't be anything serious,' she answered. 'It can't possibly be.'

The irony of her words only struck me later. At the time, bless her, she was almost laughing.

My misgivings began when I started to examine her. To begin with she was a virgin. There was no breast enlargement or discolouration of the nipples and the mass in her pelvis was not a pregnant uterus. It was a worrying mass which might be malignant.

That day was the beginning of a period of six months or so when my eyes were opened wider and wider to the sheer evil and injustice of the world of nature. Dora, a charming and attractive girl of eighteen, had an inoperable cancer.

Her father, Adam Gowland, was a senior and responsible face worker at the colliery earning the princely wage of two pounds ten shillings a week. He was a staunch chapel man, deeply religious and his family were brought up strictly but in one of those secure homes that bred some of the best of the next generation.

There is some strange relationship between suffering and an all pervading religious conviction. It is certainly true now, when conditions are so much easier for most people in this country, that I see fewer families whose life is dominated by a spiritual dimension. It makes one wonder whether the nearness of evil and hardship leads people to a better understanding of the basic truths of life.

From the day Dora's cancer was diagnosed the Gowlands closed their ranks and each one seemed to concentrate on fighting the foul disease that had stricken at the heart of the family. Mrs. Gowland could not forgive herself for her early suspicions. For several weeks apparently she had suspected a pregnancy, then hoped, then suspected again, delaying her visit to me out of fear of what the news would be. 'Dear innocent,' she kept saying, 'I shall never forgive myself. And if I'd brought her to see you sooner it might have been got rid of.'

This was most unlikely and I told her so many times. We are always too ready to blame ourselves or someone else instead of the malignant spirit that would have been held totally responsible by our ancestors. I often think they were nearer the truth.

Operation revealed a fixed inoperable growth and the outcome was grim and certain. When she left hospital she naturally expected all would be well and the task of telling her she was seriously ill weighed on me heavily. The City Hospital had of course relieved me of much direct responsibility, and the next appointment with the surgeon made a focal point that she could concentrate on with hope of further help.

During the next few weeks her condition deteriorated enough for anyone to see the gravity of the situation. Dora closed her mind to this until she had been for her review at the hospital. Then when no further treatment was arranged for her she suddenly began to realise the truth. This is a grim moment at any age but at eighteen it is almost beyond belief. Hopes and fears chase one another in a macabre sort of dance, leading to violent changes of mood, from an almost mannic exhilaration to despair. I watched Dora go through all this and could do nothing to help. It seemed kinder to allow her to accept the truth in her own way than to tell her the facts however gently. This at any rate was how I rationalised my behaviour then and many times after. I shirked being frank and letting the stark horror of the truth lie openly before us.

One day as I went into her bedroom, her mother, who was a stalwart character said, 'She's been saying she's not going to get better, Doctor. I tell her she's talking nonsense. Of course she will.'

The attempt at deception seemed too crude and I avoided comment. 'How are you Dora?' I asked.

She gave a wan smile. 'Not very well thank you.'

'She's been telling me to get rid of those lovely things she's got in her bottom drawer,' her mother went on. 'I tell her she must cheer up. It's no good getting down. She's got a lovely nightie and a bed jacket and some lovely —'

'Please Mother!' Dora interrupted. 'I'd rather give the things away. I shan't want them now and it only makes me miserable thinking of them lying there in the drawer and never being wanted. It's better to give them away.'

'Don't give anything away,' I said. 'I know how bad you feel but we haven't given up hope. No one ever knows what's round the corner.' Each of us in our own way limped through the difficult days.

She didn't want to embarrass me and let the subject drop but we both knew what was round the corner.

Why from time to time misfortune should strike so hard at one family is hard to guess. Some would say it is the working of the law of averages. I prefer to blame the devil. It was at this unhappy stage of the illness that fate struck again. Andrew, Dora's young brother had a pit accident.

I was called to the coal face at the end of morning surgery. This was unusual because injured miners were generally brought to the pit head at once and we saw them there. Andrew it appeared had been injured by a fall of roof. He had almost escaped but the fingers of his left hand had been crushed under a mass of rock and he couldn't get away.

Andrew had begun work at fourteen, and as there was no favouritism under his father he started by wearing the guss. This was a leather and metal harness which, if worn by a horse, would have had the R.S.P.C.A. furiously organising a campaign to influence public opinion against the owners. The boys had the job of dragging the coal out from under the low seams — sometimes only two feet high — for loading on to trucks. Used as small horses they would go through weeks of pain while their skins hardened to the onslaught of metal on tender flesh. The older miners were sympathetic but the best advice they could give was to 'rub th' piss into un, m'son, noight an' marnin'. Things had always been like this. Why should anyone change them?

During the journey down in the cage, which in those days always seemed to be dripping with water, I was told what had happened. Sore in the loins and encumbered by the guss,

Andrew had been caught by a fall of roof at the edge of the seam. He must have spun round and almost escaped when the rock had trapped one hand on the ground.

As soon as I had the message I had begun to think what I must do. Very little good local anaesthetic was available at that time. A spray of ethyl chloride was enough to freeze the skin to open an abscess but this would be quite inadequate for the amputation of fingers. So I had brought the midwifery bag and some instruments with all the necessities for general anaesthesia.

The prospect was not a happy one. To give an anaesthetic of chloroform and ether in cramped conditions, probably lying down beside the patient, was not easy. Then to do a hurried amputation of four fingers while one of the colliery first aiders gave more anaesthetic on my instructions was going to be a nightmare. All the same fingers would be easier to amputate than an arm or leg.

Thoughts and plans rushed through my mind like the landscape seen from a train at full speed. Then, when we reached the pit bottom, all this slowed down and my mind emptied itself in readiness to meet what came. A sort of fatalism overtook me. I could make no more preparations, I could only do the best I could.

Two guides carried my equipment and a lamp each and we hurried in the dark along the rough track beside the rail lines to the scene of the accident. When we arrived Andrew was lying face down, quietly sobbing. One arm was stretched out and pinned by the fingers under a massive lump of roof. There must have been a dozen men standing a few yards back while others were erecting stout props all round to shore up the roof which was, I suppose, about four feet above floor level. Every now and then there would be an ominous crack but I was assured the roof would hold — for a time.

If it had been in imminent danger of falling those men would have held it up with their bare hands rather than leave the boy. My pulse was pumping hard with fear but there was no time to think of anything but the job in hand. I lay down beside the boy and murmured a reassurance I was far from feeling. His sobbing stopped for a moment.

136

The patchy light and shadows from lamps and torches and the mixture of hollow sounds and echoes produced an eerie effect which I hardly noticed at the time but which appeared vividly in my memory later. Pervading it all was the smell of coal dust and sweat.

The irregular under surface of the rock had caught his fingers across the knuckles. To amputate the four fingers at the proximal joints would be a disaster at his age but better than risking another fall of roof. I slid my fingers under the rock beside the boy's and thought the little finger at any rate was not being actually crushed, only pinched. The best plan was to amputate the two middle fingers and then try to pull the hand free.

I drew back and murmured to one of the men, 'How long have we got?'

'Be as quick as you can, Doctor.' This didn't sound too good.

It was worth one quick try to pull the hand out. If the rock could be moved a mere eighth of an inch this might be possible. I suggested this and was told they had already tried. 'Try once more,' I said.

'There bent much time, but we'll try.'

They had steel bars at hand and got the ends of these under one side of the rock. Two men strained at each bar and I pulled at the arm. Whether the rock moved or not I don't know but I pulled with ruthless energy and the hand came out leaving only one finger nail behind. Andrew was too brave or too shocked to make any resistance and in a matter of seconds he was carried back. The speed with which the men moved away from the danger area was a fair indication of what the situation had been. I was glad I hadn't fully realised it earlier but the risk of another fall was evidently considerable.

We had Andrew up to the pit head in no time, dressed his fingers and got him home. I remember feeling limp and rather sick and went straight home myself. Some hot tea and a cigarette pulled me together and a part of myself attended to my work for the rest of the day.

The shock of this episode occupied the Gowland family's attention for a day or two. It was a relief to think of something with a relatively happy ending, but very soon everyone's mind settled down again to the painful prospect of the weary days that lay ahead. There is much more treatment for all forms of cancer nowadays and the relief of pain is so much more effective that it never seems so hopeless as it did then.

We watched the pink colour drain from Dora's cheeks to be replaced by a leaden cachectic greyish yellow. The rounded flesh dissolved to leave the skin loose over the young bones. Her fiancé visited her daily until the end. There is no need to dwell on her last weeks. They were spent at home under increasing doses of morphia as the growth spread to various parts of the body and the pain increased. There was no Dr. Cicely Saunders in those days, no magnificent hospices for the terminal stages of cancer. The whole family were involved as well as the neighbours and district nurses but the atmosphere was one of gloom and grim determination — of something that had to be got through. All vastly different from conditions in today's hospices where skilled treatment turns the last days of many cancer sufferers into a time of peace and calm.

Dora died one night in January. It was a relief of course. I told Tom Wyburn in the surgery next morning.

'I was out in the night too,' he said. 'Kate Reddy had her baby — a strapping boy. Unwanted but healthy enough.'

'She was married in the end, wasn't she?'

'Oh yes, she's Mrs. Willing now. They just made it.'

My mind went back to Melbrook Fair. It was no good dwelling on the injustice of life.

After Dora died the demon left the family alone. Adam became a very solid and much admired member of the community. He had a temper it was wise to keep on the right side of, perhaps because his wife irritated him a good deal. Andrew grew up to have a fine family of his own and by the time *his* grandchildren were born I had become 'the old doctor' . . .

16

One of Hannah Woodruff's joys in life was 'getting in the money'. She took a personal pleasure in making sure that every penny owed to us materialised in hard cash. Naturally enough any patient who failed to pay was her mortal enemy.

When Sergeant Sperring became our debt collector one sometimes caught a glimpse of the two of them, heads together, planning campaigns against the non-payers. They were a splendid combination, Sergeant Sperring with his large size and mild manner stirred into action by Miss Woodruff's grim determination and detailed knowledge of every family.

The private patients' records were kept in green boxes which were put away each night in a fireproof safe. Tom Wyburn was a cautious man who always expected the worst. On some of the cards was written N.G. in red ink and on a few N.B.G. The meaning of the initials is not hard to guess and applied respectively to those who seldom or never paid their bills. On one of the N.B.G. cards was recorded the name Arthur Blacket. The Blackets had been to every doctor in the district and paid none of them.

Arthur Blacket had discovered in the course of a checkered career that a doctor would never refuse to treat a patient in real need. The fact that money was owing to him might make him resentful but not neglectful. This was good enough. I imagine Arthur rather enjoyed watching the various doctors fuming under their breaths at their own helplessness. He very decently made sure the doctors in the district shared the burden of his patronage fairly equally so none could really complain. What was more, the stories told about him in the Cottage Hospital gave almost enough entertainment to balance the unpaid bills. Dr. Blaythwaite for instance told how he had once tapped Blacket's hydrocoele — a collection of fluid round the testicle. He had removed a pint from the large rounded swelling and received a large perfectly rounded turnip with a note thanking him for his kindness.

I expected that sooner or later my turn would come to treat the Blackets and I had been warned by Tom Wyburn and still more forcibly by Hannah Woodruff that he must not have any treatment without paying on the spot. No medicine. No advice. In fact Miss Woodruff would not hand an aspirin over to him without payment.

I steeled myself to be tough with him when the time came. I knew he was not a panel patient and I assumed his annual income exceeded the statuary four hundred pounds. This alone was evidence enough that he was quite capable of paying his bills. It would be a challenge and I was determined to fare better than my partners and colleagues.

Arthur Blacket was a household name in the district but I had never met him until eventually he came to see me in the surgery. I had pictured him as a small man with an ingratiating manner but the reality was different. He was tall and prematurely bald with a prominent nose and an assured manner. He spoke with a pleasant Somerset accent.

'Good afternoon, Doctor,' he said. 'My name is Blacket. Arthur Blacket. I should like you to take me and my family on as patients. We've heard a lot about you. In fact we've been meaning to put ourselves under your care for some time.'

Perhaps I didn't look as flattered and pleased as he had expected. He went on, 'I ought to say straight away sir that like a lot of other people I've been through hard times since the general strike. In fact if it hadn't been for Mrs. Blacket I tell you straight I should've gone under. Wonderful woman she's been. I may have run up a bill or two here and there that should have been paid sooner but all that's over now. I'm in the scrap metal trade you see and business is looking up at last.'

I tried to interrupt him and to find out what was the matter with him but he was determined to have his say. 'I shall very soon be able to hold my head up anywheres and let me say right away that you shall be paid full and prompt for your attendance. As soon as the bill comes in that'll be paid. I promise you that. I don't mean to take up too much of your valuable time but I thought we'd better understand each other man to man right at the start. So I won't waste no more of your time. It's my balls. That's my trouble and my only trouble I should say. Swell up with water every so often.'

After this of course I didn't feel justified in demanding payment at his first attendance. Taking things to a logical conclusion it would mean demanding money on the table before I did the minor operation of tapping his hydrocoele. I was in a strong position of course because he was getting very uncomfortable! All the same you would need a very thick skin to be able to do this and I hadn't the doubtful advantage of this quality.

So I tapped his hydrocoele.

When I told my story to Tom Wyburn and Hannah Woodruff they laughed. Evidently Blacket said the same to every new doctor. After Hannah Woodruff had forcibly expressed the inevitable righteous indignation things settled down and I accepted my position of medical adviser to the Blacket family.

It was a week or two later that I had my first call to their home. It was a large solid Victorian house which looked as though it had been built as the centre point of a rubbish dump. The garden contained untidy heaps of old iron, old bicycle frames, several old bedsteads, piles of boxes, even some rusty railway lines. Inside the house, the first thing that greeted you was a characteristic smell — not altogether unpleasant — compounded of dust, potato peelings and unwashed clothes.

The whole house was dirty, not in the same category as George Grindle's cottage in Belle Vue but pretty dirty all the same. Mrs. Blacket was a cheerful untidy woman who could under other circumstances have been good to look at. She had a pink complexion, a full mouth, ample breasts, a slim waist and blonde hair that usually hung in rat's tails about her face and neck. She always had a duster in her hand but I don't think she ever used it. She was probably in a perpetual state of being about to use it.

141

Let me confess I generally enjoyed my visits there and this may explain why I was so ruthlessly exploited by them in the next few months. If they had annoyed me my irritation would have shown and they would have spared me many of their demands.

None of the rooms gave any impression of order but the individual articles of furniture and some of the pictures were good. There were some fine Chippendale and Hepplewhite chairs in the living room as well as a large and expensive radio set. The marital bed was an old, well carved, four poster and it was fair to assume the family was far above the poverty line.

On that first visit all the children had colds, one had earache and the other two bronchitis. They all exuded floods of catarrh from nose, mouth, and eyes, that from the nose being partly taken back into the system via the mouth. The eldest, Mandy, aged eight exercised heavy authority over the boys, Billy aged six and Joe aged four.

'Are you Dr. Lane?' Mandy asked me and when I admitted it she added, 'Mum said we'd try you out.'

'Quiet Mandy'. Her mother made a mild protest but was in no way embarrassed.

'You've had a lot of doctors, haven't you?' I said.

'You'm the fifth,' said the irrepressible Mandy. 'Dad says 'e expects you'm alright.'

I examined her chest and apart from bubbling like a cauldron she was not really ill and would be better up and about so that changes of posture would help to drain the mucus from her bronchial tubes. Medicine was useless and I told the mother so.

Next came Billy, also suffering from bronchitis but running a temperature and needing a bed to himself instead of sharing one with his sister.

Joe the youngest had earache. He was enveloped in a huge bandage which held in position over the painful ear a revolting mess which had at one time been a thick slice of toast softened in hot water. After spending several minutes scraping this out of the way I was able to examine the ear drum which was red and bulging. It needed incision which should have been done a day or so earlier.

142

There promised to be plenty of work for me in the Blacket household. I got Joe into the hospital that afternoon and incised the ear drum. He soon improved but Billy got worse and developed bronchopneumonia. There followed the familiar anxious days and nights while Billy's constitution fought for survival virtually unaided by medical science which was powerless to help. We put him in a separate room with a fire in it and I did my best to have the other children kept away from him. As discipline was nonexistent in the house this was a difficult problem.

It was characteristic of the household that any child who was not ill — and sometimes even if they were — would be eating bread and jam which gave them the appearance of circus clowns with large red painted mouths. Mandy and Joe, faces covered with jam, always followed me up to the sick room where they waited outside the door, Mandy talking in a loud voice. She had an annoying habit whenever she was not closely watched of probing into my bag and pulling everything out for inspection. Her mother would tell her not to do it and when this had no effect she would aim a blow at the child's head. Mandy had learned long ago to dodge these attacks and my only defence was to shut my bag firmly and keep it near me throughout my visit.

In due course Billy recovered and somehow I gained a degree of popularity which was only exceeded by my reputation for brilliance. For all I knew every doctor who attended the family went through the same stages but the result was that Mrs. Blacket began to send for me more and more often. There was always something wrong with one or other of the children. Then one day she sent for me because of her painful feet.

I protested that we always saw patients who were not ill in the surgery.

'But how could I get there, Doctor?' she asked wide eyed.

'How do you get into the town to do your shopping?' I asked.

'Oh, Arthur takes me in the van for that.'

'Then he could bring you in the van to the surgery, couldn't he?'

'He couldn't, Doctor. He's too busy. He's over at Shepton today.'

'And you couldn't walk?' It was about a mile and a half.

'How could I Doctor with these feet?' She gesticulated her conviction.

She certainly had bad feet. As a child she must have been made to wear shoes several sizes too small for her. The result was a large bunion on each foot, a big toe at right angles to the others and four hammer toes. Operation was the only treatment for her and this she would not hear of. The only other relief was by chiropody and this I warned her would cost money.

'Oh, Arthur doesn't mind how much he spends on me,' she said which caused me some surprise. 'He'll do anything for me.'

Yes, I thought, except pay the bills.

People were less determined to avoid all discomfort in the nineteen thirties and chiropodists were thin on the ground but I gave her an address of one who would be able to make her more comfortable. She was not in the least likely to follow my advice because the chiropodist would expect to be paid. Another wasted visit, I decided, and began to feel I was just being used. They were just trying to see how much they could get out of me before they transferred their demands to one of my colleagues.

For some reason at this time Mandy became passionately attached to me. Every time I called at the house she would follow me about like a shadow and she always accompanied me to my car on the way out. This meant walking along a pathway between the junk in the front garden and her habit was to try to hold my hand all the way. Her hand was always black and often sticky but it seemed wiser to let her hold my hand which I could wash later than my coat which I couldn't. So we went hand in hand to the car every time I visited the house.

'Can I come in the car with you?' she asked each time.

'No, I'm afraid I'm too busy Mandy.' She seemed quite satisfied with the same ritual.

I was called every few weeks to see one or other of the children. Their school attendance must have been atrocious. Then one day I was called to see Arthur himself. It was during one of those cold spells that we glorify by the name of spring.

The message was to say he was in bed and couldn't move. It sounded ominous — a stroke possibly.

I went as soon as I had finished morning surgery but it turned out that there was nothing urgent after all. On my way upstairs Mrs. Blacker told me it was one of his regular attacks of lumbago. When I examined him lying down his back moved well in all directions. It flexed, it extended, it rotated, with no trace of spasm or limitation of movement so I asked him to get out of bed. As I began to test his movements he promptly staggered and fell dramatically on to the bed. A classical malingering act, but why? I spent a few minutes checking everything. It takes far longer to make a diagnosis of malingering than anything else in the realm of every day medicine — partly because one is anxious not to be unjust. However I convinced myself there was nothing wrong with him and told him so.

'But it's my lumbago, Doctor. I get it every year. It just needs a few days in bed and I shall be alright again.'

'Very well, if you like to rest in bed do so by all means.' I prepared to go.

'I'll need my certificate, Doctor.'

'What certificate is that?' I knew he was not a panel patient.

'For my insurance. Just write it on a bit of paper. That's all I want. Say you've told me to stay in bed.'

'But I haven't. I can't find anything wrong with you.'

'But the doctor always gives me a certificate. I've paid them good money, it's only fair I should have what's due to me.'

'It's only due to you if you are ill,' I said as patiently as I could, 'and you are not ill.'

He looked puzzled and hurt. He was a good actor was Arthur Blacket. I began to wonder whether I had made a mistake and felt distinctly uncomfortable. There is nothing worse for someone genuinely ill than to be told they are malingering. Perhaps his lumbar muscles went into genuine spasm as soon as he stood up. However it was no good hesitating. I had made my decision and must stick to it.

'How many attacks like this have you had?' I asked.

'I get it every year,' he said, 'every year of my life.'

I told him gently but firmly that if he got up he would soon be alright. 'You'll be alright. You can go to work tomorrow.'

145

'Then I've got to lie here and not a penny coming in.' He sighed and before I left I thought he would burst into tears.

I still wasn't happy about him. Malingerers deserve sharp punishment which they never get. But one has to be sure they are malingerers.

Mandy came out with me to the car as usual and this gave me the chance for a little underhand investigation.

'I suppose you'll have to help your mother a lot now your father is in bed,' I said. 'Do you carry the trays upstairs?'

'What trays?' she said firmly, planting a layer of sticky brown stuff on my hand.

'What you put the dinner on,' I said.

'He don't have his dinner upstairs. He was only in bed till you did come.'

'Oh I see,' I said. Dear Mandy what a help you were.

I thought this episode might be the end of my care of the Blackets but this was not yet. The children all had measles. This meant three visits and a lot of cough medicine — much to Miss Woodruff's disgust. When I made my last call at the house over the measles Arthur happened to be at home so I brought up the question of payment. He was no whit abashed by the lumbago affair.

'Funny you should mention the bill, Doctor,' he said. 'I was going to tell you I'm expecting a nice little deal in a few days and when the money comes in you shall be the first to be paid.' He beamed reassuringly.

'Splendid,' I said. I must be very gullible but I thought he meant it.

Time passed and no money arrived. Finally after discussing the matter with Tom Wyburn I decided to put the account in the hands of Sergeant Sperring, the retired police officer who had become our debt collector. He was a friendly man who knew everyone. He was not in the least likely to make demands on people who couldn't pay. The arrangement was that he should have ten percent of any money he collected and the Blackets owed seventeen pounds — a large sum in those days.

Within two weeks the whole sum was paid.

We didn't actually open a bottle of champagne in the surgery but there was a good deal of cheerful rejoicing. No one who receives regular payment from the public purse can have an inkling of the hazards and uncertainties of private practice in the years of the depression.

I asked the Sergeant how he had managed it and he was rather hesitant. 'Oh it wasn't too difficult,' he said.

'But he owes money to every doctor for miles around,' I said. 'We've all asked to be paid and he promises but does nothing about it.'

'Well,' said the sergeant, 'there was a time when he took some bits of metal from the factory yard. We knew he got away with some stuff twice but we couldn't prove anything.'

'You mean you threatened him? Blackmailed him?'

'Oh no, nothing like that sir. I did just mention that we knew about it and told him he would get a fine of more than the doctor's bill if anyone were to report him. Nowadays, I said, the magistrates are hotter on that sort of thing than they used to be.'

I wanted to tell the story at the hospital but Tom Wyburn — a cautious man as I said before — thought better of it. If we told the others they might all want to borrow him and this might somehow depreciate his value.

I continued to treat the Blackets partly because I was for a time the only doctor they didn't owe money to and partly because Mandy who was a strong character refused to see anyone else. From that time on though the calls were far less frequent. What was more, in the course of time — sometimes a very long time — all their subsequent bills were paid.

17

I had been prepared to take strong action against the Blackets because I knew they had made something of a game of their determination to defraud us. On the other hand my own childhood experience had made me only too well aware of the hardships sometimes caused by doctors' bills and I was often accused of being over sympathetic towards the non-payers. From time to time this led to sharp differences of opinion.

I attended the Kenyon family for much of one winter. The man was a surface worker at the colliery, the wife not a brilliant manager and there were four children. Persistent coughs led to a high demand for cough medicine and it was after dispensing at my prescription several bottles of syrupus pectoralis rubra — splendid name for red cough medicine — that Hannah Woodruff made one of her caustic comments to me. Her voice was low and challenging.

'Those Kenyons will never pay their bills, you know.'

'Do they owe a lot?'

'They haven't paid last year's yet.'

'Poor devils, they haven't much to bless themselves with.'

'And you are prescribing the S.P.R. in such high concentration. Dr. Ballard used to prescribe half an ounce to the bottle. You order two ounces.'

'It's not much good giving them coloured water.'

This mild implied rebuke to my predecessor was enough to bring the bright red colour to her cheeks. She turned away in disgust while I mentally shrugged my shoulders.

In case I was neglecting my duty to the partners I had a look at the Kenyons' record card afterwards. They had been paying a shilling a week for several months. So that was that. They were doing their best.

A few weeks later Hannah Woodruff broached the subject again. 'That Kenyon family are owing over three pounds. They are getting into debt twice as fast as they are paying off.'

'What do you suggest? Refuse to treat them?'

'Tell them to get a parish note.'

'That wouldn't help. We are not paid per item of service.'

'It might shame them into paying if you suggested it.'

'I'm not going to suggest it.'

Whereon she froze into silence which as far as I was concerned lasted for several days.

I had particular reason to be sympathetic with the Kenyons whom I had come to know quite well. Jonas Kenyon had worked on the coal face until a couple of years before when he was involved in an accident underground. The injury was caused by a fall of roof which struck him in the back fracturing the spinous process of one of his vertebrae. He was away from work for three months and when he returned to the colliery he was unable to do his old work at the face and was given a surface job at a lower rate of pay. For the first three months the colliery made up his pay to that of a face worker but then a difference of opinion followed which led to long arguments. The management was convinced that he was well enough to do his old job at the face, Kenyon was convinced he wasn't. Then followed the reduction of his pay to the rate for surface work which was thirty five shillings a week.

The miners' union took up his case and asked the management to make up his pay to the original forty two shillings a week or to pay him a lump sum in compensation. They refused.

I was asked to support Kenyon's claim by a certificate of partial incapacity. This wasn't too easy because the injury to the spine was superficial and the bony process had healed well. Any subsequent pain would, I thought, be due to damage to muscles and a degree of stiffness in the back. It was questionable whether this was really enough to prevent his doing his old job and I was convinced that a large part of his disability was the result of the nervous shock of the accident. In other

149

words he felt such a dread of returning to a job which might involve him in another accident that he couldn't face it.

My certificate simply stated that as a result of the accident Kenyon was unfit to return to his work at the coal face. Time went by and still his money was not made up to its previous level. At last the miners' agent representing the union decided to take legal action against the colliery owners. He obtained a surgical specialist's opinion which I did not see but which I understood backed the man's claim to some extent but not very strongly.

Mr. Speed, the miner's agent, came to see me one day. He was a shrewd man and had no intention of spending funds for a case he would not win. He believed Kenyon was genuine and I agreed. 'We shall need a forceful opinion from you, Doctor,' he said. Then he told me what the owners' defence would be against his claim.

'When you treated him after the accident you had him Xrayed and found a fractured spine?'

'He fractured the spinous process of the ninth dorsal vertebra,' I told him. 'That's one of the prominent knobs you can feel under the skin down the spine. The rest of the vertebra was unaffected so he ought to have recovered.'

'Then why hasn't he?'

'He has some stiffness still but I think his nervous system was so badly shaken that he genuinely can't return to the coal face.'

'Not much physically wrong?'

'Not a lot, no.'

'What treatment did he have?'

'Only rest and heat and exercises when the fracture had recovered.'

'You are satisfied that no other treatment was needed?'

'There was nothing else you could do about it.'

'I only bring it up because this is what you will be asked in court. They will say why didn't you get a specialist to see him.'

'It wasn't necessary. There was nothing else a specialist could do.'

'That's alright then. The next thing they always do is to try and make out that he is swinging the lead. You agree he's genuine?'

'Absolutely genuine.'

The conversation rang a small alarm bell in my mind. I didn't look forward to defending my opinion and treatment against the attack of Mr. Bull, the advocate, who generally acted for the colliery owners against the union. Not that there seemed much they could attack in this case. I had a word with Tom Wyburn when Mr. Speed left. He knew about the Kenyon case.

'There's nothing much they can criticise in the treatment of that fracture is there?' I asked him.

'Nothing at all I should say, but I don't understand why he can't go back to the coal face. With a simple fracture like that which doesn't affect the function of the spine one would have expected him to have made a full recovery by now.'

'There is a strong nervous element and I can't blame him for that. Anyone who had just missed being killed by a fall of roof wouldn't be too keen on going back again.'

Tom Wyburn was not impressed. 'Then when you had a road accident you didn't expect to drive a car again?'

'It's not quite the same. Besides I wasn't injured.'

'I wonder whether he'll get away with any compensation,' Wyburn said.

'You don't think he will?'

'To be honest I should say not. If he is just nervous, that's not the colliery's fault. It's the way he was made.' Since Wyburn had been married he had become more tolerant and had a better understanding of patients' weaknesses. All the same he evidently didn't think Kenyon was genuinely incapacitated.

Some time later all four of us — Symonds, Beverley, Wyburn and I met by chance at the hospital one morning. There were no comfortable coffee sessions in those days and we talked together in the old car park in front of the hospital. The new car park as big as a football pitch had not been built then. I asked the others if they could spare a moment to talk about a case that was worrying me. 'It's coming into court soon,' I told John Symonds.

'They can be worrying, can't they? What is it?'

I told them.

Bill Beverley was the first to give an opinion. His pronouncements delivered from his full height and with the weight of his full fourteen stone often had the authority of a papal edict. 'If he fractured a spinous process,' he said, 'he must have damaged the rest of the vertebra. You can't hit a bone hard enough to knock a bit off it without disturbing its setting — ligaments, attached muscles, not to mention nerve roots.'

'That's true,' I said. 'I hadn't thought of it like that.'

'On the other hand,' Wyburn said, 'it should surely have settled down in eighteen months.'

'If there was a more serious injury than a chipped bone,' I told them, 'I shall be asked why I didn't consult a specialist right at the start.'

'I don't see what else he could have done,' Beverley said.

John Symonds had been listening. 'The more you dwell on the physical after effects the more you lay yourself open to criticism because you didn't get a specialist to see him. What is the Xray like now?'

'The spinous process is a bit crooked but the rest of the vertebra and the rest of the spine look normal.'

'Then if you think he is genuine the trouble will be nervous. That's the view I should press. As Wyburn says, he should have recovered physically after eighteen months. There's always plenty of argument about these cases once the nerves come into it. The old railway spine and so on. No one can possibly blame you if the after effects are nervous. You see what I mean?'

Beverley backed the same opinion. 'Anxiety neurosis,' he said firmly. 'Stick to that and don't budge. I must be off. Goodbye chaps.'

The group broke up and I was left with a vague malaise. They had been thinking more about keeping me free from criticism than anything else. I supposed I had nothing to worry about but I didn't look forward to dealing with this man Bull in the County Court.

The case came up at last. Acting for the union was a barrister named Love. He was pale in appearance and gentle in manner but dogged and determined. For the colliery was a solicitor who acted as advocate — Mr. Bull — who was red faced, thick necked with a degree of confidence that gave the impression of arrogance. No doubt he was excellent at his job but he was no friend of mine over the years!

After long wearisome preliminaries about the accident there followed the examination and cross examination of Jonas Kenyon. Mr. Bull bullied poor Jonas so much that I wanted to get up and hit him. I told myself it was all a piece of showmanship, and when Mr. Love took me through my evidence I felt quite confident.

Yes, I had treated the fractured vertebra.

Yes, I had been confident that no other treatment was needed except rest.

Yes, the Xray now showed full recovery from the fracture.

Yes, the man had had a shattering experience being half buried under a fall of roof six hundred feet below ground.

No, his nervous system had not recovered and the effects might be permanent.

Yes, he was unfit to undertake his former work at the coal face.

All this was easy. Then Mr. Bull rose slowly and looked at me as though I was a particularly incompetent first year medical student.

'You said, Doctor, that Jonas Kenyon had made a complete recovery from his fractured spine?'.

'A complete physical recovery apart from some stiffness in the back.'

'So in your opinion he is prevented from going back to his old work at the coal face by his nerves?'

'Yes. He is suffering from a severe anxiety state.'

'Does that mean he is anxious not to do the heavy work he did before?'

'No, it means he is unable to do it.'

'And would you agree that the best cure for this anxiety would be a lump sum?'

'Not a cure, no. Some compensation for his disability.'

'I put it to you that he is disinclined to go back to his old work but would like to be paid for it just the same.' He smiled round the court. 'One can hardly blame him for that.'

'He is not disinclined to do it. He is unable to do it.'

Suddenly Mr. Bull changed his tactics and his manner. He seemed about to charge. 'After nearly two years he is unable to go back to his former work after a fracture of one of the spine bones?'

'Yes.'

'When he sustained an injury which according to you has left him incapable of doing his normal work after nearly two years did you ask a specialist to see him?'

'No.'

'Why not?'

'I didn't think it would make any difference. The fracture was a superficial one. There was nothing a specialist could do for him that was not already being done.'

'How old are you Doctor?'

'Twenty six.'

'And you say that someone who has spent a lifetime treating such cases as this knows no more about them than you do at twenty six?'

'I didn't say that.'

'I commend your confidence.' He bared his teeth. 'I have here a report by an orthopaedic surgeon which I am handing to His Lordship. It states that Jonas Kenyon had a severe blow on his spine which resulted in a fracture and which has caused a considerable degree of stiffness which still remains. Would you agree with that?'

'Yes.'

'I suggest to His Lordship that if this man is still incapable of work after so long he should have had the benefit of a specialist's opinion after his accident. Therefore if he has a claim for compensation it should be against his medical adviser not against the colliery owners who take every care —'

'My Lord —' ejaculated Mr. Love.

The judge interrupted. 'Those remarks would be better made later Mr. Bull. Have you finished your cross examination?'

'One more question with Your Lordship's permission. In

view of your opinion, Doctor, that this man is permanently incapacitated by his injury would you not have been wiser to have asked for a specialist's advice in the first place?'

'No,' I said as firmly as I could. 'And his incapacity is not physical it is nervous.'

Mr. Love rose to put one more question to me. 'Doctor, if this man had nothing wrong with his nervous system would the stiffness he now has prevent him from doing his old work at the coal face?'

'No.'

I stepped down feeling thoroughly uncomfortable. I was free to go but waited for a while to see how the case went.

Mr. Love called an orthopaedic surgeon who gave it as his opinion that Kenyon had made a good physical recovery but suffered from an understandable nervous condition which rendered him unfit to return to his old work at the coal face. This made me feel better.

Much later Mr. Bull called an orthopaedic surgeon who gave it as his opinion that Kenyon had made a good recovery and *was* fit to return to his old work at the coal face.

So there was one piece of heavy artillery on each side and my own small voice on the side of the man. Mr. Bull's object as I realised afterwards was to discredit me in any way he could in the eyes of the judge. With my opinion eliminated the weight of evidence was equal. He knew that any sort of 'nerve' trouble was at that time regarded as another name for malingering.

Eventually the judge decided there was insufficient evidence that the man was unfit for his old work and dismissed the appeal for compensation.

Mr. Speed was angry and said he would appeal — though he never did. 'These people don't know what nerve trouble is,' he said. 'I'd like to make some of them work lying down under a two foot seam and see how they like it.'

I soon began to feel responsible myself for the adverse result. If we had taken the line that the trouble was physical and not nervous the result might have been different. And who could really tell? As Bill Beverley had said a blow on the vertebra sufficient to break part of the bone off must do severe damage to the tissues in the area. Who was to know whether the fine nerve filaments from the spine had been damaged or involved in scar tissue enough to cause prolonged pain? Although there were no actual physical signs of such injury there was presumptive evidence of a degree of permanent damage sufficient to prevent his return to the work on the coal face. Much could then have been made of the exhausting nature of face work in low seams for eight hours in cramped conditions.

Remembering my conversation with my partners I knew I had put aside the idea of residual physical disability because I was afraid of criticism of my failure to ask for specialist advice — useless as this advice would have been. The course of the case had proved my fears well grounded. If I had said there was severe physical disability after so long Mr. Bull would have had a field day with what remained of my self respect. All the same Kenyon might have won his case. I was convinced he was genuinely unfit for his old work, but I didn't know whether the trouble was physical or emotional.

This was why I felt sympathetic with the Kenyons over their bill. I think that winter they had everything — including whooping cough in the youngest child. They had earache, bronchitis, impetigo, bilious attacks and the mother was being worn to a shred. There were of course no children's allowances and Kenyon was paying six shillings rent out of his thirty five shillings a week pay.

When I thought of the determination that produced those tiny credit marks on their record card — 1/- 1/- 1/- — I wanted to take my hat off to Mrs. Kenyon. The idea of asking them to pay more was out of the question. I suggested they might put the four children in the club which would only cost twelve shillings a year for all medical treatment but the initial outlay was beyond them.

Hannah Woodruff had no qualms of conscience about getting money from poor payers. There were no such things as extenuating circumstances. Anyone who owed money for more than a few months was her natural enemy. Perhaps it was partly because they increased her work by forcing her to send out the same bills over and over again but it was chiefly due to the fact that my predecessor had trained her in the belief that he would starve unless she made people pay up.

One day I saw one of the Kenyon children leaving the surgery with an unwrapped bottle of medicine. Private patients had their medicine wrapped in white paper and sealed. It was the outward sign of their respectability and independence. I was preoccupied at the time and said nothing about it. Some time later I came out of my room to call on Tom Wyburn in his consulting room. This meant passing the dispensary door and I heard Miss Woodruff's voice. 'Tuppence for the bottle please'. It was addressed to one of the Kenyon children who stood gaping back at her. Without thinking I took tuppence out of my pocket and gave it to the child then went on and forgot about it.

It must have been several days later that Wyburn told me Miss Woodruff had been complaining about me.

'What about?' I asked.

'She said you had humiliated her. You gave some child tuppence to pay for his medicine bottle. It made her appear to be squeezing money out of them when it is what she has been told to do.'

'How does that humiliate her?'

'I suppose she is doing her job in trying to make people pay.'

'That was one of the Kenyon children. She shouldn't charge them anyway. They are private patients.'

'Non-paying ones?' His voice was gentle but sarcastic.

'I think they'll pay in time. They haven't got much. All rather petty don't you think?' Then after a moment's silence I said, 'Did I ever tell you about my mother?'

He gave me a quizzical look that seemed to question my sanity rather than what I was going to say.

'She was ill from nineteen eleven till nineteen fourteen,' I went on, 'when she died of T.B. They sent her to Margate where the air was supposed to do her good. She was attended by a Dr. Shipley Green who was a good G.P. I should imagine but his bills accumulated over the years because they couldn't be fully met as they came in. When she died my father was owing a sum equal to more than half his annual income. He was a schoolmaster — a headmaster and earning quite a fair income for those days — but the debt was crippling.'

Tom Wyburn looked at me with exaggerated patience, the

relevance of what I was saying had evidently not struck him. Or perhaps he was thinking of something entirely different.

'What I'm trying to tell you is that I know what it's like to be at the receiving end of a doctor's bill. When I was a boy I was well aware — the whole family were well aware — that my father was making stupendous efforts to pay off this enormous bill. My sister and I felt so sorry for him, struggling along without a wife and never able to afford a luxury of any sort, that we felt we had to play our part in saving money — which we did in a hundred ways. I can honestly say that that debt to the Margate doctor dominated my boyhood. I'm not making a hard luck story, only trying to explain how I feel about doctors' bills. They can be an appalling hardship.'

'Did you explain how you felt to Miss Woodruff?'

'Of course not. She wouldn't understand.'

'She might. She has some good qualities, you know.'

'Not much consideration for poverty. This family are paying every penny they can afford and they are going to be treated as private patients. To charge them tuppence for the bottle was an insult.' I was angry now and Tom Wyburn had the good sense to pipe down.

I wondered afterwards whether I was being unfair to Miss Woodruff. She did have some good qualities. Flashing eyes and a low masculine voice went with a toughness you had to admire. She suffered from fairly severe arthritis and never complained. She came to work on foot in all weathers and however she felt. Worthy but infuriating, I concluded. I couldn't see myself telling her the sad parts of my own childhood. Anyway I was going to make sure she treated the Kenyons as private patients. They were paying a shilling a week which was three percent of their total income.

I didn't enjoy having a set-to with anyone but it had to be done. The opportunity came one evening when the surgery was empty and she was about to leave.

'I gather you didn't like my giving tuppence to the Kenyon boy to pay for his bottle,' I said. 'I know you mean well by trying to get the money in, but the Kenyons are doing their best and they are having a bad time. I want them treated as private patients. You understand what I mean? They are too proud to ask for help and they'll pay what they can.'

'He tried to get compensation from the colliery, didn't he? And the judge said he was swinging the lead.'

Why did this woman infuriate me so badly? It was only later that I thought of crushing things to say. Perhaps it was just as well. 'That's not true. And it has nothing to do with what I am talking about anyway. The Kenyons are private patients. Alright?'

'Very well.' Her voice was icy as she moved to the door, turned to say goodnight and was gone.

I watched her walking with a slight limp to the end of the cul-de-sac until she turned into the footpath that led to Church Lane. At that moment I understood her a little better, her pride and her rigid code of service and I understood why we were as far apart as the poles. People's characters were, in her mind, black or white. The good people were the strong, the energetic, the uncomplaining. They paid their way. The bad ones were the weak, the poor, the Laodiceans, the shuffling mass of ordinary self-doubting people who were to be pitied but always disciplined and kept in their places.

The word communication was less fashionable then than it is now. It was completely lacking between us.

Like Mark Twain I am astounded at how much more sensible other people become as I grow older.

There is a postscript to add to the story of Jonas Kenyon. He went back to work on the coal face about a year later. Not quickly enough after the case came into court to make me think he had been exaggerating his symptoms and not long enough to convince me that he had been absolutely genuine. Perhaps the judge was right but who can be sure?

18

By nineteen thirty four the firm had settled down into a really good partnership. Each one pulled his weight. We got on well together and the wives were good friends. After three years I had been permitted to buy a further share in the practice worth two hundred and fifty pounds a year. For this I had to pay five hundred pounds in instalments. The Symonds had no children and shaped their lives accordingly. The rest of us were producing children pretty regularly. Barbara Symonds and Jessica went off playing golf or swimming in their spare time. J. was a very good swimmer but a terrible golfer. Barbara was the opposite. The Beverleys had a lot of friends among the school staff and roped us in to some of their activities. Tom Wyburn was less sociable than the rest of us being keen on music and learning foreign languages. Bill Beverley was the life and soul of every party. Helen Wyburn being a local girl had many friends in the district. Life was good. And of course it was too good to last.

When J. and I had one maid and one baby our small house was just big enough but in nineteen thirty four our second baby arrived. The midwife in attendance on all the wives was Dragon. She was enormously popular and in great demand by doctors' and schoolmasters' wives. So much so that she had to be booked about the fourth week of pregnancy. She herself once suggested innocently to one of her disappointed patients 'Well dear, you should book me first and have your 'party' afterwards.' When Dragon had shared our little house for the usual lying in period of four weeks (two weeks strictly in bed and two weeks of gradually increasing exercise) we began to realise we should have to find a larger house.

Each doctor's wife played a big part in the practice. The surgery phone was only manned by Hannah Woodruff for only a few hours a day and most of the messages came to the individual houses. This meant that either the doctor's wife or an experienced maid had to be constantly available to answer the door bell or the phone. We had of course no refrigerator, no dish washer, no washing machine. These were merely the adjuncts of decadent living that was rapidly engulfing the American people. There was no question of the British becoming involved in such soul destroying luxuries. The result was that the wives were very fully occupied.

Bill Beverley and I did our small bit by washing the babies' nappies at the weekends but Tom Wyburn firmly refused to do anything of the sort. He soon found that soap powders irritated his skin and he was forced to withdraw. My own father had discovered an equally effective method of avoiding the need to help in the domestic work. He always dropped a cup or a plate very promptly when he was asked to help and was shortly dismissed from the kitchen.

After our second baby was born we debated for some time the question of engaging a nanny. Then a treasure became suddenly available and Gladys Beverley urged us to have her. A girl who had just left school at fourteen was on the look out for a place at five shillings a week where she could gain experience in the care of children. So Margaret joined us.

She was indeed a treasure and after six months J. made the major decision to put up her wages to seven and six a week. The reaction was remarkable — not from other employees of nannies but from Margaret's mother. This good lady was a strong minded woman and dressed in her Sunday best she was truly formidable. She called on J. one summer afternoon.

After respectful preliminaries she began, 'I don't want to complain, Madam, but I felt I really must come over and see you. I've talked it over with my husband, though he doesn't know much about young people. Then I talked it over with my neighbour and then with Mrs. Dominy the schoolmaster's wife. In the end I feel I must speak.'

J. was feeling a little embarrassed by this time and made a quick mental calculation as to whether she could afford ten shillings a week for Margaret's wages. She waited.

'I want my Margaret to grow up a good girl, Madam,' Mrs. Ayres went on. 'And I think she will be one. We don't want any fly-by-night for a daughter, nor an extravagant one who doesn't know the value of money. So I hope you don't mind my speaking up. It's taken me a long time to make up my mind but there it is.' She seemed at this point to have forgotten that she had not explained what she had come for and lapsed into silence waiting for a reply.

At last J. said, 'I'm afraid I don't quite understand. Is it about Margaret's wages?'

'Yes, Madam.'

'How much do you think I ought to pay her?'

'Five shillings a week, Madam, was what we agreed for the first year and then you were to see how she got on.'

'But she is doing so well I have put her up to seven and six a week.'

'I know Madam.'

'Then what's the trouble?'

'It's too much Madam. It'll turn her head. If you would stick to what we agreed for a year. Then after that if she's really worth it she could go up a shilling or so.'

'Too much,' gasped Jessica. 'I thought you meant it wasn't enough.'

'More than enough Madam. I hope you don't think I'm being impertinent. She's very happy with you. She tells me everything of course and what you've taught her is just what I wanted for her.'

'Then you would like me to keep her at five shillings a week till the year is up?'

'Yes Madam.'

The strange interview ended with a cup of tea and one biscuit. Mrs. Ayres was very abstemious. Margaret stayed with us until all the children had gone away to school. She still visits us of course and is one of the family. Her own daughters are married now but she still spares a hug and a kiss for each one of us when she calls.

Competition between us and the opposition still kept us reasonably on our toes but there was no ill feeling between us.

We backed our firm as we backed the Somerset cricket team against Gloucestershire with enthusiasm but no venom. Being the youngest I took on a good many of the newcomers to the district and my list grew fairly steadily. Otherwise the practices were well stabilised and there was virtually no transferring from one to the other. Until, that is, Mrs. Slater came into the limelight.

Mrs. Slater had been a patient of the opposition's for many years, but one day her husband telephoned to ask me to call. She was my first conquest from the opposition for a long time and I was quite pleased. She was a seven and sixpenny visit too — fifty percent above the average.

I rang Dr. Blaythwaite of course and apologetically asked his formal permission to take over his case. 'Of course, my dear boy,' he said. 'By all means. You need never feel embarrassed about taking over one of my patients. Mrs. Slater, yes. Her husband is a particularly nice fellow but I don't think there is anything special I ought to tell you about her. You'll soon form your own opinion. You go ahead.'

He was always a model of courtesy and kindness, but even then I ought to have spotted the fact that he was particularly cordial over this affair. Instead I marched with sublime confidence on to the new battlefield.

On my first visit it took me over an hour to get anything approaching a case history. To begin with there was Spoofy, her tiny lap dog. This small animal had the loudest bark at the highest pitch I had ever had the misfortune to encounter. She yapped till the noise lanced the air, tore at the ear drums and lacerated the brain. Had one's attention not been rivetted to the sharp little spikes of teeth that guarded the origin of the noise one would have looked round to see whether every pane of glass in the district was not shattered by the vibration. Mrs. Slater evidently regarded the newcomer's acceptance of Spoofy's aggression as the necessary passport to her attention. I am not fond of tiny dogs and this little creature became a veritable Cerberus in my imagination.

The first few minutes of my interview with the patient were punctuated by a series of tympanic assaults but eventually I was able to get down to business. As far as I can remember

Mrs. Slater had symptoms in her digestive system, her chest, her joints, her muscles, her bones, her bladder and of course her nervous system. As soon as I was on the point of clarifying the nature of her wheezing attacks she would say 'but of course it's the calves of my legs that are the real trouble'.

After about an hour I pinned her down to some extent. 'So you have to get up twice every night but have no trouble by day, you have a backache associated with pains down your thighs, there is the windy pain that comes on regularly two hours after meals and there is the pressure on the head as though you were wearing a hat that was much too tight for you. That's right, isn't it?'

Mrs. Slater sat back in her chair and wriggled into a comfortable position. She was in her late thirties, blue eyed with a rather sallow complexion, above average height with quite a good figure, and dressed in the fashion of the day. The brown hair was flat on the head though well cut and tended. A pale green twin set of jersey and cardigan matched a speckled green skirt and the shoes were good brogues.

Her eyes challenged me as if to say 'your move, Doctor'. Then in case the move should come too soon — the doctor's visit was evidently her morning's occupation — she called Spoofy. 'There darling Spoofikins, the kind doctor is going to give Mother some medicine to take her pains away. Isn't that nice my precious?'

'I'm afraid I'll have to examine you first,' I said. 'You seem to have rather a lot of problems and I'll have to be sure I know what is at the root of them.'

'Examine me?' asked Mrs. Slater in shocked disbelief. 'You mean take my clothes off?'

'Yes,' I said firmly. 'I think in your bed would be the easiest way.'

It must have been quarter of an hour later that she called to say she was ready for examination and the visit had already lasted over an hour. I made a rapid but reasonably thorough examination and found nothing. Finally I wrote a prescription for some harmless sedative and left the house in a state of near mental exhaustion. The patient on the other hand seemed well pleased and thanked me profusely for my care and thoroughness.

After this I saw her nearly every week at her own or her husband's request. We chatted and I sympathised and left a prescription. But I wasn't very comfortable over the case. I told myself that I ought to say 'Mrs. Slater there is nothing wrong with you. You are a self centred woman who is determined to buy sympathy and attention you don't need and which does you no good whatever.' But I didn't of course. I went on with my visits. As long as I went on pandering to her she seemed well satisfied but I wasn't very proud of myself. As time went on I became more short tempered with her, but the more abrupt my manner with her the more amazing symptoms she would produce. At each visit I had to put up with several minutes of ear splitting noise from Spoofy together with her playful nibbles at my ankle. I tried to push her off saying 'Alright Spoofy it's only me. You know me don't you?' Far better to have stood quite still and allowed myself to be bitten and then quietly asked for some iodine to put on the wounds.

While I was treating Mrs. Slater the news was announced that Paul King was leaving the Blaythwaite practice and joining a partnership in the City. I was sorry. We had had our differences but he was part of the pleasant and stimulating background of those early years. It couldn't be that the few patients I had taken from the opposition had had any effect on his future. They were only a handful but just then I wished there hadn't been any at all. Most of all I wished I hadn't been landed with Mrs. Slater. After King left I was appointed medical officer to the Isolation Hospital and everything seemed to go my way. It was as though in a tug-of-war the other side had suddenly stopped pulling. Surely now I should be firm enough to refuse to treat people like Mrs. Slater.

I made no decision but let things drift on. Was there anything wrong, I asked myself, with giving her the attention she wanted and was prepared to pay for? Doctors had done the same all down the ages. Even Axel Munthe describes in the 'Story of San Michele' how he had made a good living from fashionable Parisian women who suffered from nothing more than a variety of 'malades imaginaires'.

I spoke to Bill Beverley about my conscience and he was forthright. 'What are you complaining about?' he said. 'We all get aches and pains and your woman wants to be regularly reassured that she is not seriously ill. You tell her what she wants to know and charge her seven and sixpence. There's nothing wrong with that.'

So I went on with my visits in better heart for a time.

Then in the course of ordinary chat about cases I mentioned her to Tom Wyburn. 'Would you go on treating a woman with nothing wrong with her for seven and six a time?' I said to him.

'No, I should let her know what I thought about her and she wouldn't send for me again. There are too many really ill people to bother with a woman like that.'

In retrospect he was no nearer the truth than Bill Beverley but his reaction matched my own. No one in those days taught — or even vaguely understood – how the minds of patients like Mrs. Slater really worked.

We were no more lacking in compassion than the next generation but we had been indoctrinated by simplistic mechanistic theories which left us blind to a good deal of the basis for human misery. For years we had been taught that, when diseased, each organ of the body will cause specific signs and symptoms. When none of these were present there was no 'real' disease. Anyone therefore who complained of symptoms that were unfamiliar to us was either a malingerer or a fusspot. Dr. Michael Balint was already observing the strange effects of personal relationship on the whole body mind complex. He had noticed how patients suffering from agitation, anxiety, depression would often convert these symptoms into others representing physical disease because this was what the doctors understood. But we had never heard of Dr. Michael Balint. The only problem in our minds was whether we ought to pander to neurotic patients or treat them to a firm auto-cratically imposed discipline. When occasionally neurotic symptoms progressed to the ultimate manifestation of suicide we said the balance of the mind was disturbed. But there was no half way house.

One day Mrs. Slater complained of losing the feeling and most of the strength of her left hand which led me to make an examination of her nervous system. I found nothing and a few minutes later I watched her pick up Spoofy in a manner which convinced me that she was malingering.

'Mrs. Slater,' I said, 'there is nothing wrong with your hand. You just picked up Spoofy perfectly well.'

I waited for her to blush with shame at being found out but she didn't. She spoke to Spoofy. 'The doctor thinks mother is fussing, darling. He doesn't understand, does he? He doesn't understand at all.'

'What don't I understand?' I asked.

'You don't understand how much I suffer. No one does. Men are all the same. You've never really understood me, have you? I'm no better than when I first saw you. It's not much to be proud of, is it?'

'No it's not,' I said. 'But if I can't find anything wrong with you it's no good offering treatment.' I was glad she didn't remind me of the bottles of medicine I had given her.

Spoofy feeling the tension suddenly got off her lap and came at me barking furiously in a cacophony of discords. I stood up and she gave me a sharp nip on the ankle. The inevitable happened. I won't admit that I kicked the little dog but I did lift her on my shoe and deposit her a couple of feet away from me. The visit proceeded with increasing chilliness on both sides though nothing satisfactory was said by either doctor or patient. It was one of those occasions when frankness on both sides would have done a great deal of good. More disasters are caused by persisting in the veneer of polite language than by the risks of outspokenness.

I fully expected to hear from Mr. Slater that I was not wanted there again but next day an urgent message came to my house before surgery. Mrs. Slater had lost the use of her left hand and arm.

I went along to see her in a hurry. Her husband had stayed at home and she was in bed. 'I think you will have a shock, Doctor,' he said. 'You didn't think there was much the matter with her and to tell the truth neither did I. But she woke up this morning with a paralysed arm. At first I thought she had been lying on it. I massaged it and moved it this way and that but it's quite dead, quite useless. I saw the same thing in my father when he had a stroke. She can't even feel it when I pinch and scratch her.'

The first thing I noticed about the patient was the look of satisfaction. At last, she seemed to be saying, you will have to take me seriously.

I examined her carefully. An area up to the elbow was completely devoid of sensation. I pricked her with a pin to the point of drawing blood and watched her face but she felt nothing. Above a sharp line at the elbow the sensation was normal. She was just able to bend the elbow but the hand was flail and useless. The rest of her body was normal. I paid particular attention to the other hand and her feet but they were normal.

The diagnosis was fairly obvious. She had a hysterical paralysis of the arm. I was somewhat reassured until I reviewed the whole case later. I told them it was a nerve trouble which would recover in time but that we should need to consult a specialist from the City. This I thought would please her and satisfy the husband. He was relieved to some extent but the patient was quite different. She didn't seem to be in the least interested in specialists or anything else. In fact she showed the classical 'bel indifference' of the hysteric.

I telephoned Dr. McNeil in the City who usually came out in consultation with us but he was away for the day. Then I phoned the Slaters to say I would be in touch again during the evening. But after lunch Dr. Blaythwaite came on the line.

He was obviously doing his best to suppress his amusement. 'Mrs. Slater,' he said. 'Her husband has asked me to look in and see her again. Is that alright?'

'Of course,' I said. 'By all means. She has a frank hysterical paralysis of the arm. I promised to get McNeil to see her but he is away for the day. I'll leave all that to you now, shall I?'

'Yes, I'll telephone him. What went wrong?'

'I don't know. I'm afraid I didn't handle her very well.'

'She has to be helped along like a partial cripple, doesn't she. Anyway you've no objection to my seeing her again?'

'None whatever. In fact I shall be deeply grateful to you.'

'You probably brought matters to a head. That's no bad thing.'

I sat in silence by the phone after this for several minutes. A hysterical paralysis meant she had come up against a situation she couldn't face and resorted unconsciously to an act of self mutilation. The last straw had been my suggestion that she had been malingering but what the underlying cause was I never knew. Her constant complaints were signals of distress. She offered one after another outrageous symptom to gain a doctor's attention, hoping he would enlighten her about whatever fiercely repressed emotions were churning up the deep levels of her mind. If one couldn't elucidate her problems one could at least do what Dr. Blaythwaite did and treat her gently.

At the time all this was a mystery to me and I called to see John Symonds about the case. The only thing I can remember him saying was, 'You know, Lane, we are just about as ignorant about the workings of the human mind as they were in the Middle Ages.'

And he wasn't far out.

19

Soon after Paul King left the district we had the far more distressing news that Bill Beverley had accepted an appointment with the Ministry of Health. He had won the Charles Hastings prize for research in general practice a year or two earlier and I suppose it was fairly obvious that he would aim at a more academic career in due course. All the same we were badly upset by the news. It felt as though our world was disintegrating. John Symonds was only to be with us another two years and the time when I should have to carry the main burden of the practice myself in Tom Wyburn's absence grew suddenly and threateningly near. A month or two earlier it had seemed years ahead. When the Beverleys told us they were leaving Jessica and I felt deserted.

We had the news on a December day — one of those days that seem devoid of light, and its sombreness fitted our mood. And it was that afternoon or the next that I was badly shaken by a case out on the Mendips. The events are closely related in my mind.

I had an urgent call at lunch time to see Jo Grundy's wife. They lived on the fringe of the practice beyond Hinton Mendip where Tom Wyburn had taken over the branch surgeries three years before in an effort to promote his courtship. After he was married he kept most of the patients in that area — perhaps for sentimental reasons — but I still had a few old faithfuls in and beyond the village.

In the summer I enjoyed my visits out there. It was a twenty minute drive which was a pleasant rest from work and the Mendips are a bleakly beautiful countryside, loaded with history. Preddy, at one time the centre of the wool trade, is now little more than a hamlet though picturesque enough when the hounds meet there on Boxing Day. The solid dry walls of local stone zigzag in apparently pointless fashion round pasture that was feeding ground for sheep long before the Cotswolds became famous. The mist hangs there a thousand feet above sea level sometimes for days on end and at night a journey can be hazardous.

Lead mines not far from Preddy were world famous in Roman times and a legend is still cherished that Christ as a young man once walked its streets before he started his ministry. They say he came over in one of Joseph of Arimathea's ships which traded between Israel and the Bristol Channel. When you stand alone on the empty hills the legend for some reason comes to life.

Harsh stories about the lead miners fit the landscape. It is told for instance how they used to punish a man who stole from another's workings. He would be tied down in his cottage and burned alive. Life was as hard and bleak as the hills.

Jo Grundy's wife was behaving strangely, he told me on the telephone, wouldn't let him sleep and kept talking nonsense. I set out early after lunch and the mist struck me like a blanket a mile before I reached the house.

I crawled along the road in my Morris Minor hoping to get the visit done quickly enough to drive home in daylight — although there was little enough of this even at two o'clock. The mist was still and clammy, swirling a few feet as I drove through it and, as I imagined, settling down again a few seconds later. The trees had an eerie look and seemed to reach high enough above you to disappear in the gloom. No wonder the poor woman was behaving strangely. Anyone might if they had to live for long in this dark dead silence.

Jo was a labourer and they lived in an old stone cottage near the main road. You could call it a main road in the summer; there appeared to be no traffic that day. The cottage was beyond the trees and faced out across what on a clear day was a fine view of the top Mendips. I knocked the door and walked straight in. There was no one in the living room and a paraffin lamp somehow made it look darker than ever. A fire was burning and this was the only cheerful thing in the place. I stopped to warm my hands — cars like the Morris Minor had no heating at that time and driving in winter was a cold affair. From the bedroom above came the sound of voices — a monologue punctuated every now and then by a man saying 'Alright, 'oman, alright.'

I went up the narrow stair and found Mrs. Grundy lying fully dressed on the bed with Jo apparently lying on top of her, pinning her down by the elbows. Not unnaturally she was struggling to get up.

'Can't mek out what be matter wi' she,' Jo said. 'Bewitched, I reckon. Zets an ztares out thic winder noight an day. Zays she can zee 'underds of volk out there, an there bent nuboddy.'

'Alright Jo,' I said. 'Let go of her and let me have a look.'

Reluctantly he released her and she lay quite still staring at the ceiling.

'What is it, Mrs. Grundy? Are you feeling ill?'

She stared at me as though I had joined the ranks of the enemy of whom her husband was the leader. She slowly raised her head and shoulders but Jo pounced on her and pushed her down again.

'Why do you do that?' I asked.

'Can't trust 'er Zir. Never know wot 'er be gwine ter deo.'

'Let her go. She'll be alright. I'll keep an eye on her.'

I stood beside her with Jo just behind me. There wasn't much room beside the bed.

'Lie deown 'oman,' Jo said.

'She'll be alright,' I repeated.

There was no easy course in an acute mental breakdown in those days, no routine consultation with a psychiatrist before treatment was planned. The certificate of insanity which led to incarceration in a mental hospital had to be very carefully completed. It was a responsible job and a general impression that someone was insane was useless. First hand evidence of actual delusions formed a vital part of most certificates of unsound mind. For years I kept copies of all my certificates in case questions should be raised later. To get the necessary evidence it was essential to get the patient to talk and this often took a long time. In this case I needed to get from the patient herself an account of what she saw happening on the hills.

'Tell me Mrs. Grundy what has been happening?'

'Appenin', 'appenin'' she muttered.

'Tell me.'

'It's them out there.'

'Who are they?'

'Underds on 'em, over the 'ills.'

'What are they doing?'

'They'm goin' to burn 'un.'

'Burn who?'

'Im as stole.'

'Where is this?'

'Over by the Miners' Arms.'

'You can't see that from here,' I said. 'It's more than a mile away.'

'I do zee 'un.'

It took a good deal longer than this but eventually I was satisfied the certificate would be straightforward. I confess I was concentrating more on this than on what she was doing. I made a few notes and when I looked up she was smiling strangely at me. She evidently felt better with Jo's weight off her, I thought. Then very slowly like an automaton in slow motion she stood up and stared at me. She was a big woman of thirteen or fourteen stone but she appeared completely docile.

She turned slowly and looked at the mist outside, then with a movement like a flash she stepped to the window, threw open the casement and dived outwards.

Joe and I grabbed a leg each to try to drag her back into the room but most of her weight was already outside the window hanging head downwards. What was more she did her best to prevent us from pulling her in by fixing her hands on the outer windowsill. We were both fairly strong and we pulled with all our might but her weight and her powerful arms pushing her outwards and downwards were too much for us. I shall never forget those minutes of sheer effort and near panic. Ten feet below was a concrete path which would crush her skull if she fell on to it. I remember the hopeless feeling as my strength began to ebb. There was no time to blame myself for letting her get up from the bed but a thousand thoughts of disaster rushed through my head. Sudden violent death is bad enough, but sudden violent death that you are yourself responsible for is far worse. Joe had known better than I did what was in her mind.

We pulled her this way and that hoping her muscles would tire before ours but they seemed to have superhuman strength. Her weight too increased every second.

'Let her go a few inches, Joe,' I panted, 'then she can't fight against us.' Her hands couldn't reach the windowsill then but the whole of her body weight below mid thigh was still dragging her downwards. 'Give a sudden pull upwards when I say — Now.' We tried to heave together but as soon as we raised her the few inches back went her hands on the windowsill to prevent us from hauling her in. Her hips were again flexed at right angles with the sill pressing into her groins. This put us in an almost impossible mechanical disadvantage. We were pulling at right angles to the upward direction which would have saved her.

We had almost given up hope when a car came by. It was crawling through the mist with the windscreen wide open in the way they used to be made. The mist was giving the driver problems and this was a godsend to us. We both shouted at the top of our voices and he stopped. Had he been travelling at normal speed and with closed windscreen he would never have heard us. It seemed only seconds later that the man ran into the room and with the extra strength of a third person our chances improved. He was fresh and strong. He stood between her legs with a hand round each thigh and we pulled together. In a short time we had her back in the room.

Joe and I and the patient collapsed panting on the bed. The relief was overwhelming.

When we had recovered our strength and some degree of composure I gave her a sedative and went off to phone for an ambulance. She was admitted an hour or two later to the Mental Hospital. Her condition was referred to as a schizophrenic episode but she recovered in a few weeks and never had a relapse. By the time I came back after phoning for the ambulance the helper who had saved us had gone.

'Who was he Joe?' I asked him.

'Never zeed 'un afore,' Joe said.

'And I didn't even thank him as far as I can remember,' I said.

'Too flummoxed we were I reckon,' said Joe and this was no exaggeration.

By the time I drove home that evening it was pitch dark and I was feeling badly shaken. It was good to descend low enough from the hills to get out of the mist and see such sane things as lights in cottage windows. I felt very much to blame for not watching her carefully enough but the thought of her making such a swift and determined effort to kill herself never entered my head. For years after this I found myself standing between the patient and the window in all my mental cases.

I went home for a cup of tea before surgery and absorbed the healing atmosphere for a few minutes. On occasions like this, traumatic experiences and acute anxieties would fall into perspective at home. Not because it was in any literal sense a place of 'peace and holy quiet'. It was usually a hive of activity but it seldom failed to put me right.

It was too soon to talk about Mrs. Grundy's escape from violent death and I sipped my tea in silence. Jessica knew that something disturbing had happened but didn't ask what. She knew I should blurt it all out in due course. On these occasions she would bid me a more than usually affectionate goodbye to tell me she knew I was bothered about something but would ask no questions.

It is useless to try to express in a few words the intimacy of a long close marriage. The mental and emotional needs of each are fundamentally different and the other learns to supply them. A strong mutual attraction holds the bond firmly while the natural aggressions and needs of each one find expression and understanding. It is fairly clear when you come to think of it that the study of a marriage in sufficient depth ought to enable doctors to understand the emotional illnesses in their patients many of which are the result of disturbed family relationships. The high and still rising divorce rate suggests they have had little success so far.

I suppose the present hard bitten age would have regarded us as sentimental. I don't think we were. It is just as important to express your affection as your aggression and much pleasanter.

Faced with the first imminent crack in the medical partnership, as well as the first rumblings of the menace of Hitler, the fact of home — the mere knowledge of its existence whether you were in it or not — was an anchor of security. I came to learn later the devastating effect on fighting soldiers of hearing of a breakdown of home life. Some people are strong enough in character (or insensitive enough) to remain inscrutably calm in the presence of sudden violent death without a subsequent tremor of distress. I am not one of these. The professional calm in emergency is essential but it is not always free from cost. In my own case the price was paid out of the much blessed emotional reserves of our marriage.

We talked out the details of the Grundy case that evening before bedtime. The image of the poor woman crushing her skull by a fall on to concrete was not easy to dispel. It was as real as if it had actually happened.

'If I hadn't been so confident,' I said for the fourth or fifth time. 'If I had trusted old Joe to know what he was doing. If I had even thought of her diving at the window like that I shouldn't feel so bad about it.'

'How could you have known?' Jessica said, also for the fourth or fifth time. 'And she is quite safe anyway. Nothing has happened. There's nothing to worry about.'

And in the course of time the tough, strong minded doctor was ready to go out again to the next traumatic emergency.

The strangest thing of all in that Grundy episode was the way the man who arrived in the nick of time disappeared out of our lives. I tried to remember what sort of car he was driving and seemed to picture an old brown Morris but I wasn't sure. With only this to go on we tried to trace him but failed. We never discovered who he was. I would have liked to be able to thank him.

20

Night calls in our bigger house after 1935 were heralded by a crunch on the gravel instead of the clang of the garden gate of our first cottage. In those days most night calls came by messenger and this was a more kindly method of disturbance than the telephone. There was immediate contact with a human being, one moreover who was in real need and usually apologetic and considerate into the bargain.

The telephone bell on the other hand is impersonal, inhuman, a robot. The person at the other end is not stirred to compassion at seeing you leaning out of the window, bleary eyed, hair on end. As often as not he hides his embarrassment at disturbing you by putting on the voice of aggression. No matter how the bell is modified to softer cadences, even cooing sounds, it is still a detested destroyer of the peace. Tom Wyburn came to hate the sound of it so intensely at one time that when it had tortured him beyond endurance for a day and a night he threw the instrument on the floor and jumped on it. Being a man of strict honesty he told the telephone engineer the next day what had happened and did his best to pay for the damage. Such were the ways of telecom in those days that this was impossible and a replacement was made free of charge. I always felt after this that the giant in charge of the telephone system was really a benevolent fellow at heart.

The phone was always near my pillow at night and when a message came that way I would grunt into it, trying to hide my resentment. People often say to me 'of course you don't mind being called out at night because you are so used to it'. This of course is nonsense. It always seemed to me an outrage to be called from the deepest sleep, to leave my bed and the warm body of my wife to face the cold bleakness of a silent and hostile world. I always made a great effort to put on a voice that said 'how good to hear from you' because after all whoever was calling was usually in real trouble. I understood from patients who were also friends however that these efforts were singularly unsuccessful.

In my experience night calls were almost invariably genuine emergencies of one sort or another. There was one occasion though — and this has nothing whatever to do with the story I am about to tell — when I was so angered that it took me hours to go to sleep again.

A voice said one night at about 2 am, 'Is that Dr Lane?'

'Yes'

'Can you tell me what Dr. Furlong's telephone number is?'

I resisted the temptation to shout abuse and said as politely as I could, 'You will find it in the telephone directory.'

'I can't find one here. Likely someone has gone off with it.'

I gave up and told him the number he wanted but having failed to express my aggression to the voice I suffered from a bout of extreme frustration for an hour or more. 'Can you imagine? Of all the confounded nerve' etc etc. Neither of us slept much more that night!

One winter's night, by contrast, Matron Tyson phoned me from the Isolation Hospital. I had been appointed medical officer there a couple of years earlier when Paul King left the district so it must have been in 1937.

'We've got a patient in, Doctor. A gypsy child and very ill. Advanced diph. I think needs tracheotomy.'

I was awake in a flash, adrenaline squirting wildly into my bloodstream. Diphtheria was common in those days though usually controlled in the early stages by antidiphtheritic serum. It was very rare to be confronted by a case so far advanced as to obstruct the breathing. Our practice was to give 24000 units of serum in any doubtful throat infection pending the result of a throat swab. If the result of this was positive for diphtheria, a second dose would sometimes be given, but even this was often unnecessary. A tracheotomy was a very rare emergency and indeed I had never had to perform one in my life nor seen one done — even during my time at the North East Metropolitan Fever Hospital.

The operation is simple enough and as students we were often regaled by stories of colleagues who in older days, when such emergencies were frequent, had performed miracles of improvisation. The classic story was of a child seen in a bus or in the street choking with advanced diphtheria as the mother was taking it to hospital. There was not a moment to lose and the intrepid medico would whip out his pocket knife, call for a hairpin from the nearest woman bystander and proceed to cut open the windpipe. Once the opening was made it would be held open by the springlike action of the inserted hairpin. The child would be rushed to hospital where a proper tube would replace the hairpin.

I had never been called on to perform this deed of heroism. If I had I was sure something would have gone desperately wrong and the child would have died under my hand leading to a charge of nothing less than manslaughter.

In tonight's emergency all the necessary instruments would be available and all I had to do was to get on with the life saving operation. But how difficult this can be in the imagination when you have never had to do it before!

I drove through the silent streets and raced up the hill to Peterdown. The Isolation Hospital was opposite the Cottage Hospital, purpose built with large wards for scarlet fever and diphtheria and a ward of single rooms for special or doubtful cases. It was in these that a year or two later I had the joy of treating cases of cerebrospinal meningitis with the new sulphonamide drugs and watching young men and women recover from what had previously been a hopeless death coma.

I swung the car through the hospital gates and was met by what looked like a riot. There must have been twenty or more dark faced men and women all talking and gesticulating. The car park near the main entrance was full to overflowing, it seemed, with the gypsies who had brought their sick child for treatment. It transpired that the boy had been undergoing for days a sort of group therapy organised by the grand old woman of the clan. I suppose when she realised the child was dying she decided to make a dramatic event of it, at the same time throwing the responsibility on to someone else.

As I got out of the car the noise stopped respectfully and a narrow gangway was formed for me to enter the doorway. In a few seconds I was in the little operating theatre. On the table was a child of five or six struggling to breathe. His eyes were dilated and his colour blueish grey. His pulse was racing and he was, in fact, in extremis. I looked in his mouth and my torch showed a mass of stinking diphtheritic membrane over the whole throat. The neck glands were grossly swollen.

'Why in God's name?' I muttered but it was no time for asking questions.

'Nine days,' said Matron. 'They've kept him nine days.' She was a solid character, quite unemotional as a rule, but on the verge of tears at the horror before us.

I stripped off my coat and washed quickly. Oxygen was already being fed into the air around the child's face. Now for it, I thought, and may Heaven guide me.

'Make a firm incision below the thyroid cartilage,' I said to myself. 'Cut vertically downwards with the scalpel at an exact rightangle to the floor. Go through the cricoid cartilage if necessary and straight into the trachea. No problem at all.

I pressed with finger and thumb into the place where the trachea ought to be but all I could feel was a soggy mass. How did you cut into the windpipe when you had no idea where it was? My heart sank.

The whole neck was grossly swollen and when you remember that in a child of that age you are looking for a tube the size of a small pencil you realise what you are up against. Tracheotomy in a healthy patient or a dead body could be done blindfold — by feeling — but this was another matter. It was mad and maddening. The child was going to die while I failed to do my first and perhaps only tracheotomy.

There was only a few minutes in which to open the windpipe and get an airway going. A blind cut was useless; it would only complicate things by a lot of blood which would make the whole job virtually hopeless. I cursed the fools who had left the boy until he was at death's door before asking for help. I had no plan in mind but stood rooted to the spot, a finger and thumb automatically pressing over the place where the trachea must be. After a long minute the oedema swelling was gradually pushed aside by my pressure and as it dispersed I began to feel the resistance of the small windpipe. As it took shape as if by a miracle I thought I could just make out the resistance of the thyroid and cricoid cartilages.

The child was unconscious and in any case a local anaesthetic was out of the question. It would increase the swelling and the trachea would disappear again so I had to go ahead without an anaesthetic of any sort. This meant that if things went well we should have a struggling child to deal with but this was preferable to the alternative of a still and silent one.

I held the scalpel in my right hand and pressed firmly with the finger and thumb of my left on the sides of the thyroid cartilage. As soon as I was fairly confident I could cut into the trachea, I meant to cut through the surface tissues with one incision and into the trachea with the second. At this moment while my heart was beating like a steam engine Matron gasped suddenly. 'Good Heavens. Go away.' She sounded so distressed that for a second I looked up to where she was staring.

There at the top of the window was a woman's face. The lower panes of the window were opaque but the upper ones were of plain glass. Somehow the woman — who turned out to be the mother of the child — had been hoisted up so that she could see into the lighted room.

I was concentrating so hard on what I was doing that I didn't care at that moment who was looking on. All the gypsies in the world could stand and stare if they liked. My mind was concerned with only one object — to get air blowing in and out of this windpipe. I cut firmly down into what I would have sworn was the right place. Nothing happened except a gush of dark red blood. I cut deeper in the same place. Still nothing. Dark blood oozed all over the neck making things even worse than before.

At that moment the mother peering through the window screamed. I don't know what she said but the sound was agonised — horrifying. It had the effect of making my brain ice cold and my concentration even more intense. 'Tell someone to take that woman from the window and look after her,' I said.

There were murmered words and someone left the theatre. I swabbed the wound and grasped the trachea more firmly. I could feel it better, probably because the swelling was being steadily dispersed by my pressure. Then Matron whispered, 'Go straight through the cricoid, Doctor'. She was more experienced in this emergency than I was and I felt I had powerful support. I still bless her for this. I cut straight downwards in the same incision. It felt so deep that it seemed as though I must almost have reached the spine but suddenly a wonderful sound rewarded me. Bubbles of air gushed in and out blowing small jets of blood like a spray in all directions. The trachea was open.

The moment of thankfulness that fills you on such occasions makes the tense anxiety leading up to it almost worth while. But not quite. I wouldn't want to live through another five minutes like that again.

I kept open the incision into the trachea with forceps while oxygen was directed into the area. The boy was quite still and his pulse was racing so fast as to be uncountable but gradually air flowed into the bursting lungs and his colour improved. In a few minutes the blood oozing from the wound became a brighter red and we knew the immediate danger was over. Then best of all the boy began to move. This was the signal to put in the tracheotomy tube. Matron handed me one of exactly the right size and with a little manipulation I fixed it in place. We tied the tapes firmly round the neck and watched. I took a deep breath of sheer relief.

Matron was equally relieved. 'That was the nearest thing I've ever seen,' she said.

I watched the child's improvement and ordered a large dose of antidiphtheritic serum then we retired to Matron's room for a cup of tea. There is a longing to talk when you come out of an emergency of this sort — rather like the reaction to a bad accident when someone has missed death by a hair's breadth. It doesn't come on at once but follows when the mind has time to go back over the recent events. Matron was a good psychologist and encouraged me to talk which I did for some ten minutes or so.

I had quite forgotten the riot of gypsies outside and even, I fear, the mother of the boy herself. Suddenly all the gypsies outside began to talk at once. The impression was of a cocktail party in full swing.

'What's happened now?' I asked Matron.

'I told nurse to go out and say the worst is over and the boy is breathing again. They seem to be welcoming the news.'

Every patient in the hospital must have been wide awake by now but I hadn't the heart to tell them to keep quiet. Their need to talk probably equalled my own.

'How on earth did that woman climb up to see in the window?' I asked.

'Nurse said that when she went out there, she was standing on a man's shoulder. Poor thing, she didn't look much more than a child herself.'

'How long did you say the child had been ill?'

'Nine days. They had given it all sorts of remedies. They have an old woman who treats all their illnesses.'

'I wonder what she'll say now.'

Matron laughed. 'If the child recovers she'll take the credit I shouldn't wonder.'

When the flow of talk had spent itself there was a scuffle outside and a large man and an elderly woman pushed their way past a nurse and into the room. The man had removed his hat — a brown trilby I remember which must at one time have belonged to a man of fashion — and was twisting it in his hands. 'We want to thank you sir'. He held out his hand and all but crushed my own.

The woman's attitude was quite different. She stood like a queen beaming down at us as though waiting for homage — or perhaps congratulations. The main thing I remember about her is her dark brown piercing eyes.

We were too relieved to be severe with them. I advanced to meet them at the door and said, 'This is Matron's room. I'm afraid you can't stay here. We'll take care of your boy. Come back in the morning and enquire about him'.

Evidently the woman was the camp medical adviser and she was not going to be prevented from having her say. She seemed quietly pleased with herself, certainly not in the least conscience stricken over her part in the case.

'I've treated 'im night and day, young sir, but I knew the ninth day were when 'e would turn one way or t'other. Wait till the ninth day I said. Then I thought he'd better come in here for the turn. And I were right weren't I?'

I told her that he ought to have been in here from the beginning and then suddenly remembered the public health aspect of the case and asked if any others in the camp had sore throats.

'There's one or two with the white mouth,' she said.

This made me virtually speechless. Did she really think the boy was suffering from 'white mouth' — the common name for simple thrush? The thought of a vast pocket of infection carefully nurtured by the gypsies was horrifying. How many more would come to us dying of asphyxia?

'But this is diphtheria,' I said. '*Diphtheria.*' The word had no effect on her whatever. 'It's a very dangerous disease.' She looked through me in silence. I had no doubt that the medical officer of health would call on the camp later that day and would take vigorous action and I added, 'A doctor will call at your camp during the day.'

This disturbed her for a moment but she soon recovered and stood looking at us as though we were some strange animals in the zoo.

I had never met ignorance so supremely confident, so completely divorced from reality. In her own mind she had justified herself, had acted correctly according to her principles. Whether the boy lived or died was a matter for the gods, she had done her part. Indeed she had, and had almost succeeded in killing him but it seemed useless to try and make her understand and it didn't seem fair to accuse her. The brutal treatment of witches in the middle ages became suddenly more understandable. I wondered later whether the number 'nine' being to do with witchcraft, had anything to do with her strange theory.

Defeated, I shepherded them both out of the room. If there was any lecturing to do, I told myself, it was the job of the M.O.H. who at that time was Dr. Braithwaite. Meanwhile the child was likely enough to die in spite of the tracheotomy.

In less than half an hour I was back in bed. In those early years I usually slept again very quickly but that night sleep wouldn't come. I went over and over again the traumatic events of the past hour — the details and difficulties of the tracheotomy, the young woman's face at the window framed against the blackness of the night, and the Sary Gamp who had treated the boy for day after day while his chances of life slid steadily away. I regretted too that I hadn't had a word with the poor little mother. I am pretty good at remembering too late the kindly things I ought to have done and nothing is more certain to keep you awake.

At half past six or so I was still awake when the telephone rang again. It was Matron. The boy had died. His heart had failed after the appalling onslaught of the diphtheria toxin and all my efforts had come to nothing.

I wonder sometimes whether the young mothers of the nineteen eighties realise the enormous blessing of the innoculations their children receive as a matter of course. No, I don't wonder any such thing. They have no conception of what they are being saved. Not that this matters really so long as, for the children's sake, they accept the safeguards they are offered.

21

Swain Galley was what used to be called a gentleman farmer. I suppose this meant that he belonged to a family with some inherited wealth which entitled him to the description 'gentleman'. He was a farmer, and a good one at that, but he was best known for his outrageous propensity for leg pulling. By all accounts he had been handsome in his youth but he had certainly put on weight before reaching middle-age. Most of his adipose tissue was deposited in the area adjacent to his hips. In other words he had a large bottom. The diamond shaped figure that resulted was exaggerated by the voluminous breeches he always wore. In the pockets of these he carried not only pipe and tobacco but books, account books, papers and even a farm implement or two.

He was a good horseman and regarded riding as his natural mode of progression but when he left his six hundred acres and came into the town he used one of two old dilapidated and rusty motor cars. What colour these were under their coat of permanent mud is uncertain — probably a fairly dark brown.

The whole Galley family were 'characters' with huge self confidence and robust views on every problem that came their way. I had been flattered by being asked to attend Swain's mother who was as daunting an old lady as I ever met. She ruled the family with a rod of iron and was said to be the only human being with any influence on her eldest son.

'What do you think of my son Swain?' she said to me one day.

'Well he's a character,' I said non-committally and added, 'with a great sense of humour.'

186

'It's not humour,' the old lady said. 'He can't laugh at himself, only at other people. Sometimes I think he suffers from a severe inferiority complex and spends his time proving to himself that he is cleverer than anyone else.'

The thought of Swain Galley with an inferiority complex almost made me laugh out loud, but perhaps old Mrs Galley had a more penetrating insight than I had.

Swain had two labourers on his farm who might be called ordinary in that they were content to live their lives without seeking notoriety. His third helper was a man as colourful as himself. Lemuel Fields was known and recognised everywhere in the district. When I knew him he was always dressed like a scarecrow with a very wide brimmed hat that acted as umbrella or sunshade in all weathers. He would sit crouched on his cart as the horse drew him majestically along at two to three miles an hour. He carried a whip with which he would touch the horse occasionally though most of his communication with the animal was in the broadest of Somerset accents. The two were inseparable.

Lemuel, who had been a fine figure of a man in his young days was in the Life Guards in the first world war. I was told that when he came home on leave he would ride on horseback along the High Street in full dress uniform with sword at present arms. Sometimes in those days of few motor cars he would gallop at full speed uttering ferocious war cries loud enough to waken the dead. And in those tolerant days — tolerant that is of idiosyncracies — people would only laugh and say, 'Oh it's only Lem back on leave'.

There are not many people who are completely indifferent to the opinions of others but I believe Swain Galley cared not one jot for any living soul. Most people prefer to have the good opinion of their group or their neighbours or their professional colleagues, and society depends for its stability on this normal human trait. On the other hand change, progress, development, evolution, depend just as obviously on the mavericks, the independent ones who will go their own way in spite of the frowns and curses of the majority. Swain was a maverick but not one, I think, likely to lead humanity along new evolutionary paths to the greater glory of man.

I know for a fact that his dachshund — Wilhelm — slept not just on his bed, but in it, and no protest from his family had the slightest effect on him. If ever a fox on the run from the hunt came anywhere near his land he would shoot it thereby spoiling the run for the hunt. It would be charitable to suppose that his object was either to protect his land from damage by the hunt or to prevent the fox from suffering, but I must confess that my own charity falls somewhat short of this interpretation of his motives. Certainly members of the hunt were his natural enemies and the dislike was mutual. I personally never enjoyed seeing a fox torn to pieces by hounds in spite of the claim that it is the most natural way of getting rid of vermin, but it is fair to say that such qualms never entered Swain's head.

One of his practical jokes was perpetrated on a very gentle inoffensive man in the town named Percy Napper. Percy lived with his sister and kept a small shop. He wouldn't hurt a fly and aimed at being on good terms with everyone.

One day — it was a few weeks before I was first called to see him — Swain went to the post office and saw a magnificent new Bentley standing outside it. As he stood admiring it along came Percy Napper.

'What do you think of her Percy?'

'Beautiful, isn't she?' answered Percy.

'I thought it was about time I got rid of both my old cars and got something decent.'

Percy stared at him. 'You don't mean it's yours?'

'New last week. Like a run in her?'

'That would be very nice,' said Percy.

'Jump in then. Try the driver's seat first. See how comfortable the back of that seat is. Does my back good to sit in her.' He held open the door.

'May I really?' said Percy. 'It's awfully kind of you.' He climbed in.

'Feel that gear handle,' Swain went on. 'She changes as smooth as oil. And try the horn. That's something special, that is.'

Percy hesitated. 'Go on,' said Swain.

At last Percy gave a good blast on the horn and of course at that moment the owner of the Bentley came out of the post office.

'What the devil are you doing in my car?' he said.

Percy turned to Swain, only to see him sauntering off and already twenty yards away.

When I heard this story I felt really sorry for poor Percy Napper. You need to know him to realise how acutely embarrassed he must have been, tying himself in knots with apologies, blushing and sweating, wishing he could vanish into thin air. I vowed I would pay some of his debt to Swain Galley if ever I had the chance. But this was no easy matter.

It was a hot summer day when I was called to see Swain. His wife Emma, who became our good friend for many years, spoke to me before I went upstairs to the bedroom.

'You know Swain, Doctor, don't you? By reputation anyway — yes. He's — well — a little unusual shall we say.' Emma was as nearly the perfect wife for Swain as is humanly possible. Her sense of humour was enough to meet all the circumstances — which is high praise. 'For the first time in my married life,' she went on, 'I am a little worried about him. He's been ill for two days — off his food — and this for Swain is serious, really serious. Today he is feverish. I made his temperature a hundred and four this morning. But apart from that he's been behaving strangely. He must be feeling ill but this morning I heard him laughing to himself. Laughing — all by himself. I wondered for a moment whether he was delirious but he seems perfectly sensible. When I asked him what he was laughing at he looked at me as if I was mad and said he wasn't laughing. I began to wonder whether it was me that was delirious. Most extraordinary. But then you wouldn't expect Swain to have an ordinary illness, would you? Would you?'

No, I thought, you wouldn't.

His temperature was a hundred and two and he was evidently suffering from some pretty sharp infection. I examined him carefully — throat, ears, chest, abdomen and found nothing definite except a mild redness of the throat which was nothing much to go on in a heavy pipe smoker. I was puzzled and a bit irritated that there was nothing to make a diagnosis on. There had been a fair amount of flu about and I began to think of this as a possibility. Again I questioned him about symptoms.

'No particular symptoms at all then? No pain, no cough, no sore throat?'

'No.'

He was being very unhelpful and at the same time looking rather odd, as though he was almost pleased with himself. This made little sense unless it satisfied him to puzzle me. I wondered whether he was slightly confused or suffering from some mental symptoms — perhaps a rarity like early encephalitis.

'Have you any idea what the trouble might be?' I asked.

'How should I know. That's what I sent for you for.'

I checked his throat again and his chest then his reflexes and finally looked at his retinae. Then I said we should have to keep him resting for a bit and if he didn't improve do a chest Xray and a blood test. There was no typhoid about but I was beginning to consider that sort of possibility. Abortus fever was on the cards too in someone handling cattle, especially at that time when some herds were badly infected by it.

'Any of your cows dropping their calves?' I asked.

He knew what I was thinking of. 'No, there's no fever in my herd. What's this about an Xray?' he said.

'Sometimes you get virus infections in the lung that you can't detect with a stethoscope,' I said. And then I noticed a pleased expression flit across his face which quickly became a mask again.

Could he possibly be malingering? Trying some practical joke on me? Perhaps he had washed his mouth out with very hot water just as I was arriving at the house. It was becoming a perfectly idiotic battle of wits between us. I shook my thermometer down and slipped it under his tongue again. It was a hundred and two and his pulse was correspondingly high. He was genuine enough.

I looked at him again and there was the selfsatisfied smirk still playing round his features. Why should a man with a temperature of a hundred and two look so pleased with himself? I felt sure he was keeping something back. Some sort of dysentery perhaps. 'Ever had malaria in the last couple of years?' I asked him.

190

'No'. He almost seemed to be saying try again.

Then I suddenly remembered a previous case in which I had really and truly slipped up. I wonder, I thought.

I began a systematic search of every inch of his body. He had short pants on and I had these removed. I examined his back and his neck and every bit of his scalp and still found nothing. He had his socks on in bed and I asked him to take them off.

Reluctantly he did so and there on one ankle was a blazing patch of erysipelas.

'Why didn't you tell me about that? It would have saved a lot of time.'

'Thought you were never going to find it,' he said as though we were playing hunt the thimble.

He was not in the least embarrassed. Perhaps a little disappointed that he had been denied the pleasure of showing it to me after I had made a wrong diagnosis. What he would have made of the story if I had called it flu I hate to think.

It was nineteen thirty eight and sulphonamide tablets had recently come on the market. I had already used them in cases of acute inflammation of the middle ear and had read that they were highly effective in erysipelas.

My first reaction was that after his childish behaviour he didn't deserve the benefit of the splendid new drug. What he really deserved was a massive injection with a large blunt intramuscular needle into a sensitive part of his anatomy. Such thoughts however were not only unethical but impractical because soluble sulphonamide for injection was not available at the time.

I wrote a prescription for him. 'Take two of these every four hours,' I said, 'and next time don't waste my time playing hide and seek.' I grinned at him and to do him justice he grinned back at me.

Looking at him again the thought struck me that he must be feeling very ill. Most people in his condition would be reduced to silent misery. You couldn't help admiring the spirit that kept him actively leg-pulling with a temperature of a hundred and two.

When, downstairs, I told Emma about it she said, 'Thank goodness you found it — this what's it called. Thank goodness.' There was always suppressed laughter in what Emma said. In all the years we knew her it seemed to be trying to escape between the words. 'I should have heard the story every evening,' she went on, 'for weeks and weeks. All Melbrook would have heard it in three days — with embellishments. Thank goodness.'

'To tell you the truth,' I said, 'I was lucky. I had a case some time ago when the patient didn't show me the spot on his leg until I had treated him as flu for twenty four hours and he was getting worse. That man thought the spot had nothing to do with his illness. Swain, of course, knew perfectly well.'

'Thank goodness you found it,' Emma said again.

On my way out I met Lemuel Fields. He was leaning against his horse evidently waiting for news of his master.

'Wot be madder wi' Gaffer then?' he said.

It is always a problem to know how to answer people who ask quite innocently what is wrong with one of your patients. You can't say, so you have to put them off somehow without offending them. 'He'll be better in a day or two,' I said.

'Oi doan't reckon 'er wull. Oi yeard 'er 'ad the vire.'

The Vire. The fire. What on earth did the man mean. 'What do you mean, Lem, the fire?'

'Zatan's vire. You der know.'

Suddenly the penny dropped. The old name for erysipelas was St. Anthony's fire. Satan was evidently a corruption of St.Anthony.

'Who told you that?' I asked.

'Gaffer 'isself told oi. Day afore yessday.'

'He knew what was the matter then, did he?' I left Lem standing by his horse. He didn't seem very satisfied with my side of the conversation. He would have liked more details.

So Swain Galley had known all the time what was the matter. He had a final dig at me the next day.

'I didn't expect you'd have heard of sulphonamide yet,' he said. 'I was reading about it in the Farmer's Weekly. It seems to be good for a lot of things in the live stock.'

'So I believe.'

'If I could have got the stuff without a prescription I'd have treated myself.'

That Christmas Swain and Emma sent us a turkey.

22

'Where the apple reddens never pry, lest we lose our Edens, Eve and I.'

'And what does that mean?' I asked.

'You'll know when you think about it.'

There was a touch of mystery about our relationship, Jessica's and mine. You couldn't analyse it and it was better not to try. The years nineteen thirty seven to nineteen thirty nine were our best. This is the hey-day, I often said to myself. Things will never be like this again. The recurring sting of intense pleasure in our intimate world, the struggle for medical reputation, slowly gained, the laughter — it couldn't last.

From our island of family joy the outside world seemed far away, unreal, dreamlike. It was the time when German insult and degradation were being heaped upon millions. That nightmare was as real as our own happiness and gradually, very gradually, the truth dawned on us that sooner or later it would have to be tackled. With perhaps a touch of arrogance we assumed that we — the British — would have to do the tackling. The tightly woven joy and pain of those years made each emotion more intense, more vivid and more unforgettable.

Our first baby was born in nineteen thirty one and the second, another girl, in nineteen thirty four. The old cottage we lived in became too small for us and in nineteen thirty five we moved. The new house was of local stone, built at the turn of the century for the parish curate when curates were expected to have a quiverful of children. So there were six bedrooms and we had four acres of glorious Somerset pasture round us.

The children could run out through a gate at the end of the garden across the field and down to a stream dignified by the name of the River Somer. Trout flourished there. They could be 'tickled out' by the initiated but not by me. I don't know why we never fished there — perhaps because the children were wild upholders of the rights of all creatures great and small to live their own lives in peace.

Our first maid, Dorothy, who came with Jessica from London when we were married was inevitably snapped up by one of the local lads who were quick to recognise a good thing when they saw one. So we moved house taking with us Nanny Margaret and a new maid named Doris. Doris was somewhat obese with a considerable moustache and thin brown hair cut in a fringe over her low brow but disappearing into a tonsure on her crown. I remember Jan, our eldest, sitting on the stairs very puzzled on the day of her arrival. She didn't fit easily into her classification of human, vegetable, animal and mineral. When the problem became insoluble she asked her mother — is she a girl like you and me?

My own happiness depended so much on Jessica and the children that my advice to patients was sometimes coloured by it. Father Uphill was a case in point.

He was a monk at the Abbey, and one day he came to see me at my surgery in Melbrook. It was unusual because they had their own doctor at the school and Abbey. Edward Evans had replaced Bill Beverley there and he was four years younger than I was. Evidently some of the monks felt he was too young for their confidences.

I remember Father Uphill as tall, quite handsome in a way, with ruddy bronzed complexion and dark hair greying at the sides. About forty I should say. There was a gauntness about him. The furrows round his mouth were deep for his age and had a pinched look as though they were of recent origin. My first impression was that he might have some sort of cancer.

He sat there in front of me in the old surgery, the light falling full on his face. You could read the struggle that was going on in his mind. I began to wonder whether he knew he had something sinister wrong with him, but in that case why had he

194

come to me, a comparative stranger? The monks usually faced serious illness with courage and serenity whereas minor maladies were often exaggerated.

'I'm not ill, Doctor,' he said, 'and I ought not to be wasting your time'.

He didn't know of course that these were red light words. They alerted me more thoroughly than most, indicating that the patient has struggled against consulting you but has been forced to against his will. 'I have a personal problem,' he went on, 'and I want an outside opinion. My faith has never wavered. It's not that. But as I said I have a personal problem.'

I waited but he seemed reluctant to take the plunge. Presently I asked how I could help.

'It sounds absurd when I say the words. They are so trite and ordinary for any lay person but to me they are deadly serious. I have fallen in love, very seriously in love, and the struggle with my own feelings is reducing me to a state of uselessness. It's affecting my work, my whole life, and I am powerless to deal with it.'

'Have you talked to your colleagues about it?'

'Oh yes, I have talked to my confessor ad nauseam. I've fasted, prayed and struggled but it's no use. I'm like a ghost, a shadow, I don't exist any more.'

I think at this point he was wondering why he had come to see me. I was ten years younger than he was, inexperienced in problems of this sort, and probably quite useless. A look of hopelessness settled on his face and I suddenly felt desperately sorry for him. In a flash I saw myself in the same situation, wanting to marry Jessica and prevented from doing so by some insuperable barrier. Life would be intolerable. Clearly the solution of the problem lay in overcoming the barrier — in this case his vows.

'Tell me about the woman,' I said.

His expression relaxed for the first time. 'She is a pure and lovely person. She has had a hard life. Her mother died some years ago and since then she has been almost a slave to her father. If my love were not returned there would be no difficulty but she needs me as much as I need her. I could make her very happy.'

'Is a platonic friendship possible?'

'No. I think my feelings are normal. I love her very deeply and my strongest wish is to make her happy. But there is a powerful sexual element as well.'

'Of course there is. Have you discussed it with her?'

'Not fully. I dared not. We both know. We seem to read each other's thoughts without words.'

To me love between a man and a woman was the very central core of life. Without it, existence would be a living hell. 'Have you considered leaving the monastery?' I asked. 'Could you get a dispensation from your vows?'

He hesitated for a moment then said almost inaudibly, 'I've considered many things.'

'Surely that is the only thing to do. Your feelings are perfectly natural, perfectly honourable. When you took your vows you had no idea what enormous pressure you might be under. It seems to me that for your own sake and for the woman's as well, this is the only thing to do.'

We talked for some time. The lines on his face became no less sharp but there appeared an occasional gleam of pleasure replaced rapidly by a relapse into misery.

'Would there be practical problems? How would you earn a living?'

'I'm a good schoolmaster. I should have no difficulty.'

'So it's just a matter of conscience.'

He shook his head. 'That's putting it too mildly. I couldn't ask for a dispensation from my vows. It wouldn't be granted anyway and it would be wrong.'

'It would not be wrong in my view.'

'I can't break with the Church. That is my life too.'

'What do your seniors say?'

'They pray for me.'

We were getting nowhere and I was a long way out of my depth. 'You have no physical symptoms?' I asked.

'None that matter.'

'My advice is to ask for a dispensation from your vows and in due course to marry the woman you love. I see how difficult the decision is for you and I sympathise. I really do. It is so much worse than an ordinary illness. Would you like to come and talk to me again in a few days?'

'Perhaps I'll do that. Thank you for listening to me.' He held out his hand and I shook it, feeling woefully inadequate.

The interview had lasted little short of half an hour and the waiting room was abuzz with the sound of patients waiting their turn. When I thought over the case later I was convinced that he ought to leave the monastery and marry. He was so genuine in his feelings and after all, I thought, one monk more or less wouldn't make all that difference.

For days his face haunted me. His dilemma was so understandable and so sad. It was the story of 'The Cloister and the Hearth' all over again. But surely the religious outlook had changed since the Middle Ages. A man could be a good Christian while married and making some woman happy — perhaps bringing up children. Every day I hoped to see him again but he didn't come. Weeks passed and I began to forget him.

Then I was called one weekend to see a woman named Bellamy who lived with her father in a large house a mile or two out of Melbrook. I was taken first to see the father, Grant Bellamy, who was at work in his study. I had met him once or twice on a committee of which he was chairman, but I didn't know him well. He was a tall man, rather imposing, a journalist and author whose virtues certainly didn't include modesty.

There was no beating about the bush and very little in the way of preliminaries. 'It's Alice, my daughter. I'm concerned about her. She has been losing interest and vitality for some months and now she has virtually collapsed. There is something radically wrong with her and I'd like a thorough examination to start with and then whatever specialist opinion you think necessary. I don't want any delay.' He rang the bell then waited in silence, not bothering with any light conversation in the meantime. 'Mrs. Biggs, show the Doctor up to Miss Bellamy's room.'

Relating the story as I am, the connection with Father Uphill is obvious, but the two cases were related in my mind even from that moment. It seemed more than likely that Alice

Bellamy was the woman the monk had spoken of some weeks before.

The house had a wide staircase and a landing overlooking a large central hall. By the time I had reached the top — led at a dignified pace by the massive form of Mrs. Biggs — I had decided that Alice Bellamy was indeed the woman in question. It was crazy to make a diagnosis before seeing the patient, but I made up my mind that she was suffering from frustration, tension and probably depression due to obvious causes. The ghosts of all the physicians since Hippocrates must have shouted warnings in my ear, but I knew they were merely being over cautious. An emotional origin to her troubles was highly probable and the thought of acting fairy godfather and bringing them together was already uppermost in my mind. My last thought before entering her bedroom was that I must ask whether she was a Catholic and if so my presumption would be confirmed.

Mrs. Biggs announced me and discreetly left us alone. The idea of a chaperone in those days only occurred to me if I was not sure of the character of the patient and in this case it was an obvious advantage to have no third person listening to any confidences that might emerge.

I had seen Alice Bellamy several times with minor ailments but never socially. She was in her middle twenties, not pretty, but with regular features, and highly attractive to the opposite sex. Her expression was always somewhat distant and her manner never varied. She was always courteous but never warm or familiar. Treating someone for a sprained wrist or wax in the ear is not calculated to bring about any great personal intimacy and I knew nothing of her character. That day I saw her with the eyes of Father Uphill as an attractive young woman.

She was not in bed but sitting by the window in a plain silk dressing gown, reading. She put her book down with apparent regret and gave me a cool greeting. The atmosphere was distinctly chilly.

Too much heartiness on my part was out of place and I had already learned the advantage of a smile but few words. I sat opposite her. 'Your father is worried about you,' I said. 'Tell me how you are.'

'Not very well. I think I may have a gastric ulcer.'

'Pain after your meals?'

'Pain here all the time.' She indicated a wide area of her upper abdomen. 'It doesn't matter what I eat. It comes on worse in the early morning when I'm empty.'

I took a careful history and examined her, confirming my guess that the symptoms were emotional in origin — nervous was the word we used then. I told her so in a way that invited her to talk of her personal problems but there was no reaction.

'Tell me what you think yourself about your stomach trouble,' I said.

'I don't think anything about it except that it's something I've got to put up with. It's Father who is worrying about it. He sent for you.'

I wasn't very old but I was older than Alice Bellamy. I had learnt from one of the Bath physicians the advantage of sometimes taking the risk of making a dogmatic diagnosis. There are times when it does little good to a nervous patient to tell them that they might have this or that but they probably haven't, that we had better do some investigations but it was probably their nerves. It was occasionally better to risk one's own reputation than to be over cautious. The effect of firm reassurance for instance on a patient fearful that he is suffering from heart trouble is little short of miraculous. Nowadays this can only be done after extensive investigations but then we depended on a detailed case history and our five senses. I decided to be dogmatic.

'There is nothing physically wrong with you,' I said. 'These symptoms are nervous and unless you can talk about the problems of your every day life I shan't be able to help you.'

Still no response.

'You run the house and act as secretary to your father? How much social life do you have?'

'Too much at times. And I'm quite content with my own company at others.'

'Any close friends?'

She hesitated. 'It depends what you mean by close friends. I

199

have one or two, through the church.'

'You are a Catholic, aren't you?'

'Yes.'

'I'm only trying to help you to talk. Are any of your friends in the church close enough to cause friction or tension? You know how close family relationships can cause trouble sometimes.'

'There's nothing. I hoped when Father sent for you you would be able to give me something to relieve my stomach trouble. I'm not a nervous person I assure you.'

'Nervous is a silly word. It means different things to different people. I'm only saying your symptoms are due to tension, stress of some sort. And you are the only person who can see into your own mind.'

She shook her head dismissing the subject, and remained silent. Quite composed. Utterly defended. I waited but it was no use. At last she said, 'Perhaps a bottle of medicine would help. Not that I am a person for taking medicine.'

It would have been wiser to refuse palliatives. They would do no good. All the same I fell for the old escape route and prescribed a bottle of sedative medicine.

As I was leaving she asked what I should tell her father.

'I'll tell him that you are physically well. There is no point in seeing a physician but I will arrange it if you like. That you are under strain of some sort but haven't confided in me what it is.'

'Then he'll want me to go away on holiday. He's already suggested it. I have an aunt in Italy. He wants me to go there.'

'Then why not?'

'I don't want to go away. I know it wouldn't do me any good.'

'It wouldn't solve your problem would it?'

'No, it would make me worse.'

Surely she was on the verge of confiding in me. I waited again but it was still no good. At last I left her saying I would see her again in a week and if her father insisted on another opinion I would arrange it.

She didn't object to this. Evidently she felt she knew how to deal with doctors.

Downstairs I had a less pleasant interview with Grant Bellamy.

'Sherry? Or something stronger?' he asked.

'Sherry, thankyou.'

'Well what do you make of her?'

'She is physically well. I don't think she has any organic disease. On the other hand she is in a highly nervous state — tense, anxious, unhappy — and this is bringing on her symptoms. Something, some powerful emotion is distressing her and making her ill. She won't tell me what it is.'

Grant Bellamy looked at me with evident distaste. It was obvious he didn't believe a word I said. 'You are telling me that a girl with a good home, no worries, a full and satisfying life is being made ill by some unspecified emotional turmoil? That a healthy girl, fond of games, popular everywhere she goes, is suffering so badly from nerves' — he spat the word out — 'that she is too ill to go out, refuses to see her friends and is in fact a shadow of what she was six months ago.'

'Yes.'

'Then you won't be surprised if I say I want another opinion.'

'I'll arrange that for you by all means.'

'Who do you suggest?'

I mentioned the name of a Bath physician.

'Very well,' he snapped, 'but I don't want any delay. If he can't see her at once — say tomorrow — I'll get her seen in London.'

'I can't be sure of tomorrow naturally. If you prefer someone in London and will make the appointment yourself I'll refer the case to him.'

'I do prefer it. Then I shall get the opinion I want. I'll be in touch with you later in the day.'

He rang the bell and in a few minutes I was on my way back to Melbrook.

A week later Alice Bellamy was seen by an eminent London physician, admitted to a famous clinic and fully investigated. Chest Xray, blood tests and barium meal revealed no abnormality and the conclusion was that there was no organic disease and a holiday in Italy was recommended. Grant

201

Bellamy was satisfied and Alice was no worse off. The machinery of the medical establishment had done its work. On the other hand Bellamy had reckoned without the firm inherited will power of his daughter. She refused to go to Italy. She improved to some extent and in the next few weeks the case receded into the limbo of unsolved cases that form a part of the normal environment of the family doctor. Although in Alice's case, I thought, I knew what was wrong with her.

It must have been several weeks later that I saw her again. She came to the surgery and sat with a dozen panel and parish patients in the waiting room. We had no appointment system in those days and she didn't ask me to call at the house because her father was not to know she wanted to see me.

Her manner was different now, as direct as ever but more friendly. 'You haven't forgotten about my trouble,' she said. As though I could forget a case like hers or a person like her.

'Of course not.'

'You knew all the time what was wrong, didn't you?'

'I thought I did, yes.'

'Because Dominic had been to see you.'

'He hadn't mentioned your name of course. I had to guess that.'

'When you saw me we hadn't really talked about each other. We talked about every subject under the sun except — what matters. But lately we have talked properly and he told me he had been to see you and you advised him to ask for a dispensation from his vows and marry.' She blushed and I saw how very attractive she was. 'I've begged him to come and see you again,' she went on. 'Will you please try to persuade him that it is right for him to marry? I know I have no right to ask you to help me but there is no one else — absolutely no one I can turn to.' She took a deep breath. 'I'm rather desperate,' she ended miserably.

'It's a cruel thing to happen to you both,' I said. 'I'll certainly do my best.'

It was at this stage that I became really involved myself — emotionally involved as you can be with patients you feel for and with. It depends very much on whether your own experience has embraced their particular problem because only then can you really understand them. I knew what it meant to wait three years to marry someone I was very much in love with and how much that marriage eventually meant to me. I could feel the deep personal longing of these two and I knew how it focussed itself like the sun's rays through a convex lens into a consuming sexual desire.

Alice Bellamy would never have overcome her natural reserve and spoken so freely to me if she had not been driven by powerful emotions. 'I wish I could help,' I said. 'I haven't seen Father Uphill for some time. He is seriously thinking of leaving the monastery, is he?'

'Thinking about it yes. But I dread his conscience. I don't want him to do what he believes is wrong but I can't think it *is* wrong. We are both Catholics. We could live a good life together — perhaps as missionaries — or in the slums. Anywhere if we were together.'

One of her hands was gripping the arm of the chair and the other was clenched tight. I wished I had the influence she evidently thought I had. She showed no sign of going and obviously wanted to talk. 'Do you think it would be wrong?' she asked.

'No I don't. It wouldn't be wrong for me but I don't know how he feels — how much he feels bound by his vows. I suppose it depends on his superiors to some extent. If they recommended his release he would feel free.'

'It's not as simple as that. They put the whole decision back to him. That's what is so tantalising. At the same time they tell him he is putting himself before God. That breaking his vows would be wrong. If only we weren't Catholics it would be so easy. I shouldn't say that. I am a Catholic and I don't want to be lost to the Church.'

I let her talk. Poor girl she needed an outlet. 'I grieve so much for him,' she went on. 'He looks so haggard now. He is thin and his face is so lined. I feel he just wants me and I could make him so happy.'

'He said exactly the same when I first saw him — that he could make you very happy.'

'He would of course. But we aren't just being unselfish. I want him as much as he wants me.'

She stopped suddenly and seemed to gather her defences, to rebuild the great wall of reserve that kept her isolated from other people. It is not often that an adult man or woman will take down the barriers so completely. When they do the effect is profoundly moving. I watched her receding from me, putting on the clothes of her mind. I wanted to show my concern in some practical way but there was nothing I could do. For a moment we both sat completely still. I don't know how long for. Sometimes one slides outside the restrictions of time. It was probably only a few seconds. Then we looked at each other and she said 'Thankyou'. I stood up. There seemed nothing else to say.

She looked at me again and for a moment I thought she would approach and touch me. But she just said thank you again and left.

I was so full of the Bellamy case for the next few days that Jessica must have been sick of my continual references to it. I remember she spoke very firmly on one occasion. 'I do sympathise with them,' she said, 'but they shouldn't have let themselves get into this position to start with. It's the girl's fault. She could easily have prevented it happening. Most women have to put the shutters up at some time or other.'

At the time I thought she was being hard hearted but I realised in the years that followed how right she was. Her comments were like a cool douche on my overwrought sympathy and gradually I began to see things in better perspective.

I had no opportunity to help Alice Bellamy because Dominic Uphill did not consult me again. I didn't see him for several months but one day when I was doing Edward Evans' work at the school I ran into him. He greeted me cordially but the man himself seemed to have receded into the distance as though he had withdrawn from the world's battlefields into an inner sanctuary where he was unapproachable by ordinary folk like myself. I had met the same experience some years earlier when I happened to be present at the death of a very eminent Abbot. My own ministrations had been swept aside to make way for rituals that were evidently of profound importance to all those present. It was as though I had been left outside at a meeting of mysterious significance and I had the same sensation with Father Uphill. He asked politely after the health of my family and it was all I could do to get in a slanted enquiry on the subject that interested me.

'You have recovered from the problem you came to see me about?' I said.

'You were very patient with me. Yes, all is I think well now. I had help — a great deal more than I deserved.'

'From your colleagues and friends?'

'From above.' He smiled at me from what seemed a great height — a great distance — and that was the end of the affair. I could never guess how it had been resolved.

I saw Alice Bellamy once or twice in the next year or so over trivial matters but she avoided all reference to her previous visit to me and I was left wondering how much she had been hurt. She appeared unaffected, poised and completely mistress of herself.

I couldn't help wondering what would have happened to the two of them if Father Uphill had taken my advice. I suppose I had been a sort of devil's advocate and perhaps my well meant suggestion had been easily disposed of. On the other hand I may have added to the pain of his decision. I would like to have known how they parted and whether they were both leading full and satisfying lives.

And Alice Bellamy? She joined the Wrens at the outbreak of war and was killed while on leave in London during the blitz in nineteen forty one.

I had been an outside observer, glimpsing from a distance the struggle of two people wrestling with conscience. Who am I to know whether their decision was right or wrong?

23

Grant Bellamy was a materialist of the old school who believed in nothing that could not be analysed, touched and dissected. Somehow, I am not sure how, he managed to square this with his Catholic religion. When I had told him that his daughter was suffering from a disorder due to stress he scoffed at the idea. When, after extensive investigation, no physical disease was discovered, he concluded that the tests were not extensive enough. When she recovered slowly after the emotional disturbance had subsided he concluded that nature had cured her of some obscure mechanical defect.

My next confrontation with him may have been good for my patience — perhaps even for my immortal soul — but it was a trying experience not without its funny side.

He sent for me one day because he had a pain in his chest. He was fifty five and his father had died of a heart attack some time in his fifties. He must therefore, he concluded, be suffering from heart trouble.

His attitude to me was such that I often wondered why he ever sent for me. I didn't actually dislike him but my relationship with him was something like armed neutrality. I was ready to go on the defensive at a moment's notice.

'It's my heart,' he told me firmly. 'Angina pectoris.' His hand ran over an area of the left chest just below the heart.

'What makes you think it's your heart?' I asked.

He looked at me as though it wasn't worth giving me an elementary lesson in medicine if I didn't understand the rudiments of the subject. 'Fairly obvious, isn't it? Perhaps I should tell you that my father died at about my age and his first symptom was pain in the chest.'

'Is the pain worse when you exercise?'

'Yes.'

After a good many questions and a pretty careful examination I came to the conclusion that the pain was in the chest wall and not in the heart. What was more he had a mild fever.

Not long before this, Scandinavian doctors had described an epidemic disease in the island of Bornholm, apparently due to a virus which caused pain in the chest and fever lasting a week or two and usually resulting in complete recovery. Cases had been reported in Britain and I felt pretty sure this was another one.

I explained that I thought he was suffering from a virus infection that should recover in about ten days. He needed rest and relief of pain.

'How can you be sure it's not my heart?'

'There's no sign of anything wrong with your heart and what is more you have a temperature. We'll have an Xray of your chest to exclude chest trouble, but I'm pretty sure of what I've told you.'

That night he sent for me in the early hours of the morning. The pain was worse and he was clearly very frightened. If he had no faith in me this was not surprising. As patiently as I could I repeated my previous explanation of the cause of his symptoms and reassured him that all would soon be well. We even decided to postpone the Xray.

Next morning I was busy and my call to the manor where he lived was not made till late in the afternoon. As I drove through the gate, who should I run into, or rather pass on his way out, but Dr. Furlong of Peterdown, a nearby village. We waved to each other and he shouted a cheerful 'how de do' but no more was said. I supposed he must have been visiting one of the servants. Often a household was attended by two or even three doctors for different members.

An interesting old fellow, Dr. Furlong, I thought to myself. A character straight out of Tom Jones. A typical product of Somerset — if you can really have a typical product of anywhere. Shortish, squarish, blue eyed, apple cheeked with an accent that varied from slight to strong according to his company. No one knew the age of the faded green pork pie hat he always wore. To anyone who only saw him out of doors it must have seemed like part of his anatomy. In fact it covered a bald head that was as near a perfect sphere as is possible in the world of nature.

I always thought of him as my best enemy. Usually genial, he could flare into a violent temper — especially if anyone threatened to rob him of one of his patients. A grand huntsman, a skilled but impatient fisherman, and an excellent shot, he was loved by his patients in general though he often gave them plenty to put up with.

Once, for instance, when I saw a case with him (the consultation was I swear at the patient's request not his) he addressed a woman outside the house, 'Well my dear and how's the husband this long time. I ain't seen un lately.'

The woman stared at him and stammered, 'But you der know Doctor, Will died three year agone.'

'Oh ah, of course er did. Well well.' Then he put his arm round her and said very kindly, 'And how be yourself my dear, eh?' He was not in the least embarrassed. Perhaps he always forgot which of his patients were alive or dead after so many years in the practice. Yet I never heard an ill word spoken of him.

I was shown up to Grant Bellamy's bedroom by Mrs. Gibbs the housekeeper. There was not much change and I sat and talked for a time. He was rather silent — a little less aggressive I thought. Then suddenly he said, 'Dr. Furlong doesn't agree with your diagnosis.'

'Dr. Furlong,' I must have gasped. 'You mean he's been to see you?'

'And why not? Haven't I a right to another opinion if I pay for it?'

'Did you tell him I was attending you?'

'No. Doctors are notoriously touchy. I wanted another opinion. It's *my* heart after all and I pay the bills. I shall have as many opinions as I want.'

He was on the defensive and obviously knew he had behaved badly.

'And what do you propose to do if you have different diagnoses and conflicting advice?'

'Lose confidence in both of you and get someone else.'

The situation was quite funny and with anyone else I should have laughed outright but Grant Bellamy irritated me and my sense of humour was in abeyance. 'You know the etiquette as well as I do,' I said. 'You choose a family doctor and through him ask for any other opinion you like. Then your case can be discussed properly and treatment agreed.'

'You mean you can hide your differences and come to a compromise that may be no good to anyone. No, I shall get better service from several different opinions. No single one dominating the others. I can judge who to trust.'

'You put me in an embarrassing position,' I told him. 'One person has to be responsible for you. If several different doctors are giving different advice who is responsible? The situation becomes ridiculous.'

'I don't see why. If there were no doubt about what was wrong with me you would both say the same thing.'

'No one in their senses will agree to treat you under these conditions. If you will make up your mind which of us you propose to have as your G.P. we can go ahead. If you would like Dr. Furlong I will phone him and ask him to carry on. If you want me you must ring Dr. Furlong and explain what has happened, saying emphatically you want me to attend you.'

'I shall do nothing of the sort. Why must doctors be so touchy? You are worse than a lot of old women. If I want to buy something I go to several shops and decide where to put my custom. What's the difference?'

'You are not buying anything. You are asking for personal advice and you are quite incapable of deciding which advice is better if they conflict. What did Dr. Furlong tell you?'

'Ah, that's better. He said my heart was slightly affected but it should improve with treatment.

'And who are you going to believe?'

'I haven't made up my mind yet. You came when he was hardly out of the house. If you had come a little bit earlier I should have enjoyed listening to you hammering at each other.'

By this time I was thoroughly annoyed. When he started making feeble jokes it was time for an ultimatum. 'Either Dr.

Furlong treats you or I do. Will you make up your mind please?'

'I'm not sure I shall keep either of you.'

'Then you'll have to make up your mind about that too.'

He was silent for a moment and I waited.

'Alright you can carry on. Tell Dr. Furlong I shan't want him any more.'

'That I will not,' I said furiously. 'You asked him in. You must tell him not to come again. Tell him I was already in attendance and you were wrong to send for him. Make it clear you don't want to see him any more. And it wouldn't come amiss to apologise.'

'Well, well, well. I always thought you were a quiet man. There's nothing like a bit of professional jealousy to stir you up.' He put on a malicious smile.

'There's no question of professional jealousy. Only a hearty dislike of having my time wasted. Are you prepared to get in touch with Dr. Furlong or not? If you are not, I will phone him and ask him to take over the case.'

'Alright, alright. I'll send him a message.'

The next problem was treatment. The slightest suggestion that his heart was suspect would undermine the man's confidence. It would undermine anyone's confidence. With Grant Bellamy's family history it was likely to have a profound effect and could easily turn him into a hypochondriac. The only solution of course was a third opinion and as weighty a one as possible. For a moment I thought of sending for someone from London but this might have made him more suspicious than ever. And making him pay a hundred guinea fee would perhaps be too drastic a revenge.

By this time I was half ashamed of my anger. As always it evaporated like steam. After all he was a patient and not at all well. It would have been better to laugh at him or treat him as an unruly child. An occasional outburst probably does no harm and it is a quicker way of settling matters than a long winded discussion. All the same I wasn't very happy at the turn of events.

'Right then,' I said, 'if that's settled we had better go back to the beginning. As I told you yesterday and in the early hours of this morning your heart is perfectly normal and you are suffering from a viral infection which will clear up in a week or two.'

'You said ten days.'

'I can't prophecy to a day. The point is that you must get your confidence back — confidence in your heart. It's not going to let you down. One breath of suspicion that one's heart is not right takes a lot of getting over. Dr. Furlong was wrong. Now you obviously don't trust my opinion. That was why you asked him for his. To put matters right you will have to have someone from the City. If he backs my opinion, all right.'

'And if he backs Dr. Furlong's?'

'He won't.'

'And suppose I say I won't pay for someone to come out from the City?'

'That's up to you.'

'Alright. Do as you like. I should have been better off if I hadn't bothered with doctors at all. All this fuss and fury doesn't make me feel any better I can tell you.'

Just an irritating unruly child I said to myself. 'You are quite right. You would have been just as well without a doctor — except that you were worried and didn't know what was the matter. You would have got better without a doctor if you had waited long enough. Anyway I'll get Dr. McNeil from the City. He's a very good opinion. I'll phone him this evening. Meanwhile stay in bed and go on with those tablets I gave you.'

We parted with — perhaps thirty percent — amity and equanimity. A show of anger — apart from bouts of irritability of which I plead guilty — is not natural to me and I took some time to settle down. After surgery when Hannah Woodruff, the dispenser, had gone home Tom Wyburn and I were left alone. We met for a chat and a smoke. I told him about Grant Bellamy and he was sympathetic. He had nothing to say against Bellamy himself. He was after all a very good paying patient. But Dr. Furlong came in for some strident criticism.

'Disgraceful,' he said. 'Furlong had no business to go and see him. He knew very well that Bellamy was your patient and Ballard's before you. He should at least have telephoned you first.'

211

'To do him justice he's always been very correct in his behaviour. I imagine he didn't know I was attending him.'

'It doesn't matter. He should have phoned first.'

'He will have got the chuck by now I imagine.'

Tom Wyburn laughed happily. 'I should love to be able to listen in when he gets the message.'

'Bellamy won't telephone himself. He'll send a note.'

'Pity.'

Dr. McNeil came out the next day, agreed with my diagnosis and gave strong reassurance about Bellamy's heart. So that you might think was that.

But it wasn't. That evening I had a telephone call from Dr. Furlong. He was very angry indeed.

'I hear you've been seeing a patient of mine,' he shouted.

'On the contrary you saw a patient of mine yesterday. I imagine you didn't know —'

'Your patient!! Do you know young man I've attended Grant Bellamy for twenty years.'

I was flabbergasted. 'But I've attended him on and off for eight years — ever since I came here. Then I was called in the other day. I don't know what you mean by —'

'You saw my patient? Saw him? And not a word or a by your leave. You haven't heard the last of this. The ethical committee shall hear of this and pretty sharply I can tell you.'

'As I was saying I have attended him ever since I came to Melbrook and Dr. Ballard attended him before that.'

'Then why did he send for me yesterday?' My counterattack seemed at last to be registering.

'I gather he wanted another opinion and hadn't the decency to set about it in the proper way. Don't blame me for that. I told him to make up his mind who he wanted and let the other one know. He's evidently made up his mind that he still wants me.'

He began to calm down. I remember the conversation vividly. 'You've attended him for eight years you say. The swindling bastard. You mean we've both attended him and neither knew about the other?'

'Apparently, yes. And if we hadn't called at about the same time today we shouldn't have known about it still.'

'Well I'm damned. He's been payin' the both of us, thic be one thing.' He gave a shout of laughter. Then 'There's only one thing to do with a sod like that. Neither on us should go near un. What about that?'

'I can't back out of it now. I had McNeil out last night. He's got Bornholm Disease and should be right in a few days. I've already told him pretty clearly what I think of him.'

'Give him a kick up the arse when you see him again — from me d'ye hear. Well I'm damned. I wonder how many other doctors he's been calling in. We'd better ask the others.'

'A good idea. Look I'm sorry about all this misunderstanding but the thought that he was quietly getting two doctors to see him without saying a word to either about the other never entered my head.'

'Nor mine.' And the laughter that forced me to hold the earpiece a foot from my ear did me a world of good. 'What a story,' he went on, 'wait till I tell the others.'

And the story went round with unbelievable embellishments for the next few weeks.

I got on rather better with Grant Bellamy after this though we had a flare up now and then. When he was better I taxed him with Dr. Furlong's complaint. 'How often did he actually attend you?' I asked.

He thought for a moment. 'About as much as you people I suppose. I always wanted to check Ballard's opinion. That's all.'

'Next time tell me what you mean to do.'

'We shall see,' he said. 'I'm not committing myself.'

There was perhaps a quarter of a smile round the steely glint of the eyes. So I had to be content.

24

The more I have learned about the ways of young people 'then and now' the more certain I am that they had as much fun in the nineteen thirties as in the nineteen eighties. And I don't mean at tennis parties and football matches. Puberty is reached a little earlier now than fifty years ago, but adolescence was always a time of initiation into realms of exquisite pleasure. The roll in the hay was physically different but the pleasure no less. The clasp of a hand could set the pulse racing and the touch of a breast could make the walls of the universe shudder. Prolonged caressing can give more pleasure than the compulsive smash and grab raids of the nineteen seventies and eighties.

If contraceptives were not available to adolescents the amount of pleasure they would derive from each other would be very little reduced. It might well be increased. The sensitive would be allowed to develop more slowly without being regarded as freaks. The anxieties, the painful bladder infections, the fear of V.D. would be largely swept away. The ecstasies would remain but the agonies would be less. The one true social advance of the twentieth century is greater freedom of speech, the destruction of taboos, the more primitive and natural approach to the subject of sex.

There was not much teenagers didn't know in the nineteen thirties. Most of them anyway. Out of the thousands of cheerful happy teenagers that no one talked about there was one here and there who would reach the headlines — not in the media but in the pub, the club and the kitchen. Daisy was one of these. She was a pretty girl of seventeen, a little wild, inclined to be different, ready to try anything new. She came with her mother to see me one summer day in nineteen thirty eight. The story is old and familiar and before the days of legalised abortion, even more painful.

When I had examined her and made sure she was over two months pregnant the interview began by following the usual pattern. The angry worried mother and the defiant girl sat opposite me but quite soon things went off at a tangent. Daisy resolutely refused to say who was the father of her child.

Mrs. Croft had to be given a full three minutes to express her frustrations. 'I've begged and I've bullied — I simply can't understand her — and it's not because there was more than one man — she swears there was only one but she won't say who it is. She was always such a good girl — and now this. It's his responsibility as much as hers — more probably. He'll have to pay.' And so on and so on. Poor Mrs. Croft.

'Why don't you tell us Daisy?' I asked.

'I promised I wouldn't.'

'It was a strange thing to promise. Can you tell me why?'

'He's not like ordinary men. He's different. He's — well —' She stopped as though she was afraid of saying too much.

I did my best by what I thought were devious and subtle questions to get through her defences but she was altogether too clever for me. 'Well,' I said at last, 'the choice is between having the baby adopted and bringing it up yourself. Who would pay all the expense of doing that?' Her father was a factory worker with little money to spare.

'I shall have the baby adopted.' She seemed to have the whole affair carefully thought out.

'That's not easy to do you know. Not easy for you I mean. Once you have seen the baby you will want to keep it. Is marriage out of the question?'

'Yes.'

'Is he a married man?'

Silence.

'Would you marry him if he asked you?'

Silence again.

'Have you told the baby's father about it?'

'Yes, but it's my business not his.'

'It's very much his business. It's his baby as much as yours and besides he is financially responsible for you.'

'I don't want his money.'

'Then whose money are you going to take?'

'I can earn enough.'

I was becoming as frustrated as her mother. I think I was less tolerant then of the very young than I grew later. I hadn't learned that much of what the adolescent says is kite flying or asking questions in a disguised language.

I saw her for routine examinations throughout her pregnancy, which was normal enough, but the mystery of the child's father was still unsolved. The surprising thing was that the girl was strong minded enough to withstand constant pressure from her parents. I noticed that she was very well dressed with beautifully made maternity dresses that must have been far beyond the purse of the Crofts or of Daisy herself. Money was coming from somewhere and I couldn't help asking the mother about it. I was told that the unknown father was giving a generous allowance. The plan was still to have the child adopted.

It must have been soon after the eight month examination that Daisy came to see me without her mother. She came to the point at once.

'Could you arrange for me to have the baby in a nursing home in the City?' she asked.

'I expect so. What has happened to make you change your mind? I thought you wanted to have it at home.'

'I can't stand the questions any longer. Every day, at every meal it's the same. Since I gave up work it's been worse than ever. My Mum and Dad talk to each other about me — at me — all the time. They can't bear not knowing who the father is. I just can't take any more.'

I had given up hoping she would tell me her secret. 'At one time you said you wouldn't take his money. You are having an allowance from him now?'

'Yes.'

'And he would pay for the nursing home?'

'Yes.'

'Then I'll try and arrange it for you.'

'Could you come and look after me?'

I thought for a moment. I had done this once or twice but it meant dislocation of the other work because the City was half an hour's drive away from Melbrook. At the time of the confinement one might be held up there for hours. At the same time I must have been intrigued by the case and my curiosity decided me. 'I could if you'd like me to,' I said and named a nursing home. 'How will your parents take it?'

'They couldn't be any worse than they are whatever I do.'

'I am not sure all this worry and tension is good for you at the moment,' I said tentatively.

'It can't be helped.'

I admired that girl. She had fought her way through the discomforts, and in those days the disgrace, of the pregnancy all by herself. Her determination to safeguard the man might have been misplaced but it was certainly plucky.

I had plenty of misgivings about the amount of time I should have to spend away from the rest of the practice. Labour with a first baby could last well over twenty four hours.

Money appeared no object and I got her into the nursing home a day or two before she was due. Then we waited.

To begin with she was a week late in starting labour and I had to visit her several times. When she did get going the first stage was abysmally slow. After twenty four hours she was getting very tired but any interference was out of the question. In those days we had none of the modern drugs that relax and relieve the woman during this stage of labour. I gave her some chloral which now sounds as though it was standard treatment in the Ark. She rested for an hour or so but things still went desperately slowly. I raced to and fro from Melbrook attending to my other work as best I could but most of my mind was at the nursing home.

There was no real cause for anxiety. The baby's condition was excellent and the mother's too in spite of the long drawn out labour. Every few minutes she would ask how much longer it would be and all I could say was, 'you are doing very well'.

After forty eight hours she had still not reached a state in which instruments could be used without doing untold damage. By this time the midwives in the nursing home were beginning to show their anxiety. Their looks expressed a great question mark. How much longer? Does this man know what he is doing? When one of them asked whether I wouldn't put on forceps my temper began to fray but I hoped I didn't show it.

By this time I had been forced to ask Tom Wyburn to do all my urgent work in Melbrook while I stayed at the nursing home. 'No progress?' he asked in a voice that suggested it was time I began to hit a few sixes instead of stone walling.

On the evening of that third day I was called to the telephone at the nursing home. 'It's a man,' the nurse said. 'He wouldn't give his name. Just said he must talk to you.'

The voice was clear, cultured and conveyed an unmistakable hint of authority. I could have sworn I had heard that voice before.

'Who is speaking?' I asked.

'I am the father of Miss Croft's baby. I am very anxious about her. How long will this terrible business go on?'

'It's impossible to say exactly. She is safe and well and the baby is well. Interference in her present state would be dangerous and there is no alternative to waiting till she has made certain specific progress. She is doing quite well today.'

'I see.' There was silence for a moment. Then 'You are a general practitioner, aren't you Doctor?'

'Yes.'

'Would it be possible to ask a specialist to see her?'

'Quite possible but there is nothing he could do at present.'

'I should very much like you to get in a specialist.' The words were spoken as a command and for some reason my hackles rose. I suppose I was under a good deal of tension but at the same time there was absolutely no indication for asking the help of a consultant.

'I'm afraid I have to be guided by my own opinion,' I said, 'unless the patient or her parents ask for a specialist. Then of course there would be no alternative. I am afraid I can't take a request like that from a stranger.'

'I am not a stranger. I am deeply concerned.' The voice was quietly threatening and he was clearly worried. 'I am the father of this baby, Doctor. Don't you think I have a right to ask for another opinion?'

I didn't know what to say. I was right up against it but the responsibility was my own and no one but the girl's parents had any right so far as I could see to demand the attendance of a consultant. I was silent for a moment.

The voice came again. 'Are you there Doctor?'

'You have put me in a difficult position,' I said. I really couldn't accept a demand on the phone from a complete stranger who wouldn't even give his name and whose relationship to Daisy Croft I had no means of checking. 'I think the best plan would be for you to come here and we can talk the matter over. I really must see you first.'

'That is out of the question. I am responsible for this young lady and I am not prepared to allow her to suffer if it is not necessary.'

I began to feel sorry for him. I had played the part of anxious husband enough to make me well aware of his feelings. But he wasn't a husband. Only a voice on the telephone. The situation was really extraordinary. An impressive sounding man with plenty of money demanding a say in a case which he had in all probability every interest in. All the same I wasn't going to take an action I knew was unnecessary on the instruction of an unknown voice on the telephone. I told him so as politely as I could and reassured him that Daisy was in no danger and that I would get further help if there was the slightest need for it.

Perhaps I was being unnecessarily touchy. My demand to meet him face to face sounded like a device to get him off my back. And what should I do if he appeared? Take him in to see Daisy, I supposed, confirm he was the man in question and then give him the right to ask for another opinion if I couldn't satisfy him that all was well.

The conversation ended in anger at his end and embarrassment at mine but it did end and I went back to the labour room.

For the next hour or two I was sufficiently involved with Daisy to keep my mind off my dilemma but I was very conscious of the fact that I had refused to get a second opinion and was taking on that much extra responsibility. If things did go wrong I should be in trouble.

Daisy made steady progress and as soon as it was possible I decided to deliver her by instruments.

We didn't use local anaesthesia in midwifery in those days and I had to send for Edward Evans to give a general anaesthetic. He was a competent anaesthetist and I had no worries on that score. On the other hand the patient was very tired and things *could* go wrong. Up to the last moment I hesitated about getting an obstetrician to see her — just to cover myself. I had been asked to get another opinion and had refused — a very uneasy thought to nag at the back of your mind as you went into action. However by this stage of my career I had become fairly confident in my own ability and I was carried along on the tide of activity.

Edward arrived like a breath of fresh air and full of confidence. He had left Guy's a year or two earlier after doing the best house jobs and was ready for anything. He gave a light and excellent anaesthetic and the delivery was straightforward.

'Five to seven,' the nurse said triumphantly. A record of the time of birth seems to be of immense importance.

I waited for the baby to cry but there was not a sound. He wasn't breathing.

This happened from time to time and often after an instrumental delivery there was a short interval before breathing was established. It was always a tense moment but the slow increase of anxiety as the seconds passed is something that grips you by the throat, sets the adrenaline flowing and hardens the arteries.

Routine measures were taken quietly and efficiently by the midwife while I held the baby head downwards. A fine looking eight pound boy. We waited. No sound. The little limbs hung limp.

When the throat was well cleared I did what I had done many times before, put a piece of gauze over the child's mouth and my mouth over his, and gently blew into him. It is said that this doesn't work in new born infants. I can only say that by some sort of stimulus it often does. I blew and relaxed, blew and relaxed, blowing my own expired air into the baby's throat. No response.

We put him in warm water then I tried mouth to mouth again. The clock ticked on in an otherwise deadly silence. A profound silence like that on the top of high mountains, only full of menace. The waste, the appalling waste of a human life was almost overwhelming. Modern drugs to stimulate breathing were not available then and there was nothing else we could do. I went on. The child's heart was still beating though more feebly and there was still hope. I thought there was a change in his colour. Or was it my imagination? As the past is said to float through the mind of a drowning man the past few hours floated before mine. Still no breathing.

Then the world changed and the agonising tension disappeared like a dense fog penetrated suddenly by the sun. The child moved his face into the position of a cry. A gasp — so like the last sound of the dying. Another. Then the most glorious sound in the world — a full blown cry. Only the great chorus of Beethoven's ninth symphony conveys an equal triumph. Thank God, I muttered. Unbeliever as I then was I still thanked the God I didn't believe in.

We returned to normal routine as though nothing had happened. Only about three minutes had passed since the birth but they were very long minutes.

'Glad that kid is alright,' Edward Evans said to me afterwards. 'I was afraid I'd got her too deep.'

'The anaesthetic was perfect,' I told him. 'It was a long labour and I suppose the strain had been worse than I thought.' The first thought of both of us was as always 'what else could I have done? Was it my fault?' Anyway all was well.

A couple of hours later I was telling Jessica about it.

'Why didn't you let the man pay for a consultant?' she asked.

'There was nothing else he could do except share the responsibility for a fairly normal birth.'

'It would have been worth it.'

'As it turned out, yes.'

She put her arms round my neck and I knew a criticism was coming. 'Don't be too proud to call in a consultant.'

'I'm not proud.'

'Aren't you?'

'Well — '

Presumably I should hear no more of the mysterious father. As Daisy had decided when I first saw her, the child was adopted. She suffered the usual depression at parting with the baby. The identity of the father was revealed to the adoption society but not to me and I felt curiously left out in the cold, untrusted.

It was not until many years later that I found out a little more about the case. Daisy married in due course and had two daughters. When I attended the elder of these girls in her first confinement I had a good deal of time to talk to Daisy alone. The birth was to take place at home with the district nurses attending and the atmosphere of a home when you are waiting for the arrival of a grandchild is remarkably conducive to confidences — especially during the night.

Daisy and I were waiting downstairs for the call from the district nurses — not Martha and Mary now but two equally splendid performers. The daughter was having an easier labour than her mother and we drank tea and relaxed while we waited.

'You remember your first, Daisy?'

'I never told you what you wanted to know, did I?'

'No. Why not?'

'I'd promised for one thing. And I was a bit shy for another.'

She seemed reluctant to go on but I prompted her. 'Do you ever hear from him?'

'Never. He left the City a year after the baby was born and I haven't heard anything of him since.'

There was a long silence then I asked, 'Are you going to tell me any more about him?'

'I was in love. For the first time in my life. Mmmm. He lived in a big house on Burberry Hill. Three servants there were. I had to go there one day to do some typing for him. Then he asked for me again and I went there quite often.' Another silence. 'He was a wonderful looking man. Tall and very important — dignified — you know what I mean. Well we got interested in each other. His wife was away — in France or somewhere. Then one afternoon it happened. All the servants were out and it happened. Only once. He told me it would be alright. But it wasn't. That was all.'

'There was no question of your marrying him?'

'No. He could never have married me. Not a man like that. We didn't think so much about divorce in those days. Not that he could have anyway. I was mad at him when I got pregnant. He'd let me down you see. Promising me like that that nothing would happen. Then when I told him about it he started sending me money and I took it. Mum and Dad almost made me. And — well.'

'I still don't understand all the secrecy.'

'You would if you knew him. And I was so much in love I would have promised him anything.'

I told her of my dilemma when he demanded another opinion during her labour. Her response was mildly flattering. 'The cheek,' she said, 'the awful cheek.'

'But why so much secrecy? He wouldn't even come to see me when you were in labour and I asked him to.'

She laughed. 'You might have recognised him. He said it would have ruined his career. Perhaps it would have ruined his marriage as well.'

There was a call from upstairs. 'She's ready Doctor.'

And a few minutes later Daisy's grandson was born.

25

Family doctors in the country had little help from consultants
in the nineteen thirties. We depended largely on each other
but usually managed to find the right answers between us. Our
regular meeting place was the Cottage Hospital and there we
asked each other's opinion, argued and debated. The case of
George Shedlock was a typical case of muddling through.

The hospital was at Peterdown, a mile or so from Melbrook.
It had been built by the help of public subscription in 1880.
The original hospital was literally a cottage in the village and
the new building must have given rise to a degree of local
excitement equal to the discovery of penicillin half a century
later. The new hospital stood proudly at the top of a hill, facing
southward over the Mendips. It boasted a ward for men and
one for women and a small casualty department but its pride
and joy — evidence of shining modernity — was the Xray
room.

The intensity of radiation in this little room which was
about ten feet square must have been more than enough to ster-
ilise anyone who worked in it for very long. Fortunately we all
did our own Xray work and no one was there long enough to
come to any harm. Had anyone bothered to think in terms of
this particular occupational hazard, the endemic nature of
pregnancy among doctors' wives would have reassured them.
The ten doctors who used the Xray room had a total of thirty
five children between them — a figure a good deal higher than
the national average at the time — so all was well in this
respect. As to blood cell counts, the idea never entered our
heads.

The hospital records for the early part of this century show an annual turnover of about a hundred patients. A few of them died but most of them were marked with the brief but slightly arrogant comment 'cured'.

Administration, which on the introduction of the National Health Service in 1948 was taken over by eight full time clerical staff, was done efficiently and splendidly by Mr. Herbert Miles in his spare time. He said it took him the best part of two evenings a week. I must admit that these eight full timers also administered four other small hospitals but even so the increase in administrative man-hours works out at about 3000%!

I am concerned at the moment with the Cottage Hospital as it was in the nineteen thirties and a flurry of events that had to do with Matron Pang, Dr. Furlong of Peterdown and a patient named George Shedlock. It was not long after Dr. Furlong and I had met over the case of Grant Bellamy which had somehow served to improve our understanding of each other. One thing that had always warmed me to him was that he seemed to have come out of the very heart of Somerset. I imagined his ancestors had lived there since the time of Alfred the Great or earlier. When he was in a cheerful mood he certainly spoke the language of the West Country. His vocabulary was vigorous and for those days unorthodox. He was admired, feared and loved by the vast majority of his patients.

Matron Pang had by this time developed a high colour and a substantial solidity of build. Her admiration for Dr. Furlong and his partner clashed at times with a refinement that was a little too ostentatious. A large framed quotation 'Beauty is truth, truth beauty, and knowing this is love and love is duty' decorated the wall in front of her desk. This and her rimless pince-nez represented in my mind the 'refined' side of her nature. Her full lips and red face as well as her familiarity with Dr. Furlong indicated another side to her character. The wards, the corridors and the cupboards were spotless, shining and tidy, the patients heavily disciplined, the nursing staff a little cowed and Matron herself well content so long as everyone agreed with her. When flattered she blossomed and grew in size. As I have mentioned before I was not one of her favourites.

George Shedlock was fifty years old and had been admitted for operation on a gastric ulcer by Furlong's surgical partner, Frankie Bates. Frankie was red faced and jolly with a hint of aggression beneath the smiles. He was a competent surgeon who was prepared to operate on anything in the abdomen. He had a remarkable record of success and loved surgery. He believed that all 'real' disease had a mechanical origin and would usually respond to surgical treatment. Dr. Furlong and I viewed matters differently.

In the case of George Shedlock a complication arose. When he was admitted to hospital he developed a pain in his chest which suggested a cardiac abnormality. Anaesthetics at that time depended almost entirely on ether and oxygen and doubts about his heart led to some anxiety with the result that the operation was postponed for a day or two.

Now it so happened that when the situation was explained to Shedlock he asked if my opinion could be obtained about the state of his heart. I had met him frequently on a committee and we got on well together though he had never been my patient.

It must have been a hard task for Dr. Furlong to consult me — twenty five years his junior in experience and wisdom — and I can well imagine him saying, 'What do 'e reckon Lane can tell 'e that I can't?' But Shedlock was persistent and I was called in.

We had no electrocardiograph machine at that time and relied on blood pressure readings, Xray of the chest, clinical examination and above all the history of the case.

I spent a long time with Shedlock and eventually decided that his heart was sound so it was safe to go ahead with the operation. One difficulty I had was that having been trained at Guy's I should not have advised operation for the presumed gastric ulcer to start with, but this was not the question I had been asked. I told Dr. Furlong that I thought his heart was sound and the risk of a general anaesthetic was no greater than normal. My language must have been a bit too guarded because his reply was caustic.

'What do 'e mean no greater than normal?' he said. 'Think I'm not safe or summat?'

'You are as safe as anyone else,' I laughed, 'but no anaesthetic is a hundred percent without risk. I'd say Shedlock is a normal risk'.

Furlong didn't seem very pleased with my report as though for some reason he had wished the man's heart could be incriminated. I had my say and left him huffing and hawing to himself and the world in general.

I had to call at the hospital that evening for something or other and found Matron talking in the doorway of her room to a woman I didn't know. She stopped me and said, 'Doctor, may I introduce a friend of mine, Mrs. Shedlock? You saw her husband this morning.'

I shook hands with the lady but felt little warmth in her manner. On the other hand Matron was at her most gushing. 'You were very reassuring about Mr. Shedlock, Doctor, weren't you?'

'Yes,' I said, 'I don't think he has anything to worry about over his heart.'

'But you are not a specialist Dr. Lane are you?' said Mrs. Shedlock. 'Suppose there were something wrong and he collapsed at the operation?'

I wasn't sure what to say and glanced at Matron. I thought I caught a look of satisfaction at my discomfiture and I guessed she had either suggested or encouraged the idea of consulting a specialist.

'No,' I said, 'I'm not a specialist but I think his heart is quite sound. If you are not happy about my advice you must talk it over with Dr. Furlong.'

'I don't know. I don't know I'm sure. What do you think Matron?'

'It's not for me to say.' Matron laughed uneasily. 'The doctors have to decide what is to be done.'

'I thought you said — .' Mrs. Shedlock turned to me again. 'I'm not satisfied, Doctor. Not satisfied at all.'

'Then you must go and talk to Dr. Furlong. You can ask for any other opinion you like, you know. I'm sure he won't mind. It was your husband who asked for me to see him.'

'On yes George thinks the world of you I know,' she said grudgingly.

'But you have to be satisfied as well. Have a chat with Dr. Furlong.' I left her with Matron.

Next morning I met Dr. Furlong in the hospital again. He called after me, 'Lane, come here a minute.' The Somerset accent had disappeared indicating that he was in a serious mood or more probably angry. He would never quarrel in dialect. We talked in the corridor and Matron stood listening. 'I hear you told Shedlock's wife to ask for another opinion about his heart.'

I laughed. One gets used to being inaccurately quoted by patients for their own ends. 'She told me she had no confidence in my opinion so I told her to talk to you about it. If she wants another opinion she must tell you so.'

'That wasn't what I understood. She came to me this morning and said you told her she ought to have a specialist to see him.'

'I said if she wasn't satisfied with my opinion she could ask you for another — a specialist if she wants one. I didn't remind her that she would have to pay for the next one though.'

'Damn fuss over nothing,' he grumbled. 'I say he's alright. You say he's alright. So what are we waiting for?'

'I wonder if Matron can tell us what she said to Mrs. Shedlock or what Mrs. Shedlock said to her?'

Matron bridled. 'It's not my affair Doctor'. The deep flush on her face suggested to my suspicious mind that she had something to hide.

'You didn't suggest that a specialist would be a good thing?'

'We discussed the matter. It's my duty to talk things over with patients. That was all.'

I turned to Dr. Furlong. 'Well I've given you my opinion. The rest is up to you Doctor.'

On the next day and the one after that I expected to find that Shedlock had been operated on but each morning he was sitting comfortably up in bed, still waiting. I went over to him when I had seen my own patients.

'When is the operation?' I asked.

'You might well ask, Doctor,' he said. He looked round the ward to make sure none of the staff could overhear him. 'It's the women. Matron and the wife. They've settled it between them that I ought to see a specialist.'

'Has Dr. Furlong arranged anything?'

'You know what he is. A fine doctor, you couldn't wish for a better but you try and push him! He says there is no need for a specialist, that you and he are agreed. But the wife won't hear of it.'

'I imagine the doctor will go by what you say, not your wife. After all you are over twenty one!'

'The funny thing is that my stomach has been better since I've been in here than it's been for months.'

'Aren't there times when you are comfortable between the attacks?'

'No. It's been every day of my life for two or three years now. Starts about five o'clock and goes on till I'm asleep at night.'

Of course at this point I should have left him but I was fascinated by a thought that had just occurred to me. And after all I *had* been consulted over him and this gave me just enough excuse to allow my curiosity to have its way.

'What did the Xray of your stomach show?' I asked.

'An ulcer, they said.'

'Done here or in the City? The Xray I mean.'

'Here.'

I knew enough about barium meals done in the Cottage Hospital to mistrust them. We had no visiting radiologist at that time and none of us were capable of giving a good opinion on that score. Gastric and duodenal ulcers almost invariably give symptoms for a time and then have a period of quiescence. The fact that he had pain every day and that his wife was a domineering woman made me suspect that what he was suffering from was not a gastric ulcer but nervous dyspepsia due to tension in the household. I couldn't say anything to him about this and left him. 'I expect you will soon be alright again,' I said with more meaning than before.

It seemed a shame that he should have to undergo a major operation if there was nothing organically wrong with him but there was nothing I could do about it. Besides I might be quite wrong. He might have a chronic ulcer after all. If Frankie Bates operated and found nothing wrong with the stomach he would stitch him up again. He was a competent surgeon and the man would be little the worse.

Next day I met Dr. Furlong in the Hospital again. 'I want

another word with 'e about this man Shedlock,' he said. 'Frankie and I don't agree about him. I don't understand this 'ere Xray he's done. I can't see nothing wrong with it myself. Then there's this fuss about his heart. I agree that's alright but his wife keeps cussin' about a specialist. Now they get no fee for coming to the hospital and I don't like askin' for favours. I want you to have another look at 'un and say what you do honestly think. Has 'e got an ulcer or not? And should Frankie cut out half his stomach or not?'

I was delighted to be asked, especially as I had half made up my mind already. I examined him again, took a long and careful history and looked at the Xrays. I felt fairly confident that there was no ulcer. This left me with the problem of being tactful enough with Frankie Bates.

The three of us met in Matron's room. There was no staff room at that time. Tact, I said to myself. Be careful.

'I'm not much good at interpreting these Xrays,' I began. 'I think the radiologist Johnnies go more by the screening than by the pictures. So I can't offer any opinion about that. As to the man, he's very well nourished and he doesn't look like an ulcer case.'

'You think you can tell by looking at him?' laughed Bates. 'You're cleverer than I am then.' He had a knack of making himself sound simple, even ignorant, when in fact he was very shrewd indeed.

'Wait a minute,' I went on. 'He doesn't look like ulcer patients generally do. Put it that way. He has had no remissions of pain. He has pain every day starting after his tea and going on till bedtime. No waking with it during the night. That's not a very convincing ulcer story. What's more the pain is not localised, it's all over the place. Then his wife. What do you think of her?'

'What has she got to do with it?' said Bates laughing again.

'Quite a lot I should say.' Even in those days I believed that in treating any patient you had to take the whole family into account though I had no idea how unconscious people's reactions to each other often are. 'She struck me as being a bit of a bully — a nagger. Matron knows her very well. What do you think of her Matron?'

Matron spoke with a hint of defiance. 'Mrs. Shedlock is a very nice person,' she said.

'I'm sure she is but would you say she is rather — strong minded? — Domineering?'

'A strong personality if you like.'

'And does she dominate her husband, do you think?'

'I don't know about that.' She began to laugh and looked at Bates for encouragement.

I was certainly not carrying the day. Bates had made up his mind and Matron would back him whatever he said. I spoke more decisively than I felt. It was an automatic response to the atmosphere of antagonism. I looked at Dr. Furlong. 'In my opinion he has a sound heart and a sound stomach. He hasn't got a gastric ulcer and suffers from nervous dyspepsia probably due to a domineering wife. I would be against operating on him.'

'Well that's definite anyway,' said Furlong and I could see he agreed with me. 'There you are Frankie, that's two to one.'

I hadn't realised it before but Furlong had disagreed with Bates all along and the whole question of Shedlock's heart was merely temporising on his part. We were firm allies now.

'Suppose he perforates as soon as we send him out of hospital,' said Bates.

'He won't,' I said.

'I agree with Lane,' Furlong said. 'If you don't agree, Frankie, there's only one thing to do. Send him into the City for another Xray and go by that.'

At last it was all clear to me. Bates loved the Xray machine and was inordinately proud of it. He would rather trust it than any clinical assessment. Furlong had doubted the value of Bates' Xray and doubted the need for operation. Rather than have a confrontation with his partner over the Xrays he had seized on Shedlock's chest pain as an excuse for a postponement. When this had failed he had appealed to me again. As it turned out even Matron had played a useful part. By encouraging Mrs. Shedlock to insist on a specialist's opinion she had assisted in the delay.

We now had to wait for the Xray in the City Hospital and as

231

the time passed my uneasiness increased. I had been so dogmatic in my statement of opinion that my worry now was that the Xray would show a massive ulcer. Bates and Matron had seemed to be taunting me and my reaction had been too emphatic. It would have been far wiser to say that as there was some doubt about the diagnosis another Xray and a radiologist's opinion was indicated before considering operation. Instead I had plunged in with both feet and should look a complete fool if my conclusion turned out to be wrong. Dr. Furlong had shown the wisdom of his age by not committing himself on the insufficient evidence.

Days passed while I waited uneasily for the Xray report to come through. The case was made urgent by the fact that Shedlock was already a patient in the Cottage Hospital but nevertheless it was a whole week before the barium meal was done. I had been a fool and the more I thought the more I doubted my own judgement.

I met Frankie Bates one morning and he soon read my doubts. 'Not so sure now, eh?' he laughed.

I managed to laugh back. 'Well there's no harm in postponing the operation anyway,' I said. 'Better than operating and finding a normal stomach.'

'Like to bet on it?'

'A pint of beer,' I said.

'No more than that. It's not worth it. You are having doubts aren't you?'

We parted with a good deal of discomfiture on my part. Why had I not refused to be committed and asked for another Xray as old Furlong had done? The truth was that Bates and Matron had irritated me and together they had produced my immature reaction. It was no one else's fault. I had been too hasty. Right, be more careful in future.

In due course Shedlock was Xrayed in the City and the radiologist reported no ulcer. Even then Frankie Bates claimed a minor triumph. 'Why didn't you have the courage of your convictions?' he said to me. 'You might have made some money on a bet. I gave you the chance.' And again he went off laughing — quite unabashed. Why had I not been gifted with his epidermal invulnerability?

Shedlock was discharged from hospital and as soon as he got home his pain recurred.

'What do we do now?' Dr. Furlong said to me later. 'Shoot the wife?'

'It's his defence against her,' I said. 'Leave him alone — unless you are prepared to tell the woman to stop nagging him.'

'Self defence against his wife? You mean he pretends to have a pain so as to get his own way? I shall never convince Frankie about that. He doesn't believe in nerves.'

'I imagine it's more complicated than that. But didn't you notice that he had no pain in hospital and as soon as he got home it recurred? He's never had a remission before. Why should he have one in hospital?'

Furlong thought for a minute. 'You may be right,' he said.

'And anyway we've saved Frankie from operating and doing no good' I added. 'He ought to be grateful.'

But this was too much for Furlong's loyalty to his partner. 'Hm' he said.

Some weeks later I met Mrs. Shedlock in the hospital where she was visiting the Matron. She looked at me with mild distaste. 'So you weren't sure of George's heart after all,' she said.

'What makes you say that?'

'You persuaded Dr. Bates not to operate and poor George is as bad as ever.'

'We all agreed that his heart is sound and that he hasn't got an ulcer,' I said and then added on the spur of the moment, 'he needs a lot of care from you. He works very hard and gets very tired. I think you are the only one who can cure him.'

This of course was not the way of the modern psychotherapist but it was an elementary attempt to show the wife that her own behaviour had a lot to do with her husband's health.

I met Shedlock at a committee meeting some time later and enquired after his symptoms. 'Quite a bit better really,' he said. 'The wife was properly frightened by all those threats of operation and heart trouble. She's been a different woman.'

So even he related his symptoms to his wife's behaviour.

'I'm glad,' I said. I was fairly certain that Mrs. Shedlock

would hold me personally responsible for any lapses in her husband's health but undeserved blame in one case is balanced by undeserved praise in another. So on the whole we are fairly treated!

26

Dare quam accipere. To give is better than to receive. Of course, but occasionally a rather cynical interpretation of the Guy's Hospital motto comes to mind.

Presents in general practice are almost infinite in their variety — from the framed text to the bundle of bank notes. Sometimes they have embarrassing strings attached to them and sometimes they cause such a sense of obligation that one would much rather do without them. Yet how do you refuse without giving offence?

I thought I had become reasonably skilled at accepting or refusing presents when Georgie Grindle of all people taught me another lesson.

It happens with some patients who for years are absolutely regular in their demands on the doctor, that somehow, at some point, they find a new lease of life and health. I have already told how Georgie's daughter came home from Canada on holiday and by some strange logic of her own blamed me for the filthy state of his cottage. After that he remained well for some years. Even his bronchitis improved. Then in the spring of 1938 he had several recurrent attacks of chest infection. I saw a good deal of him again and my average take-home of fleas increased dramatically.

I gathered that he had been 'working' very hard. This meant that he had bought and sold a wide variety of objects from antique furniture to old iron. He certainly frequented the sale rooms but there was no evidence that he ever made much profit. His cottage was just the same, smelling of the usual mixture of boiled potato peelings and hen manure and it was as devoid as ever of any sort of comfortable furnishings.

Often, as a compensation for the fleas I took home, I took a fresh piece of Georgie's Somerset dialect. The children, who later became adept at reproducing it, were even at an early age able to make us laugh with their efforts. Jessica who had the best sense of humour in the family — including a habit of being overcome with laughter when telling her own jokes — could never master the Somerset vowel sounds.

The phrase 'wen oider boiden glutch derpenoi crool' became as familiar in the family as the famous long word from Mary Poppins became later. In English it can be translated 'When I do bide and glutch (swallow) it do pain I cruel' or it 'hurts when I swallow'.

One afternoon when Georgie seemed to have taken his daily ration of whisky earlier than usual he told me a story that indicated not only something of a sense of humour but a modicum of intelligence and conversational power that I hadn't suspected.

There were two farmers Jarge and Amos who met at the Farrington market one Monday. Jarge said to Amos, 'Did Oi yere your rowan cow were zick las' Zummer?'

'Ah that 'er were' replied Amos.

'Wot did 'e give un ver traitment loike?'

'Traitment? Oh Oi give 'er linzeed ile. Powervul good thing be linzeed ile ver a zick cow.'

'Linzeed ile? Ah. Oi got a cow near as loike yourn were by arl accounts. Linzeed ile. Roight you be Amos.'

Next week they met again and Jarge began at once. 'Yeou der know thic zick cow Oi were tellin' yer on?'

'Ah.'

'Oi give 'er linzeed ile loike you zed.'

'Ah,'

'Well 'er died.'

'Did 'er now. Zo did moine las' Zummer.'

Of course Georgie's roars of laughter as he told the story brought on a severe bout of coughing from his still convalescent bronchial tubes. It was not a very good story but looking back at it I ought not to have been so surprised by what happened a few weeks later.

I called to see him one day after the usual message that he

'had been taken with his chest again' and found him covered by old army blankets and sitting in his usual chair in front of a huge fire. His grey hair and ragged beard made a large irregular frame for the fiercely penetrating blue eyes.

'Chest again Georgie?' I asked.

Without a word he undid the top button of his shirt allowing the routine few square inches of upper sternal area on which I was supposed to make my examination. The argument over exposing his chest was as routine as his regular spitting towards the fireplace. It was part of the ritual. He knew I should win in the end but liked to show his independence as far as possible. It was nine years since I had taken him over from my predecessor but he would generally repeat the gibe, 'Doc Ballard didn't never mak all thic fuss. 'E knew what was up be jest lookin' at me.'

'Up with your shirt,' I said.

I managed to examine him in due course. He had a little fever and a good deal of bronchitis which would probably respond to the newly available sulphonamide drugs. When I had written the prescription he said, 'Open thic door.'

'This one?' I said approaching the door to the front room. I supposed he wanted some fresh cool air, I knew the probable temperature of the 'parlour'. As I opened the door I had the surprise of my life. There standing in the almost empty room were two of the most beautifully carved Hepplewhite chairs I had ever seen. I gazed at them in reverent silence and then picked one up to examine it. It was layered in dust and the tapestry on the seat hopelessly faded but it was as solid as on the day it was made. 'Where did these come from?' I asked.

'What do 'e reckon o' they then?'

'Beautiful. Have you just bought them?'

' 'ad 'em ver years,' then after a pause he added, 'two 'underd pound.'

There was no question of my buying them. I couldn't afford them. Out of politeness I said, 'For the two?'

'Each,' he said.

This was much too high a price even for chairs like these. 'Who do you think will pay that for them?' I asked.

'You can 'ave one on 'em,' he said. 'Oi dun want yer money.'

I was startled into silence for a moment. 'You mean you want to give me one?' I confess a small wave of excitement passed over me. Then I knew it was impossible to accept such a gift from someone on the poverty line. I hesitated a moment under strong temptation then said firmly, 'It's too valuable Georgie. I couldn't accept it.'

'Please yerzelf,' he said.

'It's very kind of you but I couldn't take it. If you don't mean to sell them why don't you keep them here where you can enjoy them?'

He made no reply and seemed to dismiss the subject. I was embarrassed. I didn't want to hurt the old man's feelings. If he had been even moderately well off I would have accepted one of the chairs with alacrity but to do so from a poor old fellow like this was out of the question. I carried both of the chairs into the kitchen and put them one on each side of the table. They gave the place an air it had never aspired to before. 'They are beauties,' I said. 'I shall enjoy seeing them every time I call on you.'

He coughed and spat, causing me to take smart evasive action and shortly afterwards I left him. The event stayed in my mind most of that day. I supposed he had mentioned the price of the chairs to impress me with the size of the gift he was offering. There was a kind heart beneath the squalor and I kept hoping he wasn't unduly sensitive.

I called on him again a few days later. The chairs were nowhere to be seen and I didn't mention them. His chest was better and his temperature normal and in ten minutes I was ready to go. Just before I left he reached down into the shadows beside his chair and brought up a round crocodile skin bag of the type doctors used in the old days. It was well made and in perfect condition, something I could accept without undue qualms if he meant to make me a present of it. I wouldn't risk hurting his feelings again.

'What do 'e think o' thic then?' said Georgie.

'It's a very fine bag. Very fine indeed.'

'Yer can take un away.'

'That's very kind of you.' I looked inside. It was well lined and even polished. To make up for my previous snub my praises for the bag were probably a bit fulsome. I didn't want another bag and had no idea what I should do with it but I couldn't refuse to accept it. He was evidently anxious to show his gratitude for my services and when you considered how trying he could be, not to mention the fleas, I thought perhaps I deserved some show of gratitude.

I picked up the bag and prepared to leave. 'Well thankyou, Georgie,' I said. 'It's very good of you.'

'It'll cost 'e five pun,' he said.

I stared at him in silence. 'Five pounds,' I repeated. I didn't know what to do. Should I refuse to buy the bag after I had praised it so roundly or just pay up?

The only thing was to pay up graciously. I took the necessary notes from my pocket and put them under the whisky bottle on the table. The glint in the old eyes was obvious now and I walked out with my two bags maintaining my dignity as best I could.

I couldn't pretend to understand the workings of a mind like Georgie Grindle's. He evidently understood me a good deal better then I understood him and had planned the whole operation from the start. He probably needed the money.

Perhaps in time I shall learn never to be surprised in general practice. I still have the bag. It is used for emergency first aid equipment but its value lies more in reminding me of the dear old rascal who sold it to me than anything else.

27

The Norvals' life from nineteen thirty two to nineteen thirty eight had been uneventful and, I think, as happy as most human lives can be. After his operation at six weeks, their son Martin thrived. To look at he was blue eyed and square — almost cuboidal — and very jolly. Henry and Kate were one of those couples you felt sure were happy together. Sometimes we amused ourselves, Jessica and I, by deciding which of our friends could be regarded as happily married. There were never more than a few even in those days. The Norvals were always on the select list.

Their third baby was born that spring with no complications and very soon another blue eyed, well rounded addition to the family was becoming a character in her own right. Once when I visited the farm Kate told me that sometimes she felt they had no right to be as happy as they were. I liked her for this. She was really thankful for their blessings. Not that they were rich — far from it. They had all the struggles of the rest of us in deciding whether they could afford this or that for the house, and farm machinery was very expensive even then. All the same, there was a great deal on the credit side. Their red poll herd was doing well and even brought them a prize one year at the Bath and West Show. The farm prospered, Henry was strong, Kate was attractive and the children were bouncing with good health. God was in His heaven, all was right with the world.

Until one autumn day in nineteen thirty eight.

I had to go out to the farm to put a couple of stitches in young Martin's leg. He was a great climber at the age of six and fell pretty regularly. Usually he got away with it but this time some barbed wire had left an ugly gash over his patella. When I had finished with him Kate mentioned that Henry had a migraine attack. He had had them in his teens but none for some time. This one came as a surprise.

'Shall I go and have a look at him?' I said. 'He's in bed, is he?'

'He's in bed yes, but don't bother. He'll be alright. And he hates anyone to know he has migraine. He says it makes him sound like a neurotic woman.'

Kate had one of the merriest laughs I have ever heard. I dismissed Henry from my mind and enjoyed another few minutes chatting with her. While we talked young Martin escaped, I remember, and we saw him run across the farm yard to show his bandage to one of the men.

'That won't help the healing,' I said. 'The local anaesthetic is still working and he can't feel it. He will presently if he tears about like that.'

Kate ran out to bring him in and I came away. She was to bring Martin down to the surgery in three days time.

Next morning I had a call from her during morning surgery. 'I'm just a bit worried about Henry,' she said. 'His migraine is no better which I suppose is nothing to worry about. But he's mad to get up and meet the vet over the bull. Is there anything for it? The migraine I mean.'

'When did he have an attack last?'

'Oh it must be several years ago.'

'How long did that one last?'

'Only a day as far as I can remember.'

'I think I'll come over and have a look at him,' I said.

'Are you sure?' she protested. 'I thought some tablets or something. There are some now aren't there?'

'I'll come over after I've finished here.'

I wasn't worried about the migraine but there is an old rule that when an intelligent woman becomes concerned about a complaint in one of her family that 'is not like the usual ones' you have to beware. I remembered a child who was subject to bouts of biliousness and the mother told me this one was different from his usual attacks. The case turned out to be a particularly nasty appendix. So I went over to see Henry.

He had a severe headache still and had been sick early that morning. I examined him pretty carefully but found very little except a suggestion of stiffness in his neck. He was quite clear headed and angry with Kate for sending for me.

'I shall be alright by dinner time,' he said.

But of course he wasn't.

I saw him again that afternoon. He was restless and feverish — much worse than an hour or two earlier. He was conscious but not very clear headed. His temperature was not high enough to make him delirious and his confusion needed an explanation.

'How do you feel?' I asked him.

'My head aches,' he said and tossed about in the bed, angry at being ill but not well enough now to complain at the inconvenience of it.

It was impossible now to flex his neck and any attempt to do so produced severe pain at the base of his skull. It looked very like meningitis.

There were none of the small red spots I had seen once in a case of cerebrospinal meningitis — called spotted fever in the old days. I wanted to know more about his state of consciousness and asked him what day it was. He said he didn't know and didn't care.

Kate sat on the other side of the bed holding his hand. She looked at him intensely as if willing him to get better but she wasn't unduly worried. He was so strong. Nothing could go far wrong with him. He could lift two hundred weight as if it were a pound of tea. He would soon throw off this fever whatever it was. 'Poor old Henry,' she said. 'You are out of sorts.'

I was certain now that he had some form of meningitis. The word in those days was a death sentence and I tried to avoid using it but when we went downstairs I told her that I should have to admit him to the Isolation Hospital. Then of course she demanded to know the worst.

'I may be quite wrong,' I said, 'but there is just a possibility of meningitis.'

'Oh no,' she gasped and went as pale as if I had struck her. 'Henry. I can't believe it. It can't be really. You mean it just might be?'

There were several common organisms that caused meningitis and all of them were fatal in ninety eight or a hundred percent of cases, but I had read in recent literature about the new drug which had caused such a stir. We had already used it in some common catarrhal conditions and for Swain Galley's erysipelas but there were reports that some cases, even of meningitis, had responded miraculously to it. It was sulphonamide.

'If it is meningitis we may be able to treat it with this new drug,' I told her, but without much conviction. 'I'll have to send some of his cerebrospinal fluid to the laboratory and they'll tell me what germ it is — that is if it is meningitis.' The word kept coming out in spite of myself and Kate's normally happy face took on a look of tragedy. And I don't think my own was much better.

Before I left she gave way to a brief spasm of tears. She couldn't believe me when I spoke of treatment by a new drug. Everyone knew that meningitis was incurable. Everyone knew that in the rare cases which survived, the brain was damaged and the patient became a permanent invalid — paralysed, incontinent, perhaps insane. She based what hope she had on the diagnosis not being meningitis after all. If it were meningitis she would naturally opt for treatment of any sort that gave some hope of survival, whatever the consequences. Older people would say 'better not to interfere than let him end up like that'.

I had already seen the effect of sulphonamide on the commonest of all children's diseases — inflammation of the middle ear. A child screaming with earache would, in a few hours, be pain free and comfortable after a few doses of it. But inflammation of the ear drum was one thing, meningitis quite another.

I telephoned from the farm to arrange Henry's admission to the Isolation Hospital and then for an urgent ambulance. Then I tried to console Kate but this wasn't very successful. The only case of cerebrospinal meningitis I had seen was at the North East London Metropolitan Hospital nine years before. It was a girl of sixteen or seventeen. I remembered her admission with intense headache and her sudden harsh discordant

243

screams when the pain became worse. She sank into a coma and after a day or two of increasing paralysis and incontinence she died. She was an only child and I remembered the anguish of the parents. A case here and there stands out in my memory and this was one of them. The thought of Henry dying like that was hard to face.

Mixed with my distress over past experience there was an undercurrent of excitement. The new drugs were having startling success in some cases, why not in this one? It was possible. All things were possible. Sulphonamide drugs had acted well in erysipelas and scarlet fever as well as septic abortion, and in March that year a Norfolk farmer suffering from an almost hopeless lobar pneumonia had been cured by one of them. So why not meningitis? I had read that one of the organisms commonly responsible for meningitis was very sensitive to the drug and such cases might respond very well. All the same I found it hard to believe that an acute inflammation of the surface of the brain and spinal cord could ever be cured. When I was a student great stress was placed on post mortem appearances and the post mortem appearances of meningitis could be horrifying. I hoped for a miracle but had little faith that one would be forthcoming.

Kate went back to Henry and I went to the surgery to do some more telephoning. The first thing was to get on to the pathologist at the City Hospital. I should have to ask him to examine a specimen of Henry's cerebrospinal fluid as an emergency. Once he could determine the nature of the organism we should know what prospect there was of successful treatment. He would tell me more about other reported casses too.

When he came on the line I told him my problem. 'You are pretty sure it's meningitis?' he said and when I said I was he became quite excited. 'If it's a meningococcus,' he said, 'you will probably cure him with sulphonamide. There have been some excellent reports. In the Lancet a few weeks ago Gaisford and Evans of Birmingham reported a hundred cases of pneumonia treated by it.* And the other day there was a report of a

* Report in The Lancet 2nd July 1938.

case of meningococcal septicaemia cured by it.* *How soon can you get the c.s.f. in to me?'

'I'll lumbar puncture him as soon as he arrives in the hospital and the wife could bring it in — say in an hour and a half?'

'That would make it about four thirty. Be as quick as you can. Obviously early treatment stands a better chance. I'll expect it and ring you back later. It will probably mean culturing it and I shouldn't get the answer until tomorrow. If there is plenty of pus I may be able to make a diagnosis on direct smear but I shouldn't bank on it.'

'What do I do while I'm waiting for the result?'

'Give him sulphonamide intrathecally as soon as you've withdrawn enough fluid. Then give it intramuscularly every four hours. It can't do him any harm and if it's the right organism he will be improving before I make the diagnosis.'

My next hurdle came up before me suddenly and embarrassingly. To give the first dose into the spinal column when I did the lumbar puncture meant having some of the soluble sulphonamide in hand. I hadn't any.

'I'm afraid I haven't any soluble sulphonamide,' I said weakly.

'Oh heavens,' he said. 'You'll have to get hold of some pretty smartly then. Will your local chemist have any?'

'I'll try him. If not I shall have to send in to the City. But I shall have to do the puncture straight away so I can't put any of the stuff back in the spine.'

'It would be worth waiting a little while till you get some to be able to use it straight into the spine.'

'If our chemist has any, I will. If not I shall have to do the puncture and send the specimen in to you and have the sulphonamide picked up at the same time. I'll start it intramuscularly as soon as I get it.' To give the first dose into the spine would mean doing a second lumbar puncture after the stuff arrived. The patient would be getting more rigid in the spine with every hour and I didn't relish the thought of this.

I must have sounded agitated because he spoke soothingly.

* * Publication in the Lancet 20th August 1938

'Don't worry. It'll be alright intramuscularly — if it's the right bug.'

All this, which became second nature to us in due course, was new to me then. Later we developed a quick routine for these cases and they were under treatment within a matter of minutes of their arrival in the hospital. At the time I had two problems to face. One was to make a good clean lumbar puncture so as to get cerebrospinal fluid free from contamination with blood. If the specimen was hazy without being mixed with blood this would at least confirm the diagnosis of meningitis and at the same time make the pathologist's work somewhat easier. The second problem was to lay hold of some soluble sulphonamide.

I phoned the local chemist but he had none in stock. Then I phoned the main chemist in the City and he had some but closed at five o'clock. It was then a little after three.

'I've got to have some,' I told him. 'I'll send in as soon as I possibly can but this is really a matter of life and death. Will you wait for the patient's wife to come in and fetch it?'

'There's plenty of time, isn't there. You are only twelve miles away.'

'I've got to get the patient into hospital and do a lumbar puncture. Then send the specimen to the laboratory by the same transport as comes to you. It may be a few minutes after five. Please wait until my messenger arrives.' These people seemed to think you had nothing to do except run after their drugs.

'Alright,' he said. 'I will wait a little while if necessary.'

I wasn't really agitated, I told myself as I drove up to the hospital. I kept as calm as I could but I was already thinking of the chances of doing a quick clean lumbar puncture. To be in the City by five o'clock Kate would have to leave Melbrook by four thirty. It was then half past three and Henry should be in the hospital very soon. This would give me time to do the lumbar puncture and get the specimen off in time. It all depended how long the ambulance would be. It always took longer than you expected to get someone into hospital.

As soon as I arrived in the hospital I asked Matron to get all the things ready I should need. We had a block for scarlet fever and another for diphtheria and four separate rooms in a third block for special or undiagnosed cases. Henry was to go into one of these.

I waited.

Ten to four, four o'clock. No ambulance and no Henry. I was not expert enough at doing lumbar punctures to do one in a hurry. I had as far as I remember done not more than one or two in the whole of my eight years in practice. If the chemist left his shop and Kate failed to pick up the drug I should be in trouble. She might, if the worst came to the worst, be able to get some from the City Hospital. All the same the waiting was trying.

At last some time after four the ambulance arrived and in a few minutes Henry was in bed with a board under the mattress to make the positioning for the small operation easier. He was confused, restless and very strong.

With Matron's help I set to work at once. It was necessary to flex his spine so as to get the needle between the vertebrae and this proved difficult. I tried to get him to cooperate but this was impossible. Matron did her best to hold him on his left side with his knees bent up towards his chin but the position was painful for him and couldn't be maintained for long. I put in some local anaesthetic and pushed the intraspinal needle exactly horizontally into the spine towards the spinal canal. Just before it should have entered the canal it met bone. I withdrew the needle and tried again. Bone again. Meanwhile the clock ticked on and Henry became more restless.

Be calm. Relax. Put the needle into a space higher. Make sure it is exactly at right angles to the spinal column. Now. I pressed the needle in again slowly and carefully. Suddenly with the feeling that it had penetrated through parchment it was in. The drops of cerebrospinal fluid began to flow through the hollow needle. Blessed relief. It was under pressure. I hadn't prepared to measure this but it wasn't important. All we needed was the specimen. It was free from blood, thank goodness and looked clear. Perhaps it wasn't meningitis after all.

'What do you think of it Matron?'

As I withdrew the needle she held the glass receptacle up to the light. It had a fine opalescent haze. 'It looks like pus but a nice early case,' she said. The diagnosis was confirmed and there was a gleam of hope. The earlier the treatment was started the more likely the new drug was to work. Now it was up to the pathologist to determine the organism and to me to get hold of some soluble sulphonamide.

Looking back at this first case of cerebrospinal meningitis from the wider experience of the nineteen thirty nine epidemic it is humiliating to remember the stress and strain of it all. In nineteen thirty nine the routine was polished and easy and the outcome a virtual certainty. In nineteen thirty eight it was a great and nerve wracking adventure. Had I foreseen that I might be responsible for a case of the disease I would of course have had some of the drug in stock but the thought had never entered my head. We never lacked it after that day.

It was just half past four and Kate was waiting. 'Pick up the drug from the chemist first,' I told her, 'to make sure you get it. Then take this specimen to the laboratory at the City Hospital. Don't let anyone persuade you to leave it at reception. Ask to see the pathologist and hand it to him personally.' At least I wouldn't risk any more delays or inefficiency.

As she left, the thought struck me that if she had a puncture on the way in — such misadventures were far commoner then than now — it would cost her husband his life. Ought I to follow her in my car to make sure she got there safely? What absurdities determined the course of our existence. Never again would I be without this new drug. The trade name was prontosil but it was so new that even the drug firms' representatives had not yet brought it to our notice. They were usually busy urging us to stock every new drug or mixture within hours of its appearance on the market. In fact I suppose sulphonamide was the first to warrant the now familiar name of 'wonder drug'.

After Kate left I was too excited to go to the surgery and phoned to say I should be late. Everything seemed to be hanging in the balance. Was this drug as marvellous as it was reported to be? Should I be able to get hold of some in time? Was Henry's meningitis due to one of the sensitive organisms and would it respond? Or was it one of those that wouldn't respond? Perhaps if I had been older I should have been less involved with the fate of one of my patients. But who could help being involved over the life of someone like Henry Norval or the happiness of someone like Kate?

I sipped tea with Matron (not my old enemy Matron Pang) then went to have another look at Henry. He was getting visibly worse now, comatose but restless. Left alone the course of this dreadful disease was irreversible. How long could the body stand this degree of inflammation of a vital part and still recover if the germ was eliminated? Surely the damage already done couldn't be undone? How quickly did this stuff work? I looked at my watch every few minutes.

Just before five I telephoned the chemist to ask whether Kate had picked up the drug. A languid girl answered. It was hard to understand how anyone could be languid when an epoch making event was in the process of actually happening. I waited for what seemed several hours for someone intelligent and responsible to come on the line. At last a man's voice said, 'Your prontosil has been picked up, Doctor. I've given you ten doses. You'll send a prescription? You forgot?. Yes, I quite understand. You are rushed off your feet, I'm sure. You'll post it to us? And we'll charge the hospital or yourself?'

'The hospital,' I told him. How could anyone think of money at a time like this? And was I rushed off my feet? Well, not exactly. I had been fussing and fretting most of the afternoon.

It was about six o'clock when Kate came back with the prontosil. I greeted her as if she were a long vanished Arctic explorer though she had only been away an hour and a half. I remember being surprised that the prontosil was red. After reading the instructions I gave the first dose intramuscularly myself. The second was to follow in four hours time.

I watched for another few minutes half hoping to see a miracle happen under my eyes. I knew this couldn't happen and for some reason all my doubts about the efficacy of the new drug came flooding back. Then I went to see Kate who was waiting in her car.

'Can I stay with him?' she said.

'Aren't you feeding the baby still?'

249

'Heavens, yes.' She felt her breasts and added, 'I think my milk has gone anyway. Can I stay?'

'I don't think you ought to stay close to Henry — specially as you are feeding the baby. The milk will come as soon as you start feeding her. You can telephone as often as you like and come back later and look at him through the window if you want to. I'll telephone you last thing tonight.'

'I was with him all last night so what difference does it make? I'd rather stay,' she said and I realised I was up against a very determined woman. 'They can feed Prue easily enough.'

I gave in of course although I knew Matron would object strongly. 'You'll have to dress up in a cap and gown and sit quietly in a corner of the room. And you'll have to go out of the room whenever they tell you to.'

Having got her own way she became all cooperation. She smiled for the first time for many hours. Fortunately Matron agreed to her staying under the special circumstances and I left for the surgery.

'How long does this drug take to act?' she asked as I turned to go.

'I honestly don't know. I've never used it before for this sort of case. Perhaps we'll have a change by morning.'

She looked disappointed. Under desperate circumstances hope can reach ridiculous proportions when failure is too bleak to contemplate. 'Then I shall stay all night,' she said defiantly.

'No,' I said, 'you must go home when I come to see him last thing tonight. There's nothing you can do and you may need your strength for the next few days.'

'What does that mean?'

'It means we don't know what is going to happen and you've got to face a few difficult days. I shall be back at eleven.'

It is hard for anyone used to the healing powers of modern antibiotics to realise the doubts, uncertainties and excitement of those days. As I drove down from the hospital I began to wonder what the side effects of such a powerful drug might be on the human brain and spinal cord. It must have been thoroughly tried out or it wouldn't have come on the market — or so I thought then. The tragedy of thalidamide was more than twenty years in the future.

I saw a few long suffering souls in the surgery who had waited to see me. I was interupted once by the telephone. The pathologist came on the line.

'It's a meningococcus,' he said. 'Good news. I found some on direct smear.'

'That means the drug should work then?' I said.

'According to the reports it should work in a few hours.'

'Thank God for that.'

'Better do your thanksgiving when he has recovered,' he said cautiously, 'but there should be a good chance. Let me know how things go.'

How pleasant to be a pathologist whose interest is purely academic, I thought. Not to be concerned with real people.

All that evening Henry's condition remained unchanged. He was comatose, restless and moderately feverish. And he was incontinent once. This last emphasised how ill he was though of course one might have expected it.

At eleven o'clock I went up to the hospital again. I told Kate the hopeful news about the organism and persuaded her to go home. When she had gone I looked at Henry with misgivings. He was desperately ill and it was hard to imagine how a few doses of red stuff could kill this vicious germ and wake him out of his coma. It seemed crazy to expect it.

I didn't expect to sleep that night but as so often happened I went out like a light. I woke early at five a.m. to face the problems of the day. I rang the hospital but the night nurse was not very helpful. 'Mr. Norval is about the same,' she said. 'He is quiet, his temperature is ninety nine and his pulse eighty.

I couldn't sleep any more and went to see him. I had not been so anxious about a patient since the couple from Devon in the caravan when 'John Ridd' had pneumonia.

It must have been six o'clock when I got to the hospital. At a glance you could tell he was better.

Less than twelve hours after his first dose he was cool, restful and breathing quietly. I couldn't resist talking to him. 'How is it Henry?'

251

He opened his eyes and stared at me. 'You're early,' he said and dozed off again.

He awoke from his coma as if by magic. It was the outstanding experience of my life. If I practiced medicine for a thousand years there would never be another case like this for me.

He recovered completely in a couple of weeks and went back to work on the farm. In spite of Kate's rhapsodies he pretended never to believe us when we told him he had been at death's door.

'You doctors have got to keep your morale up somehow I suppose,' he said. 'Marvellous cures. Magic drugs. I seem to have read all about that in the fairy books.'

But this was a true fairy story. The first of many. To the next generation these cases would be routine. A simple matter of a germ destroyed by the appropriate therapeutic agent. In fact they will always be fairy stories possessed of a magic no less real because it is commonplace.

This was the Autumn of nineteen thirty eight and the storm clouds were gathering over Europe. To our infinite regret John Symonds retired and a heavy weight of responsibility was already settling on my shoulders. But the triumph of Henry Norval's recovery was unforgettable. It gave this phase of my life a happy ending.

HOVEL IN THE HILLS
by ELIZABETH WEST

This is the unsentimental, amusing, and absorbing account of the 'simple life' as practised by Alan and Elizabeth West in their primitive cottage in rural Wales. The Wests – she is a typist, he an engineer – moved from Bristol to North Wales in 1965, determined to leave the rat race for good. But the daunting task of converting a semi-derelict farmhouse and turning the unproductive soil into a viable self-sufficient unit was to prove a full-time job. The author describes the very individual and resourceful ways she and her husband tackled the problems which faced them – from slating the roof, curing a smoking chimney and generating their own electricity, growing a wonderful variety of fruit, herbs and vegetables on impossible soil. With a preface by John Seymour, author of "The Complete Book of Self-Sufficiency" "Hovel in the Hills" is a heartwarming and salutary tale which will either leave you yearning for a chance to get away from it all or convince you that the comfortable security of the nine-to-five is not such a bad thing.

0 552 10907 X   £1.25

THE COMPLETE BOOK OF SELF-SUFFICIENCY
by JOHN SEYMOUR

The Complete Book of Self-Sufficiency is a book for all seasons. Whether you live in town or country, on a farm or in a cottage, in a house with a garden or a flat with a window-box, this book has something for you.

If you want to bake your own bread, brew your own beer, make your own cheese, pickle your own onions, this book will show you how.

If you want to make hay, milk a cow, smoke a ham, design a dairy, convert to solar energy, this book will show you how.

If you just want to grow your own vegetables, bottle your own fruit, dry your own herbs, this book will demonstrate exactly what to do.

The Complete Book of Self-Sufficiency is an invaluable manual, packed with illustrations, and every illustration tells its own story, shows you what you need and how to do it.

John Seymour is everywhere recognised as the expert in self-sufficiency. He has lived the life for twenty years, and here he gathers all the expertise he has acquired into one authoritative volume.

0 552 98051 X   £5.95

GO ASK ALICE
by ANONYMOUS

Alice is fifteen, white, middle-class. She diets. She dates. She gets decent grades. She thinks someday she'd like to get married and raise a family.

On July 9, Alice is turned on to acid. She digs it. Acid makes the world a better place. So do all the other ups. They open up the world of sex. They make Alice feel free. Sometimes Alice worries about taking drugs. She thinks maybe she shouldn't. But, she figures life is more bearable with drugs than without.

Alice's parents don't know what's happening. They notice changes. They have no idea she's on drugs. They cannot help her.

The difference between Alice and a lot of other kids on drugs is that Alice kept a diary.

0 552 09332 7   £1.25